Faiths, Public Policy and Civil Society

Faiths, Public Policy and Civil Society

Problems, Policies, Controversies

Adam Dinham
Goldsmiths, University of London, UK

First published 2009 by
PALGRAVE MACMILLAN

Palgrave Macmillan in the UK is an imprint of Macmillan Publishers Limited, registered in England, company number 785998, of Houndmills, Basingstoke, Hampshire RG21 6XS.

Palgrave Macmillan in the US is a division of St Martin's Press LLC, 175 Fifth Avenue, New York, NY 10010.

Palgrave Macmillan is the global academic imprint of the above companies and has companies and representatives throughout the world.

Palgrave® and Macmillan® are registered trademarks in the United States, the United Kingdom, Europe and other countries.

ISBN-13: 978–0–230–57330–7 hardback
ISBN-10: 0–230–57330–4 hardback

This book is printed on paper suitable for recycling and made from fully managed and sustained forest sources. Logging, pulping and manufacturing processes are expected to conform to the environmental regulations of the country of origin.

A catalogue record for this book is available from the British Library.

Library of Congress Cataloging-in-Publication Data

Dinham, Adam.
    Faiths, public policy, and civil society : problems, policies, controversies / Adam Dinham; foreword by Lord Tyler of Linkinhorne.
        p. cm.
    Includes bibliographical references.
    ISBN 978–0–230–57330–7
        1. Church charities – Government policy – Great Britain. 2. Religion and politics – Great Britain. 3. Church charities – Government policy – United States. 4. Religion and politics – United States. 5. Church charities – Government policy – Canada. 6. Religion and politics – Canada. I. Title.
HV530.D56 2009
361.7′5—dc22
                                                                        2008046495

Printed and bound in Great Britain by
CPI Antony Rowe, Chippenham and Eastbourne

For Christine and Dennis Dinham

Contents

Illustrations

Tables

Figures

Preface

Over the past decade, I have been struck by a growing interest in faiths as a public category once more. This has surprised me because, if there was one thing that seemed clear to me as an undergraduate in Theology and Religious Studies in the mid-1990s, it was that the public appetite for religion was minimal. I lost count in those days of the number of times people asked with incredulity what on earth I thought I was doing wasting my time with Theology at university. I mean, what was I going to *do* with that? On one noted occasion I was asked by a puzzled fellow undergraduate (in Veterinary Sciences, I think) whether Theology was 'a third year option'. On others, too frequent to recount, it was assumed that I would be a priest when I finished, and that was the end of that.

In fact, I read Theology because of a tendency since childhood to start with questions about meanings, rather than explanations about how things worked. Despite a certain precociousness ('Mother, I'm playing archaeologists') I don't suppose I thought of it that way then but, looking back, that has been the trajectory of my interests ever since. So it was to everybody's surprise when I turned as a postgraduate from Theology to Politics, Social Work and Community Development. These seemed so much more worldly to my friends and family. Perhaps, at last, I had left all that religion alone. Yet, to me the connections seem clear. These are the arena of public politics and practices affecting the lived experiences of everyday people. They seek to uncover and explore the meanings and actions with which we grapple each day of our lives. To me, community policies and practices are as fundamentally associated with 'meanings of life' as any of the questions to which Theology might lay claim. And they have the added benefit of being practically focused on what could *happen* as a result.

It has been fascinating, in turn, to experience the low-level background hum of prejudice and stigma against 'faith' and nowhere more so than in the social science academy. For some, the assertions of Neitzsche, Marx, Freud and Durkheim have left a legacy of anxiety about the legitimacy of faith at all, let alone in public space, and particularly as a subject of social scientific enquiry. What axe do I have to grind? Which beliefs do I seek to promote? What methods will I use to sneak my dodgy dogmas in through the back door of a grown up, rational and intelligent academy? The assumptions of a secularised and neutral public realm are strong. Yet philosophy has been asserting the subjectivity – for that matter the constructivity – of 'rational' knowledge for decades. In this context, and with my gratitude, many have shown great interest in the subject of faiths and public space and have given me much support in my work. Others have been simply mystified.

Whether furiously against public faith, supportive of it or merely bemused, the contests reflected by these positions make the case of public faith an interesting one for throwing light on all sorts of significant questions. They bring to the surface wider debates, many of them heated, relevant to society in general. What is private and what public, who is a citizen, how are we represented and what is legitimate in the public realm? Some of these are very 'now': about faith schools, interfaith relations, the prevention of extremism and global relations. Others have been with us for longer: the persistence of spiritual hunger, the veracity of secularism and the legitimacy of faith as a public category at all. The reappearance of public faith is often an unfamiliar experience for those already in the public realm, and sometimes for the new comers themselves, too. Dialogue between different faiths is clearly important as the parties get to know one another; likewise that between believers and others. These challenges are compounded by a curious lack of familiarity between the academic disciplines too. In particular, Social Scientists and Theologians have not always seen eye to eye. The ESRC (*Economic and Social Research Council*) network I have been involved in running in recent years has done something to bring these disciplines together and we have had fun reaching across the chasm! But chasms there are between all of these areas and it takes good will, hard work and application to build bridges which can take the weight of the debates between them.

My concern is to be working out the relationships within, between and beyond faiths in a milieu which is increasingly interested in them. I am an observer of these things, but also, I hope, one who seeks to influence and inform the dialogue and what happens afterwards. This means linking up research and theory with the policy and practices which are their context and this book has been much informed by empirical evidence gathered almost always in partnership with the policy-makers and practitioners who so generously work with me. They understand, as do I, that the much-repeated distinction between the world and the ivory tower is a false one. Academics in a field such as mine must get their hands dirty by digging in its soil. For me, as for many, libraries are not places of retreat from the world but spaces to resource my reflections before setting back out with practical and concrete ideas.

Mine is also an interest firmly located in the values of empowerment, participation and inclusion, as you might expect of a former social and community worker. I think faiths have a lot to offer to a public realm in which all sorts of interests are increasingly present and which seems to maintain a persistent spiritual appetite. But there are differences in power between faith traditions, their partners in the wider world and the groups within them, notably women and gay people. I recognise, too, that faiths can have a dark side; where dogma ends dialogue we have a problem. And this is a valid and crucial part of this book's considerations too.

Overall I come to this book interested in the academic disciplines of Theology and the Social Sciences (especially Social and Public Policy), in the practices of Social Work and Community Work and in the making of policies in civil society. My starting points are a mix of these academic, practitioner and policy interests and my methods reflect them.

As for my own position on faith, nobody starts from nowhere and just like anyone else I have my own values and beliefs. But, for the record, I respect religions as expressions of the many and varied ways in which human beings have grappled with meaning, and the wide array of deities as symbols, both of this and also quite possibly of God him, her or itself. Yet social scientist and theologian alike will be relieved that such wishy-washy liberalism and uncertainty are not my starting point, however interesting I might find them. Rather, I come to the question of faith at the public table with the tools of the social scientist: data, method, epistemology and some good old-fashioned debate.

There are a number of people I would like to thank for helping me to think about the problems, policies and controversies identified in the title. Vivien Lowndes, Richard Farnell and Rob Furbey have been generous, kind and extremely thoughtful in their conversations with me about this book and I am grateful for their professional contributions and also for their friendship. To Vivien I must also ascribe, with gratitude, the phrase 'faiths as heroes and villains'. I am also grateful to Doreen Finneron, Jenny Kartupelis and Steve Miller whose practice and policy experience have been invaluable to me. In the Faiths and Civil Society Unit the Fellows, and the Chair, Lord Tyler, have provided me with a sounding board for my ideas and my writing and I am grateful to them for the generosity with which they give of their time. And Di Mitchell and Martha Shaw have been their usual thoughtful, wise, hard-working and incredibly effective selves.

I am also grateful to my friends and family who have dutifully and lovingly enquired about progress throughout. Philip Jones, Bryony

Randall, Michael Robinson and John Tyler have been particular empathisers and inspirers and to them I am grateful. In Canada, Katherine Bradshaw and her family have been more than welcoming. Her pool, hot tub and wonderful mountain views have provided an inspiring – if distracting – backdrop for much of my writing and our many conversations have been invaluable. Finally, I should give particular thanks to the Dean, Gayla Rogers and our colleagues in the faculties of Social Work and Political Science in the University of Calgary, who hosted me for a most enriching year and where much of this book was written.

Foreword

A prominent member of the Muslim community in a northern British city recently told a group of Parliamentarians (of which I was one) that she found it much more difficult to relate to the secularism of the UK than to 'her colleagues' in the Christian and other faiths of her area. The more I mulled this over the more significant it seemed.

It is surely a tantalising paradox that the Church of England is an established state religion and yet civil society in the UK has so often treated faiths as embarrassing minority cults, while in the USA religion is officially and politically off-limits and yet plays a proactive role in all levels of governance – sometimes very controversially but never to universal condemnation. As Adam Dinham observes *'The growing trend in Europe and Canada is towards believing without belonging'*, and yet our American cousins seem to be immune from this tendency: is this indicative of some deeper societal differences?

If so, what should we conclude to achieve a more creative partnership between faith communities and wider civil society, on both sides of the Atlantic?

I do not have anything like the comprehensive, thoughtful and experienced wealth of knowledge that Adam Dinham displays in this book, but my instincts and experience tell me that his analysis is both profound and very timely. My own experience – personal as well as political – has been concentrated on the UK, and my acquaintance with these issues in Canada and the USA has been filtered through occasional visits and family contacts rather than dedicated study. However, I recognise so much validity in the Dinham comparisons: a period in eastern Canada in the immediate aftermath of 9/11, witnessing the contrast between reactions of the local media there and that of the adjoining American States, brought home to me the significance of cultural and faith differences. As he observes *'The rise of extremism along religious lines has been a noted aspect of life after 9/11'*, and nowhere more so than in the rhetoric of the George W. Bush Administration.

Comparisons are of most value if they produce positive re-examination. This book presents an especially relevant policy-making opportunity, at a time when we all need to reassess how best to reinvigorate and reconnect communities throughout Europe and North America.

Adam Dinham's emphasis on *'empirical evidence gathered almost always in partnership with the policy-makers and practitioners'* gives a solid structure to his analysis and conclusions. While we all come to any discussion with preconceived prejudices – *'nobody starts from nowhere'* as he reminds us – I believe that all decision-makers will recognise the dispassionate way in which Adam Dinham marshals his evidence.

He is right to remind us that some radicalised adherents of the various faiths have adopted disruptive, aggressive views (*'where dogma ends dialogue we have a problem'*) but his corrective is even more conclusive: *'in projects and initiatives in neighbourhoods and communities across the West, faith traditions are making a far more gentle contribution rooted in post-Enlightenment theologies, and what evidence there is suggests that these far outweigh the minority of radical interests which cause such anxiety.'* Amen to that!

It is in the balanced engagement between faiths and the rest of civil society that the 'faith contribution' can be valued, supported and put to best use. Adam Dinham shows that faiths are providers of things of economic value, yes. But he suggests that they are also reminders of what he calls 'forgotten ontological categories'. Their calling us back to human value, alongside the economic, can be an important response to the spiritual hunger which he reminds us is out there, as well as providing a positive answer to the anxieties which proliferate about public faith. Getting that balance between the two is the challenge, and it is one to which we must all – policy-maker, community member and researcher – respond.

PAUL TYLER

(Lord Tyler, Chair Faiths and Civil Society Unit)

1
Faiths at the Public Table

There is an old adage that religion and politics are topics best avoided at dinner parties. This book breaches that etiquette by talking about both. It does so for two reasons: first, to explore the notion that faith is re-emerging as a public category; and second, to wonder how this might impact upon a 'public imaginary' (Bevir and Rhodes, 2006) in which the death of religion was more or less presumed.

The main focus of the book is the UK, where policy has been steadily extending in the direction of faiths since the early 1990s. It is here that a preponderance of interest in what faiths might bring has resulted in a notable extension of the public table to include faiths as contributors to community cohesion, providers of services and participants in new forms of governance. The faith 'offer' is bound up in what New Labour in Britain has called 'active citizenship', and these are the themes around which the book is organised. But it draws too, where it is useful, on examples from Canada and the USA. There are three reasons for this: first, the UK, Canada and the USA have in common the English language, constitutional democracy (in varying nuanced forms), a mixed economy of welfare (also in varying nuanced forms) and a multicultural approach to difference and diversity. This gives them much in common on which to draw comparisons in relation to faiths.

Second, the constitutional and cultural conditions of each country are at the same time sufficiently differentiated as to make each a useful illuminator of the others' distinctions. The UK is a constitutional monarchy whose head of state is also head of an established church. In this sense, faith is already a public category. Yet politicians are notably uncomfortable with public discussion of faith. The USA, on the other hand, is a republic with a formal separation of religion and state. Yet the President concludes the State of the Nation speech with the statement 'God bless

America', and religion is widely regarded as a legitimate aspect of the identity and character of American politicians. There, then, a formal refusal of public faith is countermanded by an actual prominence of it in everyday political life. Canada stands between the two. On the one hand, it shares with the UK a monarch by divine right as head of state. On the other, it shares with the USA a separation of the religious from the state, through a popular assumption that religion and society are separate (though there this is not formally constituted).

Third, in this context, the UK has been making increasingly explicit policies for public faith. This echoes the emergence of the 'faith-based initiative' in the USA to which we shall return in Chapter 6. Yet here too, Canada stands in an intermediate space, engaging with faiths in public space, most notably through service provision and faith schools, but having little or no explicit or self-conscious policy in this direction. These are salutary considerations in the book, but they are by no means a central theme. For a detailed consideration of the situations in relation to faith in Canada and the USA, readers must look elsewhere, but this book will, I hope, help whet their appetites.

It should be acknowledged, too, that the very idea of faiths at the public table raises questions and debates, which are by no means clearly resolvable. At their root lie questions about what 'faith' is and what 'faiths' are. These issues are addressed in Chapter 2, which examines the diverse demography of faiths and the implications of this for policy, and in Chapter 3, which explores meanings, definitions and debates about faiths, public policy and civil society. This necessarily includes discussion of ideas and models of all three central notions – faiths, public policy and civil society – as well as the relationships between them. It also considers a number of related debates concerning understandings of the role – for that matter the very legitimacy – of faiths at the public table.

It should also be noted that the book uses the plural 'faiths' in order to refer to the whole range of faiths and not only Christianity, though this is the majority faith of the UK, as well as in Canada and in the USA. Baha'i, Buddhism, Hinduism, Islam, Jainism, Judaism, Sikhism and Zoroastrianism are also present. This is significant because it highlights the diversity of faiths in the UK, and in North America, as we shall see in Chapter 2. There it is argued that recognition of this diversity is essential if policy is to be effective. It also matters because faiths have differing capacities, power, resources and skills for engagement. Ignorance of this is likely to result in the accidental and institutional exclusion of some and the over-representation of others.

I must acknowledge, too, that the notion of the 'public table' is also problematic. Debates about what 'public' is are manifold, as I explore in Chapter 3. And where the boundary lies between the public and the private is an especial issue for faiths. In grappling with these ideas, I have opted for the phrase 'public table' to indicate a coming together of sometimes unlikely table-fellows to 'eat together' in the construction and negotiation of civil society. Thus 'table' rather than 'square', as is preferred in the USA, suggests that participation can be as much like a meal or a meeting as the politically orientated gatherings implied by the 'public square'.

This book is intended to be an introduction to the policy contexts within which faiths are asked to engage and the issues this raises. To this extent it is a survey of the main debates and problems. It is aimed at a range of audiences, from the total newcomer to the seasoned policy-maker, practitioner or researcher, as well as students in disciplines including social and public policy and applied and public theology. The breadth of the questions raised by the re-emergence of faiths, and the relatively limited availability of sources about this, means that many will find something of relevance and interest. With that in mind, the intention is to provide a resource for anyone trying to understand what faiths do and what they are asked to do in the 'public' we all share.

It is to the surprise of many that faith is back in public space at all. In the UK, government has stated that it is 'increasingly conscious of the importance of effective co-operation with faith communities' (Home Office, 2004, foreword) and says that it sees them as 'gateways to access the tremendous reserves of energy and commitment of their members, which can be of great importance to the development of civil society' (Home Office, 2004, p. 7). Yet throughout much of the twentieth century, secularisation theorists were sure that faith was dead. Now, as Habermas has observed, there appears to be a 'political revitalization of religion at the heart of Western society' (Habermas in Norris and Inglehart, 2004); a positive 'turn to faith'.

But 'secularisation' is a more complex notion than is often understood, and a closer analysis suggests that faith never really went away. The term 'secularisation' initially referred to 'the freeing of [certain] areas of life from their theological origins or basis' (Alexander, 2002, p. 48), reflecting the idea from the Latin 'saeculum' ('age') of an essential distinction between the immanency and time-boundedness of the world with the atemporality and metaphysicality of the heavenly. This 'freeing' of 'certain areas' may describe the beginning of those processes 'whereby religious thinking, practice and institutions lose social significance' (Alexander, 2002, p. 48). But it does not banish faith altogether from public space.

Second, it has been observed that the loss of faiths' social significance is associated with their ceding to the state certain 'specialised roles and institutions' (Alexander, 2002, p. 49) such as the delivery of education, health and social care. But these processes were driven by a vision of universal welfarism, not a dedication to the expulsion of faiths from the public table (see Prochaska, 2006). What is more, it is clear that faith-based social action has maintained a foothold in public space, often remaining present even where all other agencies have withdrawn (Dinham, 2007).

A third strand asserts that faiths lost their social significance as a result of the twin forces of urbanisation and technology. Thus, as populations centred in cities, communities fragmented resulting in the loss of platforms for social control as exercised by religious leaders. At the same time, it is suggested that technology promised ways around 'God-given' constraints. These are particularly associated with medical interventions and with telecommunications. That we can resuscitate people, transplant organs, assist pregnancy, talk to each other remotely in 'real time' anywhere in the world and fly through the skies are all seen by secularists as undermining of the claims that there are laws of God laid down in nature.

Yet these ideas must be located within their Western-centricity, originating in the urban lives and technological trends of Europeans and North Americans. They do not translate easily or simply into many other parts of the world outside of Europe and North America. Indeed, even within them there are important distinctions in types and levels of religiousness (which are discussed in Chapter 2). It is in part for these reasons that Peter Berger has replaced his earlier assertion that by 'the twenty first century, religious believers are likely to be found only in small sects, huddled together to resist a worldwide secular culture' (Berger et al., 1968), with a more recent observation that 'the world today, with some exceptions... is as furiously religious as it ever was...' (Berger, 1999). Faith is persistent, he notes. For Berger it is also a 'furious' force rather than a benevolent one.

Secularisation, then, is not as clear as is often supposed. A limited or soft form of it is argued here, on the basis that the social significance of religion has been under pressure but, at the same time, at least some of that significance has *changed* rather than been *lost*. There is a role for faith in public space, though it is nuanced.

Part of this is associated with the rather curious way in which faith is played out in public in the UK, through what has been called 'the dignified parts of the constitution' (Dinham et al., 2009, p. 2). The head of state is also head of an established church; Bishops sit in the upper house of parliament, and (Christian) houses of worship are the context for public events such as royal weddings and state services of thanksgiving and remembrance. Across and beyond all the faiths, the lifespan is frequently marked in religious buildings through rites such as baptisms, weddings and funerals. These public displays of faith may be 'red herrings' – confusing symbols with less currency than the assertion of them suggests.

Another dimension is the shift that has been noted from 'believing to belonging' (see Davie, 1999). As we shall see in Chapter 2, there is a remarkable persistence of religious affiliation in Europe and North America, although there is an equally remarkable decline in the practice of organised religion.

In these contexts, faith is well ensconced at the public table. But what are the driving forces behind this renaissance? For many, the most obvious lies in the widespread perception of a tension between Islamic religious fundamentalism, or 'Islamism', on the one hand and so-called Western values of democracy and freedom of speech on the other. This reflects in macrocosm the debate about whether religion is 'furious' or benign. For many, religion is encapsulated in shadowy collective memories of the Crusades and the Inquisition. For others it is held in the rumours and histories, for example, of abusive schools run by Monks and Nuns, the oppressive practices of feudal Bishops and the aggression of British and European colonialism originating in missionary expeditions. Another backdrop which resonates for many is the conflicts in Northern Ireland, Kashmir and Israel–Palestine. Such examples are grist to the mill of those who see faith as a furious force. It is in these contexts that Islam, since 9/11, has come to be characterised in the rhetoric of the so-called war on terror, a (wrongly) perceived clash of cultures, identities and values which goes to the very roots of meaning.

But there are more subtle, and arguably more immediate, imperatives driving an interest in faith. These are in three key areas. The first starts with government's understanding of the role of faiths as repositories of resources – buildings, staff, volunteers and relationships – which have the potential to be deployed in the direction of social and community services. This extension of the mixed economy of welfare in the direction of faith communities is presented as an opportunity for faiths to engage in the delivery of services, building on an already established tradition of welfare projects and community action over a very long time. This book addresses these issues in Chapter 5.

A second dimension is the value governments attach to faiths as potential sources of social capital and therefore of community cohesion. In the UK, this is important to a government which came to power on a wave of communitarian celebration. In response to the years of Thatcherite individualism, the UK Labour government of 1997 focused intensively on Etzionian notions of community (Etzioni, 1993) and of community participation. Over the years since then this has been extended to the idea of the 'strengthened community', lifted up by the participation of an ever wider cast of actors in something called 'civil society'. Faith groups have been embraced in this rhetoric in documents such as 'Working Together' (Home Office, 2004) and, like other parts of the social, such as residents' associations and community projects, recast as members of a newly rediscovered nation 'community'. More recently still, the notion of 'resilient' communities has emerged, to describe the positive resistance in communities to extremist elements, not only the cohesion of their parts. Faiths are therefore regarded as important contributors to community cohesion at a time when the multicultural settlement is in question and while international relations between Islamic and Western countries (if not cultures) are played out in local contexts such as the English cities of Bradford, Leicester, Luton and London. The question being asked is, how can faiths in Britain be encouraged to work in their communities to strengthen British civil society and not be agitators against it? These issues are addressed in Chapter 4.

A third area is found in the extension of new forms of participative governance to include faiths. Neighbourhood boards, Local Strategic Partnerships (LSPs) and regional assemblies are all examples of where faiths are increasingly present. This strategic level of engagement in policy and decision-making at the local and regional levels is echoed in new forms of participation at the national level, where, for example, the Faiths, Race and Cohesion Unit in Whitehall focuses on making policies affecting the role of faiths, and the 'Faith Communities Consultative Council' attempts to give voice to faiths at the heart of politics and the civil service.

This book, then, is a simple endeavour in one sense. In policy terms there is an opening up to faiths of opportunities to be at the public table in service delivery, in community cohesion and resilience and in new forms of governance. Faiths are seen as 'repositories' of resources which can contribute in each of these areas.

And yet, in another sense, it is highly complex. There are so many ideas and assumptions at the level of policy about what faiths are, where they are and what they do. Likewise, faiths themselves have their own lived experiences, values and outlooks. Like tectonic plates, as policy makes its seismic shifts in the direction of faiths, so faiths are grappling with the pressures and challenges of the new geography they find themselves in.

Each area raises a large number and a wide range of very challenging questions, the substance of which this book tries to bring to the surface. Fundamental to these is the differences in values and perspectives residing in faiths and those with whom they work, at this extended policy table.

Three perspectives on faiths and public engagement

Public faith is a complex matter – that much is clear. Part of that complexity stems from the contest of policy goals and ideas pertaining to their engagement. But in addition, there are differences in the perspectives of the 'actors' in public-faith participation which underlie the ways in which these debates are constructed and addressed, and in which they interact. These differences have been explored in terms of the 'narratives' each makes for itself (see Dinham and Lowndes, 2008) and how those narratives inform and determine the actions which result. My account here owes a debt to that analysis, though I stop short of the 'narrative' account and favour, instead, a discussion of the perspectives which pertain. This uncovers the 'stories' each tells about their engagement and shows how they arise from the particular experiences they have of that engagement and the points from which they start. This, in turn, highlights the questions which are raised.

Unsurprisingly, there are differences in motivations, values, practices and goals which centrally affect and inform the stories which emerge. Thus from the policy perspective, faith is seen instrumentally in relation to public and social policy. How is faith *useful* to society and how does this inform the interactions of public servants with faiths? The extent to which this instrumentality is legitimate, and whether it attempts to be sensitive in its engagement, is a key consideration throughout this book.

Then there is the perspective of faiths themselves, whose involvements are motivated distinctively and differentially, not only from policymakers, but also from tradition to tradition and even from one worshipping congregation to another. The diversity this enjoins is a crucial part of understanding faiths and setting policy parameters which work to best effect with faiths rather than in parallel or, worse, against them.

The last perspective comes from the faith-public partnerships which come together around particular projects and initiatives in civil society which themselves come to the table with particular aspirations, motivations and ways of working, wherein the usual contests around power, resource, goals and values are already a challenge at the best of times. How these are played out in relation to faiths is another theme of this book.

What is surprising is that attempts at surfacing these different perspectives, and the tensions and opportunities between them, are few and far between. Yet policy approaches to faiths tend to make assumptions about faiths' willingness, readiness and skills, that tend to homogenise faith at the expense of sensitivity to their diversity. This represents the danger that their enormous contribution could be frittered, or even washed, away before the great wave of public demand which is flowing around them. To make the most of faiths in the public realm it is essential that their place is understood from the range of perspectives which bear upon them.

The policy perspective

The most irresistible of these is the policy perspective, which has behind it the sheer weight of force of national political will and the structures of support attendant upon it. The policy perspective regards faiths as 'repositories' of resources of use to wider society, including staff, relationships, buildings and funding. In this 'story', faiths proffer human capital (staff, volunteers, members), social capital (networks of trust and reciprocity), physical capital (community buildings and venues) and financial capital (collections, subscriptions, donations). It is a perspective which in general terms and at first glance is highly positive about faiths in public space and is associated with a whole range of new opportunities for faiths to contribute and engage. Gone are the days of faiths seeking to influence the public realm from a parallel space, racing to keep up and calling across the divide with the faith-based equivalent of loud hailers and banners. Faiths now are invited in to sit at the policy table at national, regional, local and neighbourhood levels.

This appears to reflect a new set of attitudes amongst policy-makers towards the relationship between government and faiths and between faiths and the public table, which actively welcomes them as important actors in civil society. In this way there is a new idealism about faiths which admits them to the public realm after a sustained period of diminished relevance characterised by notions of the secular polis.

Contrarily, and at the same time, the policy perspective is also highly instrumentalist in its view of faith communities as 'useful' because of what they can 'produce' or 'provide'. It understands faiths as a general additional resource in an otherwise secular context. Thus the policy aim of faith engagement is to provide services, build community cohesion and improve governance. From this perspective the 'faithfulness' of 'faith communities' is of secondary and limited (or even no) significance.

There are a number of problems with this. First, the policy perspective assumes that faiths are somehow places or spaces in which activities occur that are all, to some degree or another, orientated towards these desired policy goals. There is a perception that there is a happy coincidence in one way or another of the aims of policy and the broader activities of faiths. From this perspective the role of faiths is seen as a simple matter of harnessing what is already coincidentally supportive and tying it into the wider context more directly.

This also suggests that there is a relationship between all the parts of faith communities, for example, between worshipping communities and the wider activities undertaken in their name, and that at the bottom line everybody in a faith community is turned in one way or another towards the goals outlined in policy. This gives no account of the diversity within and between faith traditions and of the contests and debates which inhere. Yet it is often the case that faith-based community activities have an arms length relationship with the worshipping communities associated with them. For example, many faith-based projects, even where they started as initiatives directly arising from congregations, become dissociated, even divorced, from these roots as they grow and expand. Often by the time they come to the attention of others outside of faiths they have travelled some considerable distance from the community of worshippers whose regular communion is a separate matter.

The policy perspective also assumes that religious organisations naturally contribute to the formation of networks, such as local and regional interfaith forums or national bodies like the Faith Based Regeneration Network (www.fbrn.org.uk). These are seen as an expression of a greater strategic engagement with issues of governance, for example through faith leaders sitting as representatives of a 'faith sector' in public partnerships such as community boards. But this implies a linearity and 'directedness' within faith communities which empirical evidence suggests is unlikely to be the case (e.g., see Furbey et al., 2006). In particular the assumption that there is continuity between the worshipping community and the rest is contested. It is frequently the case that there are one or two seats allocated in such bodies, which need somehow to represent up to nine faith traditions across large geographical areas.

While this is a problem for others outside of faiths, too, it raises questions about whether 'faith' can be thought of as a sector in the way that those others often are. Is the representation of faiths at the public table of the same kind as that bought forward by business, for example? Can its 'interests' be thus garnered and articulated?

At the same time the policy perspective depends upon the assumption that engagement with faiths will result in the emergence of leaders and representatives, as they are 'called forth' into processes of civil society and governance such as participation in neighbourhood boards and LSPs. This assumption may be misleading because it takes no account of the power and capacity differentials between faith traditions. Indeed, whilst engagement may be relatively easy for a large, highly organised and well-resourced faith tradition like Anglican Christians, for smaller traditions such as Jains, Baha'i or Zoroastrians, involvement may take a very different character.

Another implication of the policy perspective is that 'single faith' communities will naturally journey towards inter- and multi-faith engagements as they network with each other. While this might be the aim of policies for community cohesion – the bridging of faiths between and beyond themselves – there is evidence that faiths might bond without bridging (see Furbey et al., 2006) and that this relationship building and promotion of religious pluralism may not always, or even often, result. Sometimes, especially where individual traditions are tightly bonded within themselves, their engagement outside is more limited. Far from building community cohesion, this is more likely to result in fragmentation and tension.

More generally, policy as a 'top down' exercise may be problematic. While policy-makers expect that faiths will be in tune with their aspirations, faiths themselves may be more focused on the extent to which *they* can access *government* resources. Such a reversal of perspective is likely in a context of the ever-extended mixed economy of welfare in which faiths are increasingly asked to participate. An especial issue for some faith traditions, too, is that buildings can become as much of a burden as an asset, as in the case of the Church of England, given the costs involved in maintenance, renovation and adaptation, especially of 'heritage' buildings (Finneron and Dinham, 2002).

The faith perspective

The faith perspective provides some interesting responses to such dilemmas and debates and stands in contrast to the policy perspective in that it starts from the stand point of faiths themselves. In doing so it challenges many of its assumptions while at the same time promoting other issues and concerns as important. What is striking is that such a perspective means that faith itself is made central as a motivating force for engagement and this distinguishes the role of faiths from any other actor. This gives redress to the persistent, if unconscious, exclusion of faith *as belief* from the matrix of engagement. While it is possible, perhaps likely, that a policy perspective makes assumptions about a coincidence of policy goals and those of faiths, a faiths perspective can, on the other hand, challenge this.

One of the key concerns of a faiths perspective is that people of faith engage in the public on their own terms and for their own reasons. Contrary to the instrumentalism of the policy story, a faith angle is interested in what motivates people of faith to engage from the perspective of that faith itself. While there might be a coincidence of the goals and aspirations of policy and faiths, it is by no means essential or necessary and where it overlaps this is most likely a result of happenstance rather than design. Thus there is no necessary, or even obvious, connection between faith activity and the policies which aim to harness them.

This also challenges the assumption of a relationship between those who believe or worship and those who are also, or instead, members of faith-based organisations, or active as community networkers. There is a recognition that these links are contingent and situated. Similarly, it is not taken for granted that those engaged in faith leadership and representation have broad and deep connections with the faiths from which they come. There is a more subtle understanding, sometimes one which is tense, that leaders and representatives cannot assume that they have authority vested in them simply because they occupy positions at the top of a hierarchy or at a point of intersection with other actors. This means that it is a perspective which is not premised upon the existence of a coherent and structured faith organisation, nor on a postulated faith 'sector'. Rather, it suggests that the notion of a 'faith sector' is essentially a discursive construction of policy-makers whose need is to 'call forth' structures which are effective and visible in response to policy. Just as Henry Kissinger wanted to know who to call when he wanted to speak to Europe, so too policy-makers would prefer the convenience of a 'one stop shop' for faiths. But faiths themselves are likely to see it otherwise.

This perspective takes as its focus, therefore, faith itself. It sees places and spaces of faith primarily in terms of belief, worship and fellowship rather than as repositories of resources which can be deployed in the direction of policy goals. Faiths may undertake work in projects, associations, networks, partnerships, or any combination of these. They will probably produce leaders and representatives in public spaces. But their goals are highly differentiated and derive from the primary fact of being in or of faith. 'Goals' may therefore relate to the extension of faiths evangelistically. Or they may pursue social justice and human rights. Others might seek to meet immediate community needs such as shelter, food and comfort. Some might be politically critical.

At the same time, even where goals *are* linked to public policy, it should not be assumed that they share the same motivations, logics and modes of action. In some cases, faiths may not be externally oriented at all. Apparently similar goals may in fact be predominantly or entirely interior, focusing on the relationships, fellowship, prayer life or spirituality encountered. Thus, where it happens, participation in the public realm is understood more as the 'outworking of faith' than the coupling of faith to public policy.

But the faith perspective poses a challenge to the policy one in this way too. The idea of faith brings with it an explicit debate about values – and the possibility of conflict between values. Such debates may bring to the table values and perspectives that are usually set aside for reasons of politics, for example about the redistributive aspects of government policy. Policy-makers and practitioners may be unrehearsed in the art of discussing values, especially where explicit reference is made to faith as well. At the same time, it should not be assumed that values are not important to policy-makers, but there is clearly a gap between, for example, the idea of a public service ethos and the faith position taken as motivation for public action. This vocalisation may be one of the distinctive contributions which faiths make as they participate in the public realm, though there is frequently embarrassment at the mention of faith by people of faith in public forums, even where their participation is long standing.

In these ways, perhaps faiths have within them the capacity positively to introduce 'troubling issues' (Newman, 2007) into public space, many of which may illuminate the constructed nature of policy-makers' own perspectives, for example around the conduct of formal meetings, practices of informal networking, matters of status and personal relations. They may also bring to the table challenging meta-perspectives which are unfamiliar in public space. How will this contribute to people's sense of happiness? What is the faith perspective on how to produce the 'good' society? How does love and compassion come into this? What does faith imply for social justice?

The partnership perspective

The last of these perspectives is focused on the partnerships which arise in public space in response to initiatives and needs, and which increasingly include faiths. This perspective is framed in the assumptions of 'new local corporatism' (Lowndes and Sullivan, 2004), which draws together a range of actors in relation to particular initiatives or activities to which they all can contribute, despite and often *because* of the differing values, practices and outlooks they bring. It is seen as extending or 'topping up' community participation and representation. The partnership perspective assumes that partnerships can be divided into naturally occurring 'segments' – the public sector segment (the elected local council and other agencies like health and police); the business segment (local companies, 'chambers of commerce' and privatised providers of services) and the community segment (including 'not for profit' service providers, self-help and community action projects and citizen groups). Sitting in the 'community' segment, faith is included as one of a wider range of actors in community planning and action. To this extent it is something of a surprise to many partners to find faiths turning up at the table, even though some faith-based organisations have been involved in partnerships over long periods of time and are experienced in their participation.

As relative newcomers, an important function of faiths in partnerships can be to challenge the hold of professionalised 'voluntary organisations' upon community representation (though many faith-based activities already understand themselves as existing within this professionalised domain). In this sense faiths may catalyse what has been called elsewhere the 'renegotiation of the public imaginary' (see Weller in Dinham and Lowndes, 2008). At the same time, in some of the most disadvantaged areas, such voluntary organisations may be notable by their absence while faiths are still there. For example, the Church of England's parish system means that the local vicar is often the only 'community representative' left on some run-down housing estates. He or she may play a key role in partnership activity in such areas.

But partnership often assumes that partners will come together on equal terms in collective endeavours. Yet we know that differences in capacity and skills for engagement are significant even within faiths, let alone between traditions and beyond them. The largest, most organised and best resourced faiths may be experienced and effective in their engagements in formal processes of partnership. But smaller faiths and those which are newer to Britain may have a harder time being seen and heard. The partnership perspective is capable of glossing over these differences and often ruthlessly assumes a language and ethos which is aggressively businesslike and formal. While faiths themselves would not want to participate in an *un*-businesslike way, at the same time their 'logics' may differ from others in terms of their 'whole human' views of the world and this can be reflected in practices and thought worlds which challenge other logics.

Contests and debates

So the question of faith at the public table is controversial, to say the least. Their very presence is sometimes disputed. The concepts and language used by the various partners are often disorientating and sometimes confuse. And each debate is handled differently by each of the participants and interests involved.

This means that, though the strands in the public and policy context can be set out and unpicked with reference to documents and positions in government, the relationship between them and the questions they raise are far more problematic. The potential for major controversy arises from the different starting points of the various actors on the stage of faith-based engagement in the public realm. There is no one story, only a number of perspectives. Thrown into the mix too, are a welter of further complicating dimensions: the range of faith traditions and their differing views and beliefs; intergenerational and gender differences; the intersection of ethnicity and faith, and the distinctions between them; the relationship between the local and the global in a so-called war on terror; methodological and epistemological differences between those trying to research, reflect upon and understand faiths in public space; and the relationship between disciplines and sectors in doing so. This book seeks not to synthesise these perspectives, but to 'surface' them in an attempt to unravel the tangle of issues and challenges.

It is amongst these tangles that faith engagement in the 'public' can also be understood as a critical case in the renegotiation of boundaries and processes between the state and civil society and between the public, private and personal. This analysis of faith engagement is not intended to suggest that faiths are a problem at the public 'table'. On the contrary, the controversies which pertain may actually prove to be a positive phenomenon, opening up new and fruitful debates and ways of thinking. It is these controversies, and the ways in they are played out in public space, with which this book is concerned. The surfacing of different perspectives and controversies, and the interrogation of the tensions between them, is a vital first step in seeking to harness the potential creativity of faiths at the public table. It is to these controversies that we now turn.

2
Who? Faiths, Diversity and Localism

It would be convenient, to say the least, if faiths were all the same. For a start, I would not need to have written this book, or at least it would have taken fewer pages. More importantly, governments and policy-makers would have a much easier time engaging with faiths because they would quickly be able to work out where they are coming from and what they are about. But actually, like most things in the social, faiths are far more complex than that. Understanding this is a difficult business, because, since they are so diversely active and motivated, it is hard to get a handle on which faiths are doing what, where and why. Yet it is precisely their diversity that makes them valuable in civil society and in the making of public policy because, at their best, they respond to and reflect the widely varied views, hopes and needs of people in communities in the everyday and in all their colourful differences.

Policy on the other hand has a tendency to homogenise faiths, as we have seen, and often talks about them as though there is one observable and graspable 'thing' called 'faith' which represents something of value to society. Thus in the UK, the *Working Together* report (Home Office, 2004) refers to 'faith communities' five times in the foreword alone and makes 'recommendations to faith communities' (ibid., p. 5) and later to 'faith bodies' (ibid., p. 5), talks about 'faith experts' (ibid., p. 22), encourages engagement in 'faith awareness training' (ibid., p. 5) and wants the active pursuit of 'faith literacy' (ibid., p. 7). None of these terms are explained. In the US, too, the 'faith-based initiative' is put forward as though everybody knows what 'faith-based' means. But none of these terms is defined or even discussed and their contentiousness is unacknowledged. The implication is that policy-makers think these terms will do – that they sufficiently grasp what faith *is* and what faiths *are* for the purposes of social and public policy. This in turn suggests that their engagement with faiths can be insensitive to the lived experiences of the people in them. This can have a damaging effect on people in faith communities, and in faith bodies or organisations and limit the very usefulness of faiths to which policy-makers aspire.

Any attempt at understanding faith in the public space of civil society and public policy should start then, with the assumption that faiths are diverse. There are a number of approaches and sources for understanding this diversity in the UK. The Canadian sources differ methodologically somewhat, and I make some attempt at presenting them here by way of shoring up the general case for diversity. In the US, the First Amendment preoccupation with separation of religion and state means that public data are both scarce and sceptically received, though there are some sample-based data which I also present here, for the same purpose.

All of these data are illuminating in making the case that faiths are highly diverse and are understood and 'researched' in differentiated ways from place to place. At the same time, I suggest that the UK example in particular stands as a general lesson that diversity of faiths must be taken into account if policy is to respond to and engage with faiths to best effect, here and elsewhere in the developed world.

So where are the data? First there is census material, which locates the 'where' and 'how many' of faiths. This applies in Canada and the UK, though not in the US where no 'religions' question is asked and where we must rely on smaller sample-based studies, often conducted by faiths themselves. This highlights the contested nature of faiths at the public table in the first place which results in debates about whether it is valuable to measure it or not. It also demonstrates how variable are the research approaches which are used, making comparability a serious challenge and difficulty.

It should also be noted that the census data on religion are new to the UK where it has only been included since 2001 (except in Northern Ireland where the politics are different). Then there are other sample-based data, historically and more current. Some of this seeks to do the work of a census but via statistical inference and projection, as in the case of the US data which I use here. Others focus more on particular areas and incidences to illuminate religiosity more widely, as in the case of the Anglican data I use subsequently. What emerges is a tale of the sheer diversity of faiths and the potential value of that diversity to civil society if public policy 'handles' it appropriately. For faiths, that almost certainly means a degree of localism, for that is where the energy and action is primarily to be found. This is a matter for discussion in Chapter 7, where I discuss faith in relation to new forms of governance, though the argument begins here.

Faiths in the UK

The religious make-up of the UK is extremely complicated and very diverse. The political landscape which forms its context is one part of this complexity. The history and traditions of the four nations that make up Great Britain, England, Wales, Scotland and Northern Ireland are distinctive and the religious landscape reflects this. In their enormous undertaking, the *Religions in the UK Directory*, the Multi-Faith Centre at the University of Derby, UK, surveys this. It begins by acknowledging that 'the United Kingdom has a Christian inheritance that remains the predominant religious tradition' (Weller, 2007, p. 21). At the same time it emphasises that the UK has '...a greater degree of religious diversity than is found in any other country of the European Union' (ibid., p. 21). This reflects a history of empire and immigration stretching back, not just to the Victorian and colonial era of the nineteenth century, but also way back into the ancestral histories of the Romans (who first brought Christianity to Britain), the Normans whose invasion in 1066 led to the immigration (and later expulsion) of Jews from Spain and Portugal, then the Vikings and the Saxons (see ibid., pp. 23–6). In particular the events of the Tudor and Elizabethan era in England and the rise of Protestantism in Western Europe produced a uniquely English religious settlement wherein the Church of England was established as distinct from the then dominant Catholic Church of Rome, with the Monarch at its head as well as at the head of state. At the same time, the English story is one of the acceptability of what was originally called 'dissent' (from Rome) and is now better described as 'diversity'.

It is in this context that religious diversity and pluralism have grown in the UK even while secularism has been argued during the twentieth century as a force for the marginalisation and eventual annihilation of religion in the public sphere. Indeed it is argued that 'the trend towards a greater religious diversity is unlikely to be reversed' (Davie, 1999, p. 3) and that, for example, 'churches...have maintained a persistently high public profile' (ibid., p. 2). That secularism appears to have lost the argument is suggested by evidence of faithfulness and religiosity in abundance (see Furbey et al., 2006). Indeed, it has been observed in the British context that 'relatively few British people have opted out of religion altogether: out and out atheists are rare' (Davie, 1999, p. 2).

The census data support this. In 2001 for the first time, the England, Wales and Scotland census included questions about religious affiliation alongside that in Northern Ireland where a question on religion was asked in previous censuses. Prior to this 'there had been no generally comparable data available on the size of the various religious groups in the UK' (Weller, 2007, p. 26). Earlier data had been gathered only from voluntary surveys such as the English Churches Census conducted by the Christian organisation MARC Europe (now the Christian Research Association). In addition, there had been a number of 'small sample-based studies on such questions as the nature and extent of religious belief, affiliation and practice' (ibid., p. 27). This is reflected in the US context too, where voluntary surveys, though extensive, take the place of a national 'religions' question in the census. This contrasts with Canada, however, where a 'religions' question has been asked since 1971. The focus there and in the UK is on religious affiliation and not on belief or belonging in particular. This is an important distinction which I shall return to later. It is also noteworthy that the Canadian data take the exploration a little further by using a 20 per cent sample of the whole census to dig down into issues about gender and ethnicity.

All the 'faiths' data are highly debated, however, and it has been observed that 'sociologists are always suspicious of statistics...even more [so] of religious statistics' (Davie, 1999, p. 45). The main issue is that measures which might be considered at first glance unambiguous, such as 'membership' or 'affiliation', may mean very different things to different people. This 'meanings' problem is a challenge for all research into the social, it might be argued, for the social is complex. But, as we have seen in the previous chapter, faith is amongst the most contentious of categories at so many levels. After all, as we have noted, politics and religion are the two topics of conversation best avoided at the dinner table – at least if the host wants the guests to depart in harmony.

There is also 'grey' research in the UK and in our two other Western, English speaking comparisons, often commissioned by churches and other traditions themselves to identify and demonstrate their activities. One of the largest examples of this in the UK context is the Church of England, which continues to publish its own account of religious activity under five headings: church attendance, education, ministry, community involvement, and church buildings.

The Church of England data – one example of 'grey' data

A brief account of this data illuminates both of the sorts of 'grey' research which are available and of the trends they indicate. In terms of church attendance and visits, its data indicate that

> 1.7 million people take part in a Church of England service each month, a level that has been maintained since 2000. Around one million participate each Sunday. More than 2.8 million participate in a Church of England service on Christmas Day or Christmas Eve. Forty three per cent of the population attends church at Christmas, rising to 48 per cent in London and, nationally, 22 per cent among those of non-Christian faiths. In 2005 47 per cent of adults attended a church or place of worship for a memorial service for someone who has died and 21 per cent were seeking a quiet space. Both these proportions are increases on 37 per cent and 19 per cent respectively in 2003 and 29 per cent and 12 per cent respectively in 2001. Eighty six per cent of the population visits a church or place of worship in the course of a year for reasons ranging from participating in worship to attending social events or simply wanting a quiet space. Every year, around 12.5 million people visit Church of England cathedrals, including three hundred thousand pupils on school visits. Three of England's top five historic 'visitor attractions' are York Minster, Canterbury Cathedral and Westminster Abbey. (Church Statistics 2003/04 and 2004/05, www.cofe.anglican.org)

On education, the Church of England's research shows that seven in ten of the population agrees that Church of England schools have a positive role in educating the nation's children. One in four primary schools and one in sixteen secondary schools in England are Church of England schools. Approximately one million pupils are educated in more than 4,700 Church of England schools.

In terms of Ministers, the Church of England has more than 27,000 licensed ministers including 9,000 paid clergy, 3,000 non-stipendiary ministers, 10,000 lay Readers, 5,000 active retired clergy and 11,000 chaplains in colleges, universities, hospitals, schools, prisons and the armed forces.

Regarding community involvement, the Church of England claims that

> more people do unpaid work for church organisations than any other organisation. Eight per cent of adults undertake voluntary work for church organisations while sixteen per cent belong to religious or church organisations. A quarter of regular churchgoers (among both

Anglicans and other Christians separately) are involved in voluntary community service outside the church. Churchgoers overall contribute 23.2 million hours voluntary service each month in their local communities outside the church. (Church Statistics 2003/04 and 2004/05, www.cofe.anglican.org)

The Church of England also claims to provide activities outside church worship in the local community for 515,000 children and young people (aged under 16 years) and 38,000 young people (aged 16 to 25 years). It also claims that more than 136,000 volunteers run children and young-people activity groups sponsored by the Church of England outside church worship.

Finally, in terms of church buildings, the Church of England's research claims that 46 per cent of British people think that public money in the form of central taxation, local taxation, the National Lottery or English Heritage should be 'primarily' responsible for providing funding to maintain churches and chapels, which they claim indicates a strong foundation of support for church 'presence'. Forty-five per cent of the country's Grade I listed (heritage or protected) buildings are parish churches maintained by the Church of England. There are at least £378 million of major church repairs outstanding, 87 per cent of which are for listed churches.

Faith as persistent?

The Church of England's data are highly positively presented, as might be expected, and shows the church as a healthy going concern for religiosity in the UK. It suggests that there is a fairly robust, or at least a significant degree, of faith engagement in the UK, at least amongst Anglicans. At the same time, 'Statistically there can be little doubt about the trends; they go downwards' (Davie, 1999, p. 52). Davie suggests that this can be accounted for in terms of three big changes in the UK since the Second World War: first, there have been economic and social transformations which have recast people in terms of consumption rather than production so that 'not only do we purchase our material requirements; we also then shop around for our spiritual needs' (ibid., p. 39); second, there have been demographic changes which have 'produced a constantly evolving environment in which the churches are called to minister...' (ibid., p. 22); third, and included in this, is immigration, resulting in a pluralism which is noted to be 'an urban phenomenon and differs from region to region' (ibid., p. 25). But in terms of the stories which accompany the statistics, what is also noted is the persistence of belief, attributed in the case of the Church of England at least in part to the parochial structure which is observed to be 'crucial in this respect, that it continues to give the Church of England a unique foothold in English society' (ibid., p. 55).

This foothold is not available in the same way to other faiths and in the other countries looked at, however. Nevertheless, faith appears to be present more widely and across other traditions too. This is clear in the census material in both the UK and Canada, which itself indicates a convincingly strong 'faith presence' and what we can say with a degree of certainty is that most people remain believers, if not 'belongers' (to borrow Davie's memorable phrase).

It is, though, 'important to recognise that the census questions were to do with religious affiliation...rather than saying anything about either religious belief or religious practice' (Weller, 2007, p. 27) and the distinction between affiliation and belief is very important. This relates to debates about what faith *is* and how it is expressed (which are discussed in the next chapter). It is also a reason why the data across the piece shows that there is a crucial mismatch between the statistics relating to religious practice and those which indicate belief levels. Davie observes that

> ...on the one hand, variables concerned with feelings, experience and the more numinous aspects of religious belief demonstrate considerable persistence...; on the other, those which measure religious orthodoxy, ritual participation and institutional attachment display an undeniable degree of secularisation...(Davie, 1999, pp. 4–5)

This tends to suggest 'high levels of belief and low levels of practice' (ibid., p. 5), though there are exceptions to the trend, for example in Northern Ireland and Scotland, where there are manifested 'markedly higher levels of religious practice than almost all other European countries' (ibid., p. 14). But this general phenomenon of 'belief without belonging' is not merely an academic question, of interest only in abstract terms. In many ways it goes to the very root of what makes faiths valuable or otherwise, in civil society terms, to public policy and to its constructors. For example, if governments rely on indications of high levels of affiliation as a basis for mobilising policies for active communities, they may find that the foot soldiers they envisaged do not come forward because the 'faith community' does not really have the 'members' or numbers expected. Affiliation may suggest identification with an articulated 'body' of some kind, but in practice it may turn out to mean something rather different – a 'sense' of belonging to something rather vague and in a rather vague way which is not translatable into civil society outcomes.

Nevertheless, we cannot ignore the stark facts of the sheer volume of faithfulness which has been reported, whatever we might then make of it. In the UK, 45,162,895 people reported a religious affiliation in the 2001 census. This represents 76.8 per cent of the total population, of which the vast majority is Christian, followed (numerically) by Muslims, Hindus, Sikhs, Jews, Buddhists, Jains, Baha'i and Zoroastrians, as Table 1 shows.

UK census analysis also reveals an interesting story in relation to those professing faiths other than the nine 'major' traditions, or who state that they have no religion. There were 9,103,727 respondents claiming this position (15.5 per cent) while a further 4,288,719 made no response at all (7.3 per cent). At the same time, 39,127 respondents in England and Wales felt prompted (in response to an internet campaign) to indicate affiliation to the 'Jedi' or 'Jedi Knights'. A further 58 said they were 'free thinkers', 8,296 were 'Humanists', 3 'internationalists', 37 'rationalists', 104 'realists', 11 'secularists' and 269 'Heathen'. This adds up to what has been described as 'three dimensional [religion]: Christian, secular and religiously plural' (Beckford et al., 2006, p. 7).

Table 1   Religion responses in the UK 2001 census

Religion	England	Scotland	Wales	Northern Ireland	UK total	UK%
Buddhist	139,046	6,830	5,407	533	151,816	0.3
Christian	35,251,244	3,294,545	2,087,242	1,446,386	42,079,417	71.6
Hindu	546,982	5,564	5,439	825	558,810	1.0
Jewish	257,671	6,448	2,256	365	266,740	0.5
Muslim	1,524,887	42,557	21,739	1,943	1,591,126	2.7
Sikh	327,343	6,572	2,015	219	336,149	0.6
Other	142,811	26,974	6,909	1,143	178,837	0.3
Total	38,190,984	3,389,490	2,131,007	1,451,414	45,162,895	76.8
No Religion	7,171,332	1,394,460	537,935	*	9,103,727	15.5
Not stated	3,776,515	278,061	234,143	*	4,288,719	7.3
No religion/ not stated	10,947,847	1,672,521	772,078	233,853	13,626,299	23.2

Note: * in Northern Ireland separate statistics for those of 'No religion' and 'not stated' are not available.

Source: Table reproduced from Interfaith Update 21:3, the newsletter of the Inter Faith Network for the United Kingdom. Due to rounding percentages may not total 100 per cent.

These levels of religious affiliation are reflected too in Canada where 24,738,945 people reported positively in their national census in the same year (see Table 2). This represents the higher figure of 83.5 per cent of the total population, of which, as in the UK, the majority is Christian. In Canada religious diversity goes further within the Christian tradition in particular, however, and this makes for a significantly more differentiated Christian 'count'. Indeed, the census includes 63 Christian denominations, of which four are Catholic (Roman, Ukrainian, Polish and 'other') and 59 are Protestant.[1] This reflects the fact that, unlike the UK, Canada has no established church and the Protestant and Nonconformist traditions are far more diverse within themselves. In general, though, Christians overall constitute the largest religious group in Canada by a large margin, as in the UK, followed numerically by Muslims, Jews, Buddhists, Hindus, Sikhs, other Eastern religions (including Zoroastrianism, and Taoism and Confucianism from China and Japan) and 'other religions'. The 'mixes' are similar with Christians and Muslims forming the largest faith traditions in each country. The statistics for the other faiths also follow very comparable trajectories, though if anything Canada demonstrates greater levels of affiliation (83.5 per cent compared to 76.8 per cent in the UK) and slightly broader diversity in terms of minority faiths (6.2 per cent compared to 5.4 per cent in the UK). Whichever way we look at it 'it is evident that between two-thirds and three-quarters of British people indicate fairly consistently that they believe in some sort of God' (Davie, 1999, p. 75)

Table 2   Religion responses in the Canadian 2001 census

Religion/Tradition	All Canada	All Canada %
Catholic	12,936,905	43.6
Protestant	8,654,850	29.2
Christian Orthodox	479,620	1.6
Christian not included elsewhere	780,450	2.6
Muslim	579,640	1.9
Jewish	329,995	1.1
Buddhist	300,345	1.01
Hindu	297,200	1.0
Sikh	278,410	0.9
Eastern religions	37,550	0.1
Other religions	63,975	0.2
No religious affiliation	4,900,090	16.5

Source: Data derived from the table 'Population by religion, province and territory' (2001 Census) Ottawa: Statistics Canada, 13 May 2003. 2001 Census of Canada. Catalogue number 97F0022XCB2001005.

and this is also true of Canada. At the same time, overall there are also significant reports of 'no religious affiliation' of which higher levels are reported in the UK (23.2 per cent) than in Canada (16.5 per cent).

In the US, there is no federal or governmental census question on religions and the data are drawn instead from independent non-governmental sample-based studies, the most widely used, trusted and consistent of which are analysed and disseminated by the Association of Statisticians of American Religious Bodies (ASARB). A useful source is the Glenmary Research Centre in Nashville, Tennessee, whose primary goals are 'to collect and maintain databases of current conditions and trends, cultivate a research library for use by Glenmary priests and brothers and ... design and conduct specific studies of an applied nature' (see www.glenmary.org). It conducts the Religious Congregations and Membership Survey (RCMS) which presents data reported by 149 religious bodies that participated in a study sponsored by ASARB. It originally invited 285 religious bodies in the US to participate, including 139 Christian denominations, two specially defined groups of independent Christian churches, Jewish and Islamic figures; and counts of temples for six Eastern religions.

Groups were asked to provide data for the year 2000, by county, on the numbers of congregations, members, adherents and average weekly attendance. The minimum return necessary to participate was the number of congregations in the county. Guidelines were provided as to the definitions of congregations, members, adherents and attendees, but, as we have seen elsewhere, meanings are vexed and contentious. The definition guidelines given were

Congregations: Any churches, mosques, synagogues, temples or other local meeting places (as defined by each religious body).

Members: Individuals with full membership status (as defined by each religious body).

Adherents: All members, including full members, their children and the estimated number of other participants who are not considered members. If unavailable, the study will estimate the number of adherents from the known number of members. (The RCMS estimation procedure computes what percentage of the county's population a group's membership comprises. This percentage is applied to the country's population for those under age 14. The membership total and percentage of children under 14 are added together for the estimated adherent figure. This procedure was done for 67 groups.)

Attendees: Average weekly worship attendance. (www.glenmary.org)

Because the study *invites* participation, not every group chooses to participate, or is able to do so. The Glenmary Research Centre notes that most of the largest groups do participate, so that 'the authors are confident in saying that the vast majority of people associated with a congregation are represented within the study' (see www.glenmary.org). There are, however, an additional 14 groups that reported more than 100,000 inclusive members to the Yearbook of American and Canadian Churches that did not participate in the Religions and Congregations study in 2000 (all of which are Protestant or Free Church Christian), many of which are historically African American religious bodies. The absence of these bodies must be considered when studying religious adherence in general in the US.

The study also provides estimates of both Jewish and Muslim numbers and, overall, finds 140,000,000 'religious adherents' claimed by 149 religious bodies across the US. It indicates that half (50.2 per cent) of all Americans are associated with one of the 149 religious groups who participated in this study. It finds that the three largest religious bodies in the US are all Christians, distributed between Catholics (62,000,000), Southern Baptists (20,000,000) and United Methodists (10,000,000). The reporting bodies are classified in the study as shown in Table 3.

The Religious Congregations and Membership Survey 2000 in the US, from which this table is derived, is the fifth in a series of such studies dating from the 1950s (Bradley et al., 1992; Johnson, Picard and Quinn,

Table 3   Overall faith traditions in the US religions and congregations survey 2000

Faith tradition	Number of adherents	Number of congregations
Protestant	66,000,000	222,000
Catholic	62,000,000	22,000
Jewish	6,000,000	3,727
Mormon	4,000,000	12,000
Muslim	1,600,000	1,000
Eastern Christians	1,000,000	2,000
Eastern religions	150,000*	4,000
Unitarian Universalist Association	180,000	1,000

Note: *The study notes that 'Many Eastern religions do not have a concept of formal membership in local congregations, so the adherent figure is not completely comparable to the other religious families'.

Source: Table derived from data published by the Glenmary Research Centre Religious Congregations and Membership Survey 2000.

1974; Jones et al., 2002; Quinn et al., 1982; Whitman and Trimble, 1956). As with other faiths data, the series has certain limitations, primary among which is that the data refer to participating bodies only, not to all religious adherents in the US. That said, the main findings of the study are summarised by Grammich in the following terms:

> Evangelical Protestants are nearly twice as prevalent in the South as elsewhere. Mainline Protestants are more prominent in the North Central states. There are more Catholics in the Northeast than all other groups combined. Catholics and Jews are about twice as prevalent in the Northeast as elsewhere. (Grammich, 2004, p. 5)

Muslim mosque and adherent data were also estimated from a survey conducted for the Faith Communities Today project of Hartford Seminary (see Jones et al., 2002, pp. 536–37). These data indicate there are 1,559,294 Muslim adherents in 1,209 mosques nationwide. Grammich notes that 'other estimates of the US Muslim population range from 1.5 to 9 million' (Grammich, 2004, p. 23). RCMS 2000 indicates that there are Muslim adherents and mosques in all 50 states of the US.

The 'Other Faiths' category in RCMS 2000 includes seven non-Christian traditions – Baha'i, Buddhist, Hindu, Jain, Sikh, Tao and Zoroastrian – and these were not previously included in this series of surveys. Of these, only the Baha'i, with 1,198 assemblies and 146,756 adherents, provided data for numbers of adherents. Religious congregation counts by county for these bodies were provided by the Pluralism Project of Harvard University. Grammich notes

> 1,656 Buddhist centres are in 359 counties that are home to 89 per cent of the U.S. Asian population (and 59 per cent of the total population). 629 Hindu centres are in 206 counties that are home to 78 per cent of the Indian population (and 47 per cent of the total population). 211 Sikh gurdwaras are in 118 counties that are home to 57 per cent of the Indian population (and 35 per cent of the total population). 92 Jain centers are in 71 counties that are home to 43 per cent of the Indian population (and 23 per cent of the total population). 38 Tao temples are in 24 counties that are home to 41 per cent of the Chinese population (and 12 per cent of the total population). (ibid., p. 24)

The nature of the data in the US makes it impossible to determine the exact levels of all religious adherence, and, as is the case in the UK and Canada, meanings are anyway debated. Some evidence suggests that the number of adherents reported in 2000 represents only two-thirds of the real population of religious adherents. Kosmin, Mayer and Keysar report that 80 per cent of US adults claimed religious affiliation in 2001. Davis and Smith (annual) report that 85 per cent of US adults claimed religious affiliation in 2000. Research by Cieslak, 1995, indicates that, at least in the case of the Catholic Church, survey estimates of religious adherence may overstate actual adherence by at least one-tenth.

Nevertheless, the data show that, despite the arguments of the strong secularisation theorists, religion in some definition or another remains a strong part of the everyday experiences of hundreds of millions of people in Western English speaking countries – and these are precisely the places where secularism most expected faith to decline. At the same time, they indicate that in the last half of the twentieth century there has been 'significant change in the cultural and religious composition of the UK' (Weller, 2007, p. 29) and this is reflected in Canada and the US, too. Of the UK in particular, this is a view echoed by Davie in her observation of 'the profound economic, social and political changes in British society that have taken place...' (Davie, 1999, p. 2). This has seen a major trend towards the diversification of faiths across the UK, though of its four nations England has the broadest and most numerous variety of religious traditions, while the Celtic nations have the highest levels of religious *practice*. While Christianity is by far the largest trad- ition, Islam is the biggest minority religious tradition in all four nations of the UK, and in the comparison countries of Canada and the US. This is highly pertinent in a global context where the relationship between Muslims and Christians is often constructed – and misconstrued – in terms of conflict and competition between the call to Godliness and the decadence of consumerism.

It should be noted, too, that the data do not always agree. The British Social Attitudes Survey and the European Values Survey show an appar- ent discrepancy from the UK census data so that '... self-identification with religion would seem to be less widespread than indicated' (Beckford et al., 2006, p. 7). Thus the British Social Attitudes Survey data seem to show that 41.5 per cent of respondents had 'no religion' (compared to 15.5 per cent in the UK Census and 16.5 per cent in the Canadian). Similarly, the European Values Survey reports that 12.6 per cent of respondents in the UK said religion was 'very important', 24.8 per cent said 'quite important', 33 per cent said 'not important' and 29.7 per cent said 'not at all' (Halman, 2001, p. 33).

At the same time, there are some specific cities and towns where the religious make-up differs considerably from the national profile. Thus the oldest established minority traditions in the UK are to be found in the seaports of Cardiff, London and Liverpool, whilst the industrial cities of Bradford and Leicester are enormously diverse as a result of Commonwealth immigration since the 1950s and 1960s. In Leicester, only 45 per cent of people identify themselves as Christian (compared with 71.6 per cent nationally); 15 per cent identified as Hindu, 11 per cent as Muslim and 17 per cent as of no religious affiliation (2001 Census, www.leicester.gov.uk). Including these 'pockets' of difference, therefore, 'the main concentrations of minority religions are found in the areas of greatest general population density, including London, the West Midlands, the Leicester–Nottingham area and the conurbations of the Pennines' (Weller, 2007, p. 29). At the same time, 'for all…[non-Christian]…religions the highest proportion of their regional populations is to be found in London, with the exception of the Sikhs whose share of the regional population is at its greatest in the West Midlands' (ibid., p. 29).

This suggests that the common perspective is that minority faiths are to be found primarily in the inner urban neighbourhoods of the major cities and, as has been observed, '" parallel lives" adequately describes their inter relationships' (see Cantle in Furbey et al., 2006, p. 7). However, there is an additional set of UK data approximating to 'neighbourhoods' which provides a systematic small-scale geographic analysis of the distribution of faiths across England, which is also instructive. This derives from the reallocation of the 2001 Census information to the 13,000 ecclesiastical parishes of the Church of England (see Wilkinson in Furbey et al., 2006, pp. 12–18). This analysis shows that just under 80 per cent of all parishes (or 'neighbourhoods') in England have some proportion of their population as people of other faiths than Christian, in contradiction to the suggestion that minority faiths are separated off somehow in urban areas and living 'parallel lives'. The distribution is given in Table 4.

Table 4 Distribution of population of faiths other than Christian in England

% other Faiths	No. of parishes	% all parishes
>0 to 1	4,371	35.6
>1 to 5	3,624	29.5
>5 to 10	637	5.2
>10 to 25	554	4.5
>25 to 50	227	1.9
>50	61	0.5
Total	9,474	
Total all parishes	12,264	77.20

The study notes that the 8.8 per cent of parishes with more than 10 per cent of their population as people of other faiths constitute 23 per cent of the total population. These data indicate the extensive dispersion and diversity of faiths in communities.

This contrasts with Weller's observation that 'overall, minority religious diversity can be seen to be an aspect in particular of city, metropolitan and large town life' (Weller, 2007) where the trend is clearly towards an urban concentration of faith diversity, as Table 5 demonstrates.

Though a close analysis by Wilkinson does acknowledge the overall trend towards urbanism which Weller has observed, it also digs a

Table 5   Top five areas of representation by faith tradition, UK

MUSLIM – top 5 areas of representation, UK	
London Borough of Tower Hamlets	36.4%
London Borough of Newham	24.3%
Blackburn and Darwen	19.4%
Bradford	16.1%
London Borough of Waltham Forest	15.1%
HINDU – top 5 areas of representation, UK	
London Borough of Harrow	19.6%
London Borough of Brent	17.2%
Leicester	14.7%
London Borough of Redbridge	7.8%
London Borough of Ealing	7.8%
SIKH – top 5 areas of representation, UK	
London Borough of Slough	9.1%
London Borough of Hounslow	8.6%
London Borough of Ealing	8.5%
Wolverhampton	7.6%
Sandwell	6.9%
BUDDHIST – top 5 areas of representation, UK	
London Borough of Westminster	13%
London Borough of Camden	13%
Royal London Borough of Kensington and Chelsea	11%
London Borough of Hackney	11%
Ribble Valley	11%
JEWISH – top 5 areas of representation, UK	
London Borough of Barnet	14.8%
Hertsmere	11.3%
London Borough of Harrow	6.3%
London Borough of Redbridge	6.2%
London Borough of Camden	5.6%

Source: Table derived from the Religions in the UK Directory 2007.

little deeper in demonstrating that the numbers of minority faiths are not the only factors in the diversity mix we are considering. The fact of any mix at all is also of interest and that it extends so widely, if not numerically, across so much of the UK is something to be noted by policy-makers.

The data have been assembled on the basis of the 44 dioceses of the Church of England, which between them provide a range of mainly urban, mixed urban and rural, and mainly rural contexts. The following graphs (see Figure 1) provide information for Wilkinson's own selection of five different dioceses in a study on faith and social capital (in which I was also involved), which I use here to indicate the diversity of patterns between them. They provide the religious composition of each parish within those dioceses with more than 10 per cent of the population coming from faiths other than Christian and are intended here as useful snapshots and evidence for the diversity of faiths' presence in a broader range of places than the 'urban and parallel' thesis allows.

Wilkinson observes from these data that

> ... across the five areas – and across the other diocesan areas – there is a similar pattern: Sikh and Hindu communities associate geographically with each other; Christian communities for historic reasons are present in all neighbourhoods; Jewish and Muslim communities generally do not inhabit the same neighbourhoods but Jewish communities *are* associated with Sikh and Hindu communities. In turn these latter communities tend to be located apart from the Muslim communities. (Wilkinson in Furbey et al., 2006, p. 13)

One striking message from this is that Muslims are living geographically more apart from all the other faiths than any other tradition. At the same time, their predominant co-location is with Christians, whose omnipresence in the UK, Canada and the US ensures it. This exposure could be regarded as the condition for the construction of tension between Muslims and Christians laid down in the fabric of social space. On the other hand, it could provide the basis on which understanding and cohesion are formed. Either way, diversity may appear to be an urban issue at first glance, and probably it primarily is. But Wilkinson's study suggests that it goes considerably further than the cities. There is much to be gleaned here for policy-makers in terms, especially, of community cohesion. I turn to these questions in Chapter 5.

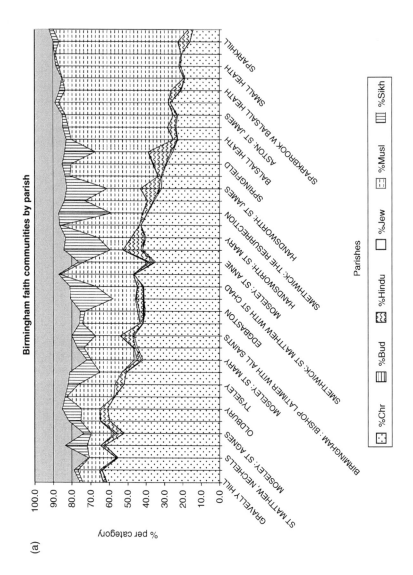

Birmingham faith communities by parish

(a)

% per category

Parishes

%Chr   %Bud   %Hindu   %Jew   %Musl   %Sikh

100.0
90.0
80.0
70.0
60.0
50.0
40.0
30.0
20.0
10.0
0.0

GRAVELLY HILL
ST MATTHEW, NECHELLS
MOSELEY: ST AGNES
OLDBURY
TYSELEY
MOSELEY: ST MARY
SMETHWICK: ST MATTHEW WITH ALL SAINTS
EDGBASTON
SMETHWICK: ST MATTHEW WITH ST CHAD
BIRMINGHAM: BISHOP LATIMER WITH ST MARY
MOSELEY: ST ANNE
HANDSWORTH: ST MARY
SMETHWICK: THE RESURRECTION
HANDSWORTH: ST JAMES
SPRINGFIELD
BALSALL HEATH
ASTON: ST JAMES
SPARKBROOK W BALSALL HEATH
SMALL HEATH
SPARKHILL

32

(b)

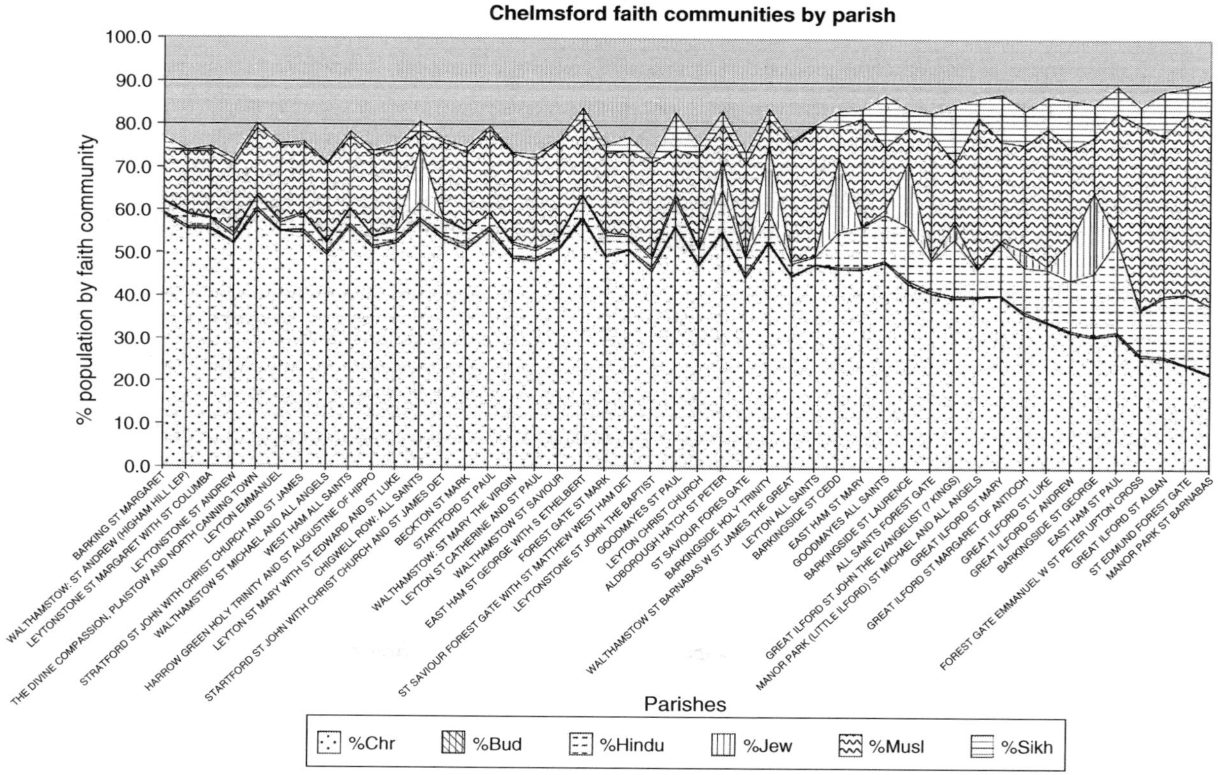
Chelmsford faith communities by parish
% population by faith community
100.0
90.0
80.0
70.0
60.0
50.0
40.0
30.0
20.0
10.0
0.0
BARKING ST MARGARET
WALTHAMSTOW: ST ANDREW (HIGHAM HILL LEP)
LEYTONSTONE ST MARGARET WITH ST COLUMBA
LEYTONSTONE ST ANDREW
THE DIVINE COMPASSION, PLAISTOW AND NORTH CANNING TOWN
LEYTON EMMANUEL
STRATFORD ST JOHN WITH CHRIST CHURCH AND ST JAMES
WALTHAMSTOW ST MICHAEL AND ALL ANGELS
WEST HAM ALL SAINTS
HARROW GREEN HOLY TRINITY AND ST AUGUSTINE OF HIPPO
LEYTON ST MARY WITH ST EDWARD AND ST LUKE
CHIGWELL ROW: ALL SAINTS
STARTFORD ST JOHN WITH CHRIST CHURCH AND ST JAMES DET
BECKTON ST MARK
STARTFORD ST PAUL
WALTHAMSTOW: ST MARY THE VIRGIN
LEYTON ST CATHERINE AND ST PAUL
WALTHAMSTOW ST SAVIOUR
EAST HAM ST GEORGE WITH S ETHELBERT
FOREST GATE ST MARK
ST SAVIOUR FOREST GATE WITH ST MATTHEW WEST HAM DET
LEYTONSTONE ST JOHN THE BAPTIST
GOODMAYES ST PAUL
LEYTON CHRIST CHURCH
ALDBOROUGH HATCH ST PETER
ST SAVIOUR FORES GATE
BARKINGSIDE HOLY TRINITY
WALTHAMSTOW ST BARNABAS W ST JAMES THE GREAT
LEYTON ALL SAINTS
BARKINGSIDE ST CEDD
EAST HAM ST MARY
GOODMAYES ALL SAINTS
BARKINGSIDE ST LAURENCE
ALL SAINTS FOREST GATE
GREAT ILFORD ST JOHN THE EVANGELIST (7 KINGS)
MANOR PARK (LITTLE ILFORD) ST MICHAEL AND ALL ANGELS
GREAT ILFORD ST MARY
GREAT ILFORD ST MARGARET OF ANTIOCH
GREAT ILFORD ST LUKE
GREAT ILFORD ST ANDREW
BARKINGSIDE ST GEORGE
EAST HAM ST PAUL
FOREST GATE EMMANUEL W ST PETER UPTON CROSS
GREAT ILFORD ST ALBAN
ST EDMUND FOREST GATE
MANOR PARK ST BARNABAS
Parishes
%Chr
%Bud
%Hindu
%Jew
%Musl
%Sikh

Continued

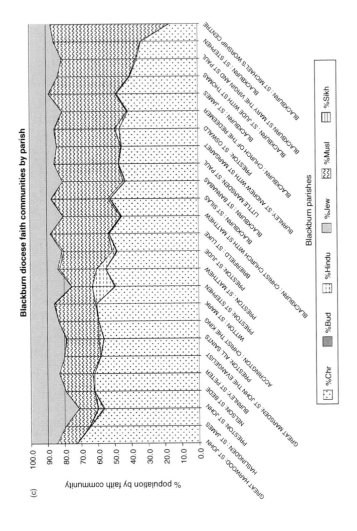

Blackburn diocese faith communities by parish

(c)

% population by faith community

Blackburn parishes

%Chr %Bud %Hindu %Jew %Musl %Sikh

34

St Albans faith communities by parish

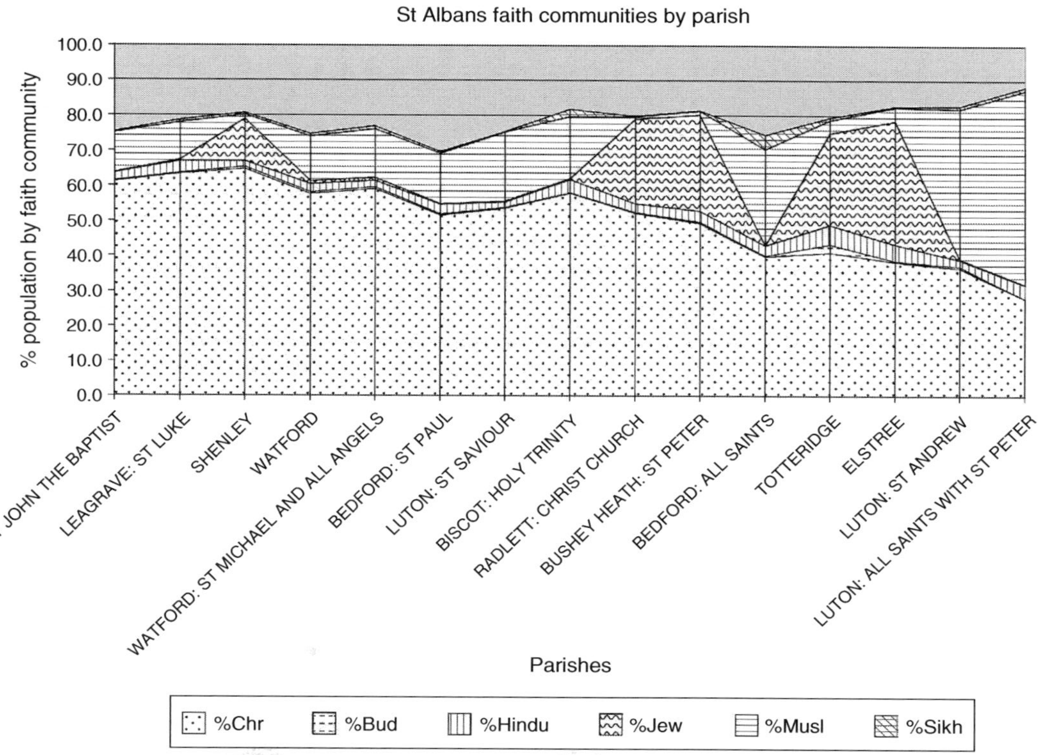

Figure 1 Diversity of faiths in five Anglican parishes in the UK

35

Faiths, diversity and ethnicity

The diversity of faiths is well demonstrated, therefore, in terms of the range of traditions and their quite broad geographical dispersal. At least 13 faith traditions are identifiable, with the vast majority being Christian denominations, followed numerically by Muslims in all three of the countries considered. While the minority faiths tend to be concentrated in urban and metropolitan areas, we have seen that they are present much more widely in rural areas too. But there is another important dimension to the diversity of faiths which should not be overlooked. This is associated with the relationship between faith and ethnicity as aspects of identity. Weller observes that 'religion is an important marker of identity' (Weller, 2007, p. 30) and this is often particularly true for minority faiths which may locate their recent histories and cultural inheritance in other geographical situations. It is all too easy to make assumptions, therefore, about someone's faith on the basis of their ethnicity, or indeed the other way round, so that a Muslim is assumed to be from the Middle East, India or Pakistan, and a Christian to be from the 'West'. Whilst the data to some extent demonstrate such trends and correlations, there are significant divergences and we cannot assume that faith and ethnicity are so easily related. There is also evidence to show that the significance of religion to identity in individual and corporate life is relatively higher for minority religious groups so that '95 per cent of Muslims, 89 per cent of Hindus and 86 per cent of Sikhs considered religion to be "very" or "fairly" important in their lives' (Modood et al., 1997, p. 301) compared to 46 per cent of White members of the Church of England. This is another crucial aspect of the diversity within and between faith traditions with which policy-makers must come fully to terms: that the intersection of religion and identity is complex. Though it is often associated with ethnicity and language, this is because traditions tend to have started within the locations and cultures which are characterised by them. Whilst the overlap between faith, race and ethnicity may sometimes seem obvious, there are many divergences from the trends, and faith does not always follow what seems to be the obvious connection. Somebody may 'look like' a Sikh, a Jew or a Christian but the assumption should not be made that they therefore *are* one. Weller's table of 'religion by ethnicity' demonstrates this (see Table 6). Though the clear trend is towards a correlation between ethnicity and religion, there are significant and notable divergences. In particular, there is a relatively large number of White Buddhists and Muslims even though the correlate trend is towards Chinese and Asian ethnicities, respectively.

Table 6 Percentages of 'religion by ethnicity' among 2001 census respondents in England and Wales

Ethnic Group	Christian	Buddhist	Hindu	Jewish	Muslim	Sikh	Other	No religion	Not stated	All people	Base
White	96.3	38.8	1.3	96.8	11.6	2.1	78.4	94.5	90.9	91.3	47,520,866
Mixed	0.9	3.2	1.0	1.2	4.2	0.8	2.5	2.0	1.9	1.3	661,034
Asian	0.3	9.6	96.6	0.7	73.7	96.2	13.7	0.4	3.1	4.4	2,273,737
Black or Black British	2.2	1.0	1.0	0.4	6.9	0.2	3.3	1.1	3.1	2.2	1,139,577
Chinese or Other Ethnic Group	0.3	47.3	0.6	0.9	3.7	0.7	2.0	2.0	1.0	0.9	446,702

Note: Due to rounding, figures may not total 100 per cent.

Source: Weller, P. (2007) Religions in the UK, p. 31, derived from Census, April 2001 National Statistics website: www.statistics.gov.uk

So caution is advised in the handling of faith and ethnicity in public policy terms because

> ...while there are often clear areas of overlap between aspects of religion and aspects of ethnicity in both the self-understanding of people and in their experience of unfair treatment, disadvantage and discrimination, for an appropriately rounded understanding and approach to policy development and impact assessment it is important that the dimension of 'religion' should not be completely collapsed in to that of 'ethnicity' nor vice versa. Rather, their complex relationship needs to be borne in mind and teased out in each specific context that is under consideration. In some matters (such as housing) it is likely that ethnicity will be to the fore, while in others (such as community participation) it may be religion. (Beckford et al., 2006, p. 8)

The Canadian data on religion by ethnicity highlight this too and, if anything are more complex, in part because Canada is a majority first, second or third generation immigrant population. Its census measures are therefore highly detailed and contain multiple Christian traditions as well as entries for each of Islam, Judaism, Buddhism, Hinduism and Sikhism. There are also data for 13 other faith traditions, including (in their order of incidence), Shinto, Taoism, Zoroastrianism, Aboriginal Spirituality, Paganism, Unity New Thought Pantheists, New Age, Scientology, Gnosticism, Rastafarianism and Satanism, and for five categories of 'no religious affiliation' including agnostic, atheist, humanist, 'no religion' and 'other' (see Table 7). I include them here to highlight and shore up the case for the sheer diversity of faiths which must underpin any policy approach to faiths at the public table.

Ethnicity, then, should not be taken for granted in relation to faith. It is too easy to stereotype faiths and their ethnic affiliations on such a basis. The elision of faith and race is one very important pitfall into which policy-makers can fall in their engagement with faiths in an extended civil society. But faith should be understood as a distinct and distinctive variable in identities if the most is to be made of the participation of faiths. This is also key if damage is not to be done to those faiths through an insensitive ethnicity-focused canter through those communities in the pursuit of policy outcomes. This was well exemplified when the UK government consulted with the Muslim Council of Britain (MCB) after 9/11, only to discover that, despite its claims to the contrary, the MCB at the time represented only a limited constituency of Muslims and that traditions originating in other geographical locations in the UK and across the world frequently held very differentiated views and beliefs. So faith is different from ethnicity, even though the categories may often have a lot in common. Faith encompasses culture and tradition which frequently reaches into different and often 'extra' parts of the social than does ethnicity. It can also make links to and affect encounters with people, stories and ideas across time and space which might otherwise not form part of the arena available to people through the ideas of ethnicity or nationhood alone. Policy engagements which do not grasp this tread on extremely fragile ground.

Faiths, diversity and generation

It has also been noted that for significant numbers of young people, Muslims in particular, faith is increasingly regarded as an important part of their identity (see Gale and O'Toole in Dinham et al., 2008) and faith seems to be increasing in importance for young people, therefore, especially for those from ethnic minorities. Weller notes that 'on average the oldest populations are the Jewish and Christian ones, while the Muslim population is the youngest and most rapidly increasing faith group' (Weller, 2007, p. 32). Indeed, more than 30 per cent of the Muslim population is under 15 years of age compared to the England average of 20 per cent.

One explanation is that this is an expression of political agitation for a fairer distribution of power and wealth in favour of countries which are currently disadvantaged in these terms. This assumes that there is a concurrence of faith and ethnicity which gets put to political purposes. It has been suggested that this is sometimes associated with the desire for the implementation of an 'Islamic State' and of Sharia law (see Hussein, 2007). Another possibility is that young people in the second or third generations of immigrant families see their faith as an important part of identifying both with their ethnicity and with the cultural inheritance from which they feel cut off or removed. A related and counter-current suggestion is that their faith becomes an expression of their ethnicity in the face of the many cultural directions in which they feel themselves to face and that taking a faith position helps to locate and pin down this diversity and thereby to curb personal dissonance and confusion. One curt observation is that an identification with faith is in some cases a form of teenage rebellion by a third generation against the Godlessness of the second (see Gale and O'Toole in Dinham et al., 2008).

Table 7   Religion and visible minority groups in Canada

Religion	Total in population overall	Chinese	South Asian	Black	Filipino	Latin American	South-east Asian
Christian (Catholic)	12,936,910	120,420	75,095	176,510	252,995	148,190	41,455
Christian (Protestant)	8,654,850	92,220	30,450	274,210	33,050	30,975	7,520
Muslim	579,640	2,150	212,805	51,680	810	890	4,440
Jewish	329,990	755	660	1,455	145	540	65
Buddhist	300,345	144,555	8,630	525	275	180	93,330
Hindu	297,205	715	260,535	1,950	100	905	2,700
Sikh	278,415	300	272,220	170	65	25	1,870
Eastern Religions	37,545	3,230	6,500	685	80	70	1,200
Aboriginal Spirituality	29,820	20	585	75	0	10	20
Pagan	21,080	110	55	325	50	30	45
Unity-New Thought-Pantheist	4,000	40	0	125	0	10	10
New Age	1,530	10	10	20	0	25	0
Scientology	1,525	30	10	10	0	0	15
Gnostic	1,165	0	3	15	0	30	0
Rastafarian	1,135	10	25	585	20	10	0
Satanist	850	15	10	35	0	0	0
Other religions	2,870	10	65	420	0	35	10
No religious affiliation	4,900,095	60,315	30,610	80,430	6,990	20,775	39,915

Source: Table derived from *Religion (95) and Visible Minority Groups (15) for Population, for Census – 20% Sample Data* Ottawa: Statistics Canada, 13 May 2003. 2001 Census of Canada.

Arab	West Asian	Korean	Japanese	Other visible minorities	Multiple visible minorities	Total visible minority population	% of total minority population per faith
33,800	3,020	24,720	4,895	23,825	24,275	930,215	7.2
3,555	1,370	32,120	17,425	16,250	10,380	549,540	6.3
122,130	81,360	155	100	13,815	6,935	497,275	85.8
730	360	105	110	240	115	5,275	1.6
40	120	3,860	12,955	1,200	10,615	276,275	91.9
110	1,305	70	55	21,595	1,465	291,495	98
45	315	20	30	60	595	275,715	99
305	7,425	135	745	170	800	21,170	56.4
0	0	15	10	0	0	740	2.5
30	0	10	0	25	25	720	3.4
0	0	0	15	0	0	215	5.4
0	0	0	20	0	0	60	3.9
0	0	0	0	0	10	70	4.6
45	0	0	0	0	0	140	12
10	0	0	0	60	10	710	62.5
0	0	10	0	0	20	95	11.2
10	0	0	10	0	15	585	20.4
5,435	9,940	20,040	34,660	9,320	13,875	875,095	17.9

Canada, Provinces, Territories, Census Metropolitan Areas and Census Agglomerations, 2001
Catalogue number 97F0022XCB2001005.

What is also clear is that different generations within the same faith traditions may experience that faith, and its relationship to their identity and practice, in highly differentiated ways. So in this, too, youth becomes a significant dimension of the diversity of faiths. In our Faith and Social Capital study (Furbey et al., 2006), we asked several second-generation immigrant faith leaders to reflect on the attitudes of their parents' generation, informed by the experience of migration to the UK some 50 years ago. They saw their own children exhibiting rather different attitudes to their own, observing that

> 'Today in our community the younger generations will accept individuals for who they are, irrespective of colour, creed, religious belief or cultural understanding. That fear within our elder generations is almost gone' (African Caribbean church leader). (Furbey et al., 2007, p. 31)

At the same time, the study observes that

> On various occasions leaders of all the main religions in the UK have indicated their concern at the loss of Faith among young people or, perhaps more accurately, an unwillingness on the part of young people to follow in their parents' Faith tradition. In relation to Hinduism, one woman commented: 'I think in the way that we were brought up, on a very practical level, going to the temple, doing the worship, we didn't have the understanding. We were told stories about Ram and so on. We weren't relating that to how that impacts on our lives. We know that we shouldn't be consuming alcohol and drugs, but we don't know why. We don't know whether the religion is telling us not to do it, or whether it's customary or tradition, or because that's how it was in India or wherever.' (ibid., p. 31)

This indicates the potential for a certain confusion or dislocation of faith in terms of identity and certainly our study found that often the young people we spoke to did not distinguish between ethnicity, culture and religion and in fact use these terms relatively interchangeably. This appeared to be borne out of the experiences some of them had of other people's confusion about faith and ethnicity too. The study observes that

> One of the young people remarked upon the extent of suspicion between groups at college: 'In some cultures, I think it's a bit beyond

help in a way. The college that I'm at, I hate it there because there is so much racism to the Sikhs and the Muslims. If you walk into the room you have a corner of Sikhs and a corner of Muslims and if you speak to the Sikhs then you don't speak to the Muslims on that day. You can feel the tension.' (Christian, male) (ibid., p. 32)

If people of faith are themselves making this elision of faith and ethnicity, it is hardly surprising if public policy does so too. But public policy can and must learn a great deal from the differences between faith and ethnicity, and those between different generations within faith traditions in order to produce contexts in which those differences can be celebrated and worked with rather than problematised and exacerbated. This is fragile ground which will only yield fruit in civil society terms if it is approached with great sensitivity and care. Differences can help in the construction of civil society but only if they are identified, recognised and celebrated.

Faiths, diversity and gender

These differences of experience of faith apply as much to gender as to generation and ethnicity and this, too, is an important dimension of the diversity of faiths. In our Faith and Social Capital study, many of the interviewees observed that women do most of the work in community activity but 'nevertheless become less visible the further one moves from grassroots activity, and the higher one goes up the ladder of decision making' (Furbey et al., 2006, p. 30). The study also observed that

Women are clearly engaged in generating bonding social capital in faith organisations and were present in every venue and project visited. However, when it comes to engaging in bridging and linking, it is mainly the men who are involved, or at least it is the men who speak about this on behalf of the organisation. (ibid., p. 30)

This clearly suggests that the role of women in faith settings is very different from that of men. Women tend to fulfil roles which engage with one to one and face to face relationships. The focus is associational and personal. Men, on the other hand, seem to focus on the strategic and formal. What we see is that faith is most certainly a gendered issue. The study also notes that this is frequently expressed organisationally so that '...some Faith groups have separate, parallel organisations for women and men' (ibid., p. 30). It reports that

> One respondent who had been associated with a Faith-based community organisation for many years, and had taken a leading role in developing its bridging and linking work, spoke with sadness about her decision to resign from the management committee because of the attitude of some of the men in positions of power. She said she had received support from a few, and that had sustained her for a while, but the overwhelming experience was of being blocked when she tried to have an influence at strategic and policy levels. (ibid., p. 30)

At the same time, the Faith and Social Capital study also provides useful examples of the changing role of women within faith settings:

> [in one] ... Black-led church in East London ... the constitution allows women to be active in all aspects, including being ministers, but not to be members of the decision-making pastoral council. This leads to the anomaly of a woman minister not being part of the pastoral council that governs her church. This church has decided, in contravention of the constitution, that women should play a full part on the pastoral council. (Furbey et al., 2007, p. 31)

Similarly, in a New Deal for Communities (NDC) area in London, UK, Muslim women have been working together to change the cultural restrictions that prevented them from participating in community processes. The timing and venues for the meetings meant that they could often not attend as they were expected to be at home. A group was started that met at a time and place that the Muslim community found acceptable. Their views were then fed into the NDC process. This meant that 'gradually, the women developed the confidence to start to challenge some of the traditional cultural constraints. Others in the community, chiefly the men, came to appreciate the contribution of the women, and to realise that it was not a threat' (Furbey et al., 2006, p. 31).

What this shows is that, as well as there being enormous diversity in terms of which faiths are present in Western societies, this diversity also goes much deeper than at first might seem apparent. There are important divergences within and between faith traditions. The experience of faith is also notably diverse across generations and gender. Though we do not have the data to show it, this almost certainly applies to other oppressed and minority groups on the basis of disability and sexual orientation, too.

Faiths, diversity and theology

In addition to numerical diversities (as shown in the census and else-where) and diversity on the basis of ethnicity, age and gender, faiths are also diverse in terms of their theological outlooks and missions, many of which may be correlated with some of these other factors. For example, O'Neil's work in Canada demonstrates the relationship between faith, gender and voting practices (O'Neil in Dinham et al., 2009). It would not be an exaggeration to say that for every faith tradition there is, and in turn for each denomination or 'school' within them, there will be a distinctive theological and missiological perspective informing their position in relation to engagement in public space and civil society. Sometimes these differences will be radical. Mostly they are subtle and this makes them all the more difficult to apprehend. This poses a con-undrum for policy-makers and other potential partners in the construc-tion of civil society: who should be turned to in that engagement? Who represents the beliefs and values pertaining to a tradition? Can these beliefs and values be determined sufficiently to arrive at such represen-tation? How do we deal with dissent from those positions? What is the intersection between diversity and the representation which public pol-icy requires as part of the practical processes of policy-making? These questions are returned to in Chapter 7.

In many ways what faiths 'believe' is the very thing which distin-guishes them and this goes to the very heart of the engagement of faiths in public space, therefore. But it is often the experience of faiths that what they believe – that in which they have faith – is the last thing of interest to the policy-makers and civil society partners around them. But faiths are highly diverse in this regard, too. Of course the ways in which this is the case are so many as to be beyond the purview even of the most distinguished theologians. For a social scientist, it is treading on dangerous terrain to attempt to grasp it at all. Yet a key theologic-ally based distinction between faiths does seem to lie somewhere in whether they focus on beginnings (causes), middles (events; what *hap-pens*) and ends – what could be called 'the three "E"s': etiology, ethics and eschatology. These are categories which at a very general level are likely fundamentally to affect the ways in which different faith trad-itions see themselves in relation to the social, the public and the civil.

Etiology is concerned with how things began and what caused them. In some senses this is about a source, being or principle which is the precondition for existence and being. It is an ontological category which seeks to ascribe meaning to being and, depending upon which meaning is given, being is determined therein. For example, in the earliest major Eastern traditions (Hinduism and Buddhism) the universe is made meaningful in terms of its source being the sum of all there is and its parts being its matter, in which we share. The Western traditions, on the other hand, see it in terms of a state of perfection to which we can aspire, rendering the world an arena in which that state can be practised.

Clearly such ontological contingencies are fundamental to how we see the world and our parts in it and therefore they affect utterly the decisions we take, the values we hold and the actions which result. This, in turn, underpins our ethical engagement with the world and informs our behaviours in moral terms. What motivates us to behave in one way and not in another is, at least in part, determined by what we believe about the ethical imperatives inherent in the world we see and make meaning of. In some cases, where being is understood as governed by an almighty creator, then the ethical might be determined in terms of laws issuing from such a being and a sense of our own ontological inferiority in relation to that being. In others, an understanding of our essential unity might lead us to a different ethical conclusion – that what we must do is to act altruistically, for example, or with concern for the environment as much as for one another.

Finally, eschatology is concerned with questions and meanings about our destination and how we end. Different emphases may be placed on ends according to what we make of causes and ethics beforehand. If this world is seen as an important and relevant arena for love and unity, our interactions with it will be radically different from those who see it as a painful holding pen, a test of endurance and moral fibre, in which we store up rewards and riches in the hereafter. These dimensions of theological thinking are an important aspect of understanding the diversity of faiths, and policy-makers should not be blind to their relevance and significance in the framing of civil society. People are motivated and will act differently according to them.

Multi-faith and interfaith working – diverse together?

In all this, faiths themselves have been effective in celebrating their own diversity together in various and varying structures of multi- and interfaith working. It has been observed that, 'while the use of "*multi*-faith" highlights variety, use of the term "*inter*-faith" points more to the relationships *between* religions and the people who belong to them' (Weller, 2001, p. 80). This distinction is a useful one. In turn, it also once again draws attention to the importance of what has been called 'faiths literacy' (see Baker and Skinner, 2006) wherein non-faith part-ners wishing to engage with faiths in civil society should come to terms with the language used by and of faiths, just as is the case with other unfamiliar faces at the policy table. This, too, is an important part of understanding the diversity of faiths and the localism with which pol-icy might best respond.

The Inter Faith Network records 25 interfaith organisations operat-ing at national level within the UK (Inter Faith Network for the UK, 2007, pp. 14–38). These include a Scottish Inter Faith Council, an Inter Faith Council for Wales/Cyngor Rhyng-greyfyddol Cymru and a Northern Ireland Inter-Faith Forum. In England, all the English regions except the North-East have established regional faith fora which are engaged with structures of regional government through the Regional Assemblies where they exist and through the Regional Development Agencies (RDAs). At local level, there are recorded details of 207 local interfaith initiatives throughout the UK. These include 3 in Wales, 10 in Scotland and 1 in Northern Ireland. In England, details of 193 groups were recorded including 15 in the East of England, 15 in the East Midlands, 38 in London, 7 in the North-East, 30 in the North-West, 30 in the South-East, 17 in the South-West, 19 in the West Midlands and 22 in Yorkshire and the Humber. In itself the breadth of this activity is a clear indication of the diversity of faiths. In addition, the fact that so much interfaith activity is in existence also suggests that there are many opportunities for and examples of working together with which policy-makers, if they approach with care, can engage.

So diverse, so what?

Diversity is key because each strand within it comes with an organ-isational infrastructure, constituent members or affiliates and a culture, mission or approach to working with others which funda-mentally affects the ways in which it engages in civil society. Often faith traditions struggle with clarity about their own organisational culture and these cultures differ in scope and capacity very widely. For example, the Church of England is highly organised and resourced whereas some of those faiths which are newer to the UK, Canada and the US, and which are numerically 'minority', are considerably less equipped, resourced or influential. How do they engage? What part should and could they play in civil society? How can public policy support them?

It is in the observation that faiths are diverse that policy's best hope for effective and sustainable engagement lies, for it is in understanding the heterogeneity of faiths that a realistic approach can emerge. The term 'faith community' may not be so ephemeral after all. Indeed, it is with faiths in communities – situated, local and real – that the motivation, the values, the skills and the resources lie. And just as one person differs from another, so faith communities have their own unique personalities and characters. This places importance on engaging with faiths as they are, in all their diversity. And in turn that means getting to know them in their situations – locally and from the 'bottom up'. Only this way can faiths as communities be recognised. It is to these ideas that we turn next.

3
What? Meanings, Definitions and Debates

We have seen that governments mean business when it comes to faiths, and we have asked whether they know who they are talking about when they think of 'faith'. In this chapter we ask, too, do they really know *what* they are talking about? The answer at one level – the policy level – is in many ways most certainly 'yes'. The general principles informing their interest, and the aspirations governments have for faiths in the UK (as well as in the US), as sources of all sorts of social 'goods', are more or less clearly articulated, for example in 'Working Together' (Home Office, 2004) in the UK and in the Faith-based Initiative in the US (see Wuthnow, 2004). This policy awareness is highlighted by the contrast in Canada where, despite significant faith-based activity in local neighbourhood-based projects and in the provision of faith schools, 'no self-conscious policies for faiths are articulated and public awareness is very limited' (Wilson, 2007; personal correspondence).

At another level, even where they are strongly aware of their engagement with faiths, policy-makers are nevertheless swimming in new waters. These are associated not only with what 'faith' means but also with three other feral concepts, and these will need exploring too. First, there is the question of what have been called 'non-religious belief systems' (Home Office, 2004, p. 8), such as secularism and humanism. Are these too in some way 'faiths'? How do they fit in, and what do we make of what they sometimes see as the privileging of religious belief systems over their own? Second, there is a danger that there will be an elision of faith, race and ethnicity which demands that we know what we mean when we refer to one and not the other. Is faith aligned with race? Are Jews a 'people' but Sikhs a 'tradition'? Where is the interface between religious culture and the cultures accruing to particular ethnicities? Third, there are debates about what we mean when we talk of faith in terms of 'multi-faith' and 'interfaith' contexts. Is engagement between and across faiths about working together in practical partnerships? Is it about dialogue but not co-activity? Is the focus theological, missionary, evangelical, social or something else? Which is to be desired, and when?

Even having grappled with these slippery ideas, further ones reveal themselves. In particular, an exploration of faith, civil society and public policy ought to give some account of what we mean by civil society, public policy and the relationship between them, and what this means for the role of faith in these public realms. This is where we will start.

Faiths, civil society and public policy

Wuthnow observes that 'When social scientists write about the relationship between public policy and civil society, they usually emphasise how civil society can shape public policy' (Wuthnow, 2004, p. 286). In this understanding, public policy is understood as resulting from or arising in civil society. Thus the public policy matrix, that area of policy which gives shape to public space, is intimately linked with the civil society actors who inform and influence it.

Thus civil society is understood as that intermediate realm somewhere between the nation state and the individual so that '...in contemporary academic explorations, "civil society" is usually defined to refer to the level of governance between the state and the governed' (Cohen and Arato, 1992). But the space between nation state and person is wide and deep. Where does 'civil society' reside within it? Where does it begin and end? What are the boundaries and parameters of the 'civil society' imaginary?

It is usually said to be located in organisations such as non-governmental organizations (NGOs), charities, foundations and professional associations. These exercise, influence and help shape the formal layers of gover*nance* which are usually referred to as govern*ment*. Their activities include campaigns and initiatives focused on specific issues in which they have an interest. Faiths have a long tradition of activity in these areas and their presence at the public table is, in this sense, not new. An example is the Church Action on Poverty (CAP), a Christian-based organisation in the UK which engages in influencing anti-poverty policies as well as undertaking its own activities in this direction. Their role in civil society is typical of this intermediacy in taking an interest already current in wider society, organising it and working with that to shape public policy.

This conception closely and inextricably relates civil society and public policy in a democracy of policy-making wherein politicians are informed and influenced by people and groups who have a claim to know what they are talking about. They are experts and professionals working in particular fields in the public realm – places where people interact, not through the exercise of their democratic right to elect representatives in Parliament and on councils, but as providers of services such as health, education, housing and police. They are also thinkers and actors on public issues such as environmental sustainability, security, global economic relations and world migration and asylum seeking. Their democracy is associational (see Hirst, 1997) and depends upon expertise, skills and experience conferring the informal right to contribute through the processes of civil society to the construction or making of the political through such mechanisms as lobbying, consultation, campaigns and private discussions. Here a new dimension of the democratic opens up which allows for voices to be heard on the basis of what they do in public space, not on a universal right to be represented and to decide who represents.

But, just as suffrage confers only limited democratic power on the individual – powers which differ from country to country – so too the presence of civil society actors such as NGOs and charities in intermediate space distributes power unevenly. The big, well-resourced, organisations are heard. But are they given 'voice' (Lukes, 1974) at the expense of smaller voices whose capacities do not necessarily match the skills and expertise they offer? This is a particular issue for faiths whose organisational capacity and resources differ significantly from faith to faith. The Church of England has the greatest capacity in the UK, for example, where a system of synods, dioceses and parishes covers the entire country in a tiered system of organisations. But the faiths which are newer to Britain, and to the US and Canada, often have limited capacities and this can impede their engagement in the intermediate activities of civil society. This can compound the disadvantage experienced by minority ethnicities, too, since there is frequently a correlation between minority ethnicity and minority faith.

However, one argument has been that the big players got there because they are good – a sort of 'earned civil society'. This is the evolutionary 'natural selection' approach to the civil society matrix which understands it as a market in which the strongest thrive. It raises questions about what is valued and therefore regarded as 'strong', who decides this, and how it is measured. Its counteractive position is that being big is as much a mark of happenstance and opportunity as of skill and expertise and that other dimensions should be taken into account when power is distributed. For example, skill and experience, a long 'reach' into unvoiced communities, or innovativeness and risk might be just as valuable to civil society. This follows a more interventionist social democracy model which understands civil society as a dialogue of the talents, not a competition of the strong. It also requires a more designed form of civil society than the organic one which exists.

But 'civil society' resides in other places too. Increasingly it could be said to be inherent in 'informal networks of association and friendship, kinship groups... [and]... communities of interest...' (James, 2007, p. 3). These less formal arrangements of people and interests come about, not so much at an intermediate level between nation state and person, which implies a middle-ground and a capacity for 'mediating' between the two to influence public policy. Rather they are rooted much more in local relationships, experiences and needs and are associated with the difficult but popular notion of 'community' which has been used so much in public policy since the early 1990s in the US and the UK (see my discussion in Dinham, 2005a). Faiths have shown themselves to be particularly good at these associational forms and their capacity for building social capital has been noted (see Furbey et al., 2006). Additionally, a desire to extend participatory governance horizontally via community, for example by giving voice to residents' associations and neighbourhood 'boards' for policing and urban regeneration concomitantly extends civil society vertically into local areas and issues. These new forms of governance have resulted in much increased levels of faith representation in the UK, for example on Local Strategic Partnerships (LSPs) and neighbourhood boards (see Berkeley et al., 2006), as we shall see in Chapter 7.

Thus community projects and neighbourhood protagonists take their place in civil society alongside the traditional actors in large NGOs and charitable organisations. Oxfam and Save the Children are joined by food banks and family centres. In this sense, civil society is shifted from the '... schematic liberal division of state, market and civil society' (James, 2007, p. 3) towards 'a wider mosaic of human inter relationships' (ibid., p. 3). Reforms to the shape and type of governance, and particularly local government, to include these neighbourhood levels promise to give them voice in shaping public policy where this had formerly belonged only to the much bigger, more organised, bodies such as NGOs and others.

There is a further extension of civil society in this conception which values the voices, not only of experts and professionals, and providers in communities, but also of users of services. The user involvement dimension has been growing in strength since the early 1990s when it was seen as a mechanism for driving up standards by recasting service users from clients to consumers (see Beresford and Croft, 1986). Under New Labour since 1997 it has been promoted as a device for generating greater relevance and ownership at the very local level and is frequently measured against targets for 'effective user involvement' in service delivery and development. There is potential here for the voices of users at the very local level to have their (small) say in an extended sphere of civil society.

In these contexts, faiths have always been part of the civil society domain, certainly at the intermediate level and especially in the UK. Here for example the established church, the Church of England, has long influenced the shape of public policy through its statements, lobbying and campaigns on specific issues. The landmark *Faith in the City* report (ACUPA, 1985) is a famous example.[1] Many of the other Christian churches have exercised similar influence through consultation and lobbying and many of the faiths which are newer to Britain have taken their place, too, in the construction of public policy through civil society. This has particularly been the case through the work of the Inner Cities Religious Council (ICRC) in the UK civil service with a remit to advise government on matters of faith. This has since been replaced with the Faith Communities Consultative Council.

But faiths have also contributed through the provision of services in the UK, and this is part of a wider trend in the US and Canada too. Indeed in the US and Canada this is the focus of the faith contribution, though this is more formally recognised in the US through the faith-based initiative (as we shall see in Chapter 6) than in Canada where policy for faiths is as yet largely unself-conscious.

As public policy becomes more interested in matters of faith, the civil society sphere is extended to embrace them and faiths are now increasingly self-consciously taking their place in a growing space for a type of civil society which embraces the 'soft powers' inherent in being able to 'persuade and negotiate, input to policy development and deliver services ...' at local, neighbourhood, regional and national levels (James, 2007, p. 4). The model, below (see Figure 2 parts A and B), is an attempt to describe this extended domain and to locate the role of faiths within it. In part A we have concentric circles of activity with individuals, groups and families at the outer circle, followed by users and providers, experts and professionals and finally government. Part B of the model shows that faiths correspond to these categories through congregations,

A: Civil society spaces

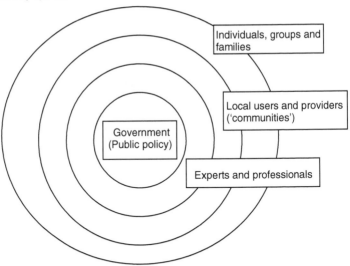

B: Where faiths fit in civil society space

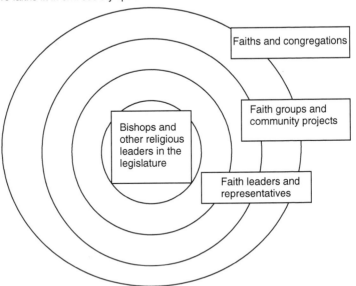

Figure 2   Faiths and civil society – an extended sphere of engagement?

community projects, their leaders and representatives, and through political representation in the legislature.

In practice, faiths are exercising these 'soft powers' primarily through engaging in service delivery through the provision of community projects and initiatives for child and youth work, care of older people, work with the homeless and so on. Thus in my review of faith-based community activity in England (Dinham, 2007) up to 48 categories of activity were found to be taking place across tens, perhaps hundreds of thousands of small, very local, civil society initiatives. I look at this in more detail in Chapter 5. That review also found that in the UK, faiths are increasingly participating also through governance activities such as participation in Local Strategic Partnerships[2] (Berkley et al., 2006) and Regional Assembly membership.

But a word of caution: civil society definitions which refer to services and strategic initiatives as that 'intermediate realm' tend to assume that those activities will always be good for society. But it has been noted that they can also sometimes have 'very uncivil outcomes' (James, 2007, p. 3). Such bodies and organisations can challenge nation state just as much as support or influence it. Certainly at the time of *Faith in the City*, UK Prime Minister Margaret Thatcher would not have seen the Church as a civil society actor. Indeed her biting retort was that the Bishops were 'Marxist'. When she made the surprise appointment of George Carey as successor to Archbishop Runcie, on whose watch the report had been published, it was widely gossiped that his elevation was 'Thatcher's revenge' on a too-powerful church. However, such engagement may well be seen by others outside of government as a highly valuable contribution to a civil society which has as its focus the well-being of human beings more roundly, and not only the achievability of specific and time-bound policy and political programmes and ambitions. Certainly many millions of people in the UK shared the Church of England's opposition to the Iraq war in 2003 and will have valued the 'civil society' contribution this organisation was able to articulate on that matter.

For faiths, public policy has itself called forth their engagement in civil society quite explicitly. In the UK and the US this has been through asking faiths to consolidate their well-established traditions of delivering social services. In the UK, this has also meant inviting faiths to take part in new structures of governance designed to support a greater engagement between 'real' people and the nation state via pockets of increasingly local participation. In turn, by engaging, faiths are themselves changed by their experiences. And others too are affected by the new involvement of faiths. This is a major theme of Wuthnow's work in which he explores how faith-based social services in the US have influenced civil society there, concluding that 'Whether they like or dislike the policies, citizens are paying attention' (Wuthnow, 2004, p. 286).

This could well be an enormously creative engagement, which demands of participants new understandings of self and the other. At the same time, there is potential for tension and conflict and the civil society 'mix' must be handled with care. Faiths are part of civil society not only at the intermediate levels envisaged by Wuthnow but also increasingly at the local level where civil society is extended into the daily lives of everyday actors and it is the realities of those lived experiences which has so much to offer and so much to risk.

What is 'faith'?

All of this raises the key question, what is faith? That faith might be 'useful' is the dominant starting point of any policy view. Therein lie buildings, resources, relationships and people, all of which can be put to 'good use' in the strong society. But faith is also something lived by individuals and groups standing in a tradition of their own, one which long predates the needs and wiles of policy or even of society, itself a contested idea. The so-called major faiths have histories of centuries and millennia and their traditions incorporate, indeed imbibe, myriad twists and turns in all that time. To act in ignorance, wilful or otherwise, of these realities may be dangerous and unwise for, at best, such an approach will fail to make the most of faith communities. At worst it will damage them. A golden goose, faiths may well be, but we know how that story ends.

As well as these historical or narrative dimensions, faiths are also 'in time' right now. They have current traditions or cultures of their own which are uniquely derived from the whole welter of positions in time and place from which they come, and the deep knowledge of all that they carry within themselves. Bourdieu's notion of 'habitus' is a useful tool for capturing this 'located' dimension of faith communities as 'a system of more or less well assimilated or more or less transposable schemes of thought' (Bourdieu, 1991, p. 5). This is intended as a means of linking subjectivity (personal and individual experience) with structure (culture, society) without reducing either one to the other. 'Habitus' is thus understood as an entity, and not merely a concept, whose form derives from the sum of individual experiences expressed in a collective social outcome. In Bourdieu's view 'habitus' is practically a physical reality in the sense that otherwise amorphous and interior individual-isms take on external expression in the social world which they add up to form. In relation to faith communities, both their 'history' and their 'habitus' are essential realities with which policy must engage and inter-act. Perhaps they themselves would call this their 'tradition'.

Faiths occupy space as well as time, and this, too, is an important part of their experience of themselves and of how they should be experienced by others, including governments. Easy talk of a 'faith community' belies the diversity and differentiation of faiths, even within denomin-ations, let alone between entire traditions. This pertains both in relation to theologies and systems of beliefs and to the structures, memberships and organisational capacities of faith communities. Distinctions within and between traditions are one way in which 'faith community' may be a gross oversimplification therefore. We shall explore these issues in Chapter 4. Compounding this is that the place in which people of faith find themselves will influence, perhaps determine, the character of that 'community' in such ways as to further preclude the sort of homogenising which policy finds so helpful. This is true of local and regional differentiations, so that Christians or Muslims in one town or neighbourhood will have their own cultural tradition and charac-teristics which are distinctive to them. It is also true of national and transnational differences, wherein whole denominations, 'schools' and sometimes sects will find expression, informed at least in part by the social, political and human geography of their contexts.

Faith, then, is a very complex thing. Its 'bread and butter' is human being: its purposes, its trajectories, its values and hopes and ultimately its transcendence. It is not easily captured from just one perspective (as we saw in Chapter 1). 'Faiths' (notwithstanding our unresolved explor-ation of its meaning) understand this well and are interested in 'stories' and 'narratives' – the flesh on the bones of policy. These may not grap-ple with 'explanations' so much as 'understandings' and they give us a different 'window' on the world.

'Faith' and epistemology

Yet, discourse on faith derives from academic disciplines arising from predominantly 'rational theory' approaches (Allingham, 2002; Sen, 1987). For this reason, treatment of the idea of 'faith' needs to take some additional starting points which may be unfamiliar to a policy audience. Thus, from one perspective, 'faith' is stories and experiences beyond or outside the 'rational'. In this sense it is an epistemological issue concerned with questions about sources and motivations, explanations of knowing and the various ways in which faith finds expression. In these ways it is associated with how and what we 'know'. For example, we might ask 'what drives us to have faith?', 'where does it come from?', 'how is it experienced?' and 'what is belief?' Theological responses might appeal to the three strands typical of the major organised religions – the Holy Book ('the word'), tradition (the historical communion of people of faith) and the 'Spirit' or internal experience of faith. Within this, theology is interested in major ontological themes about creation, theodicy, salvation and eschatology.[3]

At the same time, the allied discipline of Religious Studies is concerned more with philosophical dimensions of faith such as the nature of belief, sources of authority and morality and the construction of ethics. This tends towards a more abstract engagement with the religious and in itself highlights a distinction between 'faith' and 'religion'. This is a key distinction which is highly relevant to an understanding of 'faith communities', not least because it points up the differences between the interior and exterior dimensions of faith and of the organised versus informal. This has been called 'implicit' and 'explicit' faith (see Watts and Williams, 2007) and highlights a distinction between formal and informal faith. Hence 'faith' can be lived internally and informally at one end of a putative spectrum (e.g. through a vague sort of spiritualism or awareness of a 'higher being' or 'other') and externally and in an organised context at the other (e.g. as a priest in a major established church or in a monastic setting). Census data in the UK suggest that most people live somewhere midway between the two, and that in the memorable phrase of Grace Davie there is a high frequency of 'believing without belonging' (Davie, 1999). In the US, too, there is a similar trend.

Phenomenological approaches to 'faith'

For some, these accounts of faith will be regarded as 'wishy-washy' and 'soft'. This has often been the concern of social scientific perspectives which focus on social, socio-economic and psychological explanations of faith, many of which arise out of a context sceptical after Nietzsche, Marx, Freud and Durkheim. These perspectives question faith phenomenologically and tend to be critical and often negative. Thus Durkheim gives a sociological explanation which sees faith as a functional dimension of the social – though not actively negative, faith is no more than a useful construction for organising certain experiences and desires in social space (Lewis, 1977). Marx anticipates this with a socio-economic critique which sees faith as the much noted 'opiate of the masses' (McKinnon, 2005); a mass delusion engineered and sustained by a church and state which needs to harness the dangerous ambitions of an unequal proletariat. Freud explores the same 'delusion' but from the internal perspective of the psychological self, whose desperate response to 'mother–separation' – the post-breast 'oceanic feeling' – is to reach for an imagined 'God' to fill the terrifying gap (Dicenso, 1999). Nietzsche's bleak observation that in its rationalism, humankind had 'killed God' – 'we are his murderers, you and I' (Neitzsche, trans. Kaufman, 1966) – forms a starting point for these critical enquiries of 'faith' which shift the key question away from 'What is the nature of God?' to 'Does God exist in the first place?' Such accounts of 'faith' have frequently been seized upon as highly critical of it, suspicious of its role and function and dismissive of its potential as a force for social or psychological well-being.

Empirical approaches to 'faith'

From another point of view, the idea of faith is an empirical question associated with what 'characterises' it. What do faiths 'look' like? What do they do? How might they be described? A number of studies take this approach, often using social scientific methods to describe activities or phenomena arising out of faiths. One significant body of work relates to faith-based community development and tries to map and critically engage with what faiths do in the areas around them (Dinham, 2007 in the UK; Sherman, 2002 in the US). Another looks at how faiths engage in governance, for example in new extended forms of participative governance in the UK such as Local Strategic Partnerships,[4] Regional Assemblies and Neighbourhood Renewal Community Boards.[5] A third looks at things people of faith do, for example rates of worship (Church of England, annually, see www.cofe.anglican.org), faith-based volunteering (Home Office, 2005) and the relationship between prayer and well-being (see Watts and Williams, 2007).

Faith, belief and belonging

From another perspective, the defining characteristic of faith is religious belief, a factor much overlooked by many others in public space who are often suspicious of this difficult terrain. This is exemplified in the words of the UK prime minister's spokesperson, Alistair Campbell, in 2001 when he memorably commented, 'We don't do God'. This is a position mirrored in Canada but strangely contradicted in the US where, despite the formal separation of state and religion, presidents traditionally end their State of the Union addresses with 'God Bless America'.

Belief seems to be at its most graspable when it is relatively systematic or organised, as in the case of the major world religions. Notwithstanding the enormous range of debate, dispute and difference within, between and beyond these traditions, it has been suggested that all the major faiths have certain core principles in common: 'community service, co-operation, peace-making, pursuit of social justice and the acceptance of others' (Furbey et al., 2006, p. 18). Once again, we are on contentious ground here and theologians and social scientists alike may wince as I attempt to navigate the ground between them. This, in itself, is indicative of one of the difficulties for faith at the public table: that the languages between traditions, practices, academic and policy disciplines are not shared and there is much scope for misunderstanding and confusion. Nevertheless, while it is clear that the same words may well have different meanings, McTernan concludes that, despite their significant differences, there are 'important resemblances in belief that exist between the mainstream world religions' which include

> affirmation of life, ... inherent respect for individual choices, ... acknowledgement that religions should not coerce, ... [and that] faith rests essentially in the freedom of the individual to say yes or no ... (McTernan, 2003, p. 148)

Thus the Abrahamic religions (Judaism, Christianity and Islam) share monotheism and a vision of one God of justice and mercy who calls human beings to commit to the same. Though they do so in their differing ways, shared themes are detectable. Thus Judaism emphasises the way in which God expresses his love for humankind through Law as the source of his call to God-likeness, wherein God spells out what is required to do his will. It sees the Torah as a history of God's repeated reaching into history to bring his people back to his will in this way. The Jewish God emerges in the Torah as a 'jealous' God who mourns the failure of his people to turn to him, yet who is abounding in mercy – forgiving his people where they embrace his Law and punishing them as recalcitrant children where they do not. The story of the idolatrous worshipping of the Golden Calf at the foot of Mount Sinai while Moses is up the mountain collecting the very essence of the Law, the Ten Commandments, is indicative (The Torah/The Old Testament, Book of Exodus:20).

Christianity resolves humankind's persistent failure to respond to this call by locating the will of God, not in the Law but in the love exemplified by the figure of Christ who is explained as the incarnate God – the love of God made flesh in a man. The God of the Law is one whom Christians understand as eventually sending his son, Jesus Christ, to exemplify that Law by living in perfection. Thus it becomes the human task to follow that example through forgiveness, compassion, neighbourliness and love.

Islam in turn resolves the Christian dilemma of the Trinity – how God could be both one and yet three, having a son (and later, Holy Spirit to carry that son's spirit forth in the world) – by having Jesus stand, not as God incarnate, but in a tradition of great prophets, culminating in Mohammed who tells of Allah and his will in one single narrative written down in time. Like Judaism and Christianity, Islam emphasises the oneness of humanity, the compassionate and merciful God and an obligation for believers to act for peace and justice. As in Christianity, the call to give alms, or charity, is strong in Islam where *zakat* is one of the Five Pillars of Islam. There is also a collective responsibility to strive (*jihad*) to submit to the will of God. In Judaism this is revealed primarily in the Law, in Christianity in the love of Jesus, and in Islam, in the words of the prophet.

In the Eastern religions, there is also much in common. Sikhs emphasise the unity of humanity and the equality of all people. They are expected to develop in honesty, compassion, generosity, patience and humility. A central principle is the care and service of others and there is a call to combine action and belief.

Hinduism, while defying characterisation as the least unified of traditions, enjoins the qualities of 'forgiveness, compassion, the absence of anger and malice, peace and harmlessness' (ibid., pp. 45–6). It regards the world as of 'common ancestry' (ibid., p. 33) and the one ultimate reality, Brahman, as having 'all the diversity of the cosmos as part of itself' (Ward, 2004, p. 134). These themes of community and justice are strong here as in the other world faiths.

The major traditions, then, can be seen as sharing important fundamental common ground around themes including peace, justice, honesty, service, personal responsibility and forgiveness. They seem to contain the 'hope and possibility of tolerance and obligation to the "other"' (Furbey et al., 2006, p. 20). In these ways, an understanding of faiths on the basis of what they believe might be one starting point.

Yet, they also differ importantly in various ways. Many would themselves want to emphasise the differences in their specific theistic (or non-theistic) conceptions. Abrahamic monotheism stands in stark contrast to the non-theistic and polytheistic traditions of the East. More significantly, it has been noted that 'competing claims on the exclusivity or superiority of one interpretation of truth over the other have often led to abandonment or outright violation of these principles' (McTernan, 2003, p. 148). Common values may not therefore be a useful definition of 'faith' after all. In this it is possible to note a distinction between the theology expressed within a tradition and the religious practices which pertain and which are based very much on how those theologies are interpreted and experienced. In turn, it may be useful to draw a further distinction between religion and belief – those beliefs that hold true in the minds of individuals within religious practices and theological traditions. These distinctions encapsulate a key insight – that what people believe may not 'match' with what they 'do' (religion) and where that comes from (theology).

Non-religious belief systems

The debate is like stepping on egg shells and the more one moves about the terrain the more one is aware of the sound of them breaking underfoot. Here we find ourselves at a particularly contentious part of the debate. In many encounters as I travel all over UK, Canada and the US, I hear the voices of those in non-religious settings asking 'why do they get listened to when we do not?' The concern they have is about the privileging of faiths in public space while their own systems of values and belief are ignored. What is it that makes a faith tradition valuable in the formal reaches of civil society but not a non-faith system of beliefs and values, such as humanism or secularism?

In a complicated way, this seems to imply that public policy-makers accept the idea that faith is defined by belief in a consciously creative source or force (whether they think it or not). For what else separates the religions that increasingly have a seat at the policy table, and the non-religious systems such as humanism which do not?

Within this, belief may be divided into theistic and non-theistic belief. What is more it might be monotheistic or polytheistic. A further complicating dimension is the distinction between belief which finds expression in relatively systematic or organised contexts like churches, mosques and temples, and beliefs which do not. This phenomenon – 'believing without belonging' (Davie, 1999) – has been observed across Europe and the US, as we saw in Chapter 2, and is located in post-secularisation arguments which challenge the idea that secularisation 'happened'. This 'draining of social significance from religious thinking, practice and institutions' (Wilson, 1966) was expected to have led to a decline in the public significance of religion but it has been noted that 'the kind of inexorable and comprehensive secularisation predicted and hoped for by secular writers has not occurred even in advanced Western societies and that religion remains a significant presence in the public realm' (Parekh, 2006, p. 323). What seems to have happened is not that belief or religiousness has declined but that its expressions have changed.

Clearly, these are complex questions which can be explored from a dizzying array of highly competing perspectives. In my postmodern way, I offer the range of alternatives as widely as possible and have tried to make the links or possible links between them. But I do not seek to promote one understanding of 'faith' over another. Rather, I favour an approach which uses each of the ideas in turn to understand more fully the others and to follow that somewhat circular journey in order to develop a *sense* of faith rather than a *knowledge* of it. This perhaps reflects the difficulty for the rational theorists amongst public policy-makers who are looking for a clear definition and an objectivity about faith, preferably accompanied by a handy telephone number of the person they can refer to when they need to *know answers* about these 'faiths' with which they wish to work. This complexity can only be compounded when the idea of faith is melded with that of community. It is the idea of the 'faith community' to which we now turn.

4
Faiths and the 'Faith Community'

Just as the idea of faith is debated so, too, is the concept of 'community' with which it is frequently conjoined. It has been said to construct 'connotations which may be pleasing' (Demaine and Entwistle, 1996, p. 35) and to imply some unifying characteristic of space, identity or interest (Mayo, 2000, pp. 39–48) which may, in the end, be misleading. Others have argued that the idea tends to refer to groups 'which do not occupy positions of high status' (Barnes, 1997, p. 33) and that the designation 'community' conceals in its cosiness the realities of poverty and disadvantage. Thus, though it has been suggested that 'we are always dreaming of community' (Phillips, 1993, p. 6), the notion is amongst 'the most contested within sociological material' (Allan, 1991, p. 2) and it has been argued that 'it is doubtful whether the concept refers to a useful abstraction at all' (Stacey, 1969, p. 11). Certainly it has been identified as a 'cosy idea; as much an ideological construct as a description...' (Popple, 1995, p. 5) and Williams points out that 'community is a warmly persuasive word' (Williams, 1976, p. 65). Others have wondered why, despite decades of work by sociologists to 'expose the myth of community', the idea 'refuses to lie down' (Pahl, 1995, p. 13). Its appropriation over time across a variety of discourses and persistently in public policy is both a symptom and a cause of the contests in meaning associated with the term. Yet in the UK, the Labour party has said that 'community is the governing idea of modern social democracy ... [and it was said that] a key task for our second term is to develop greater coherence around our commitment to community' (quoting Blair in Isabelle Fremeaux, 2005, p. 2).

If talk of 'community' is so vexed, what, then, are we to make of the 'faith community'? Yet we see in the *Working Together* report (Home Office, 2004) references to 'faith communities' five times in the foreword alone. It goes on to refer to 'recommendations to faith communities' (ibid., p. 5) and later to 'faith bodies' (ibid., p. 5). It talks about 'faith experts' (ibid., p. 22), encourages engagement in 'faith awareness training' (ibid., p. 5) and wants the active pursuit of 'faith literacy' (ibid., p. 7). The ideas of 'faith' and the 'faith community' bear much weight.

The re-emergence of public faith is also asserted in the wider context of government's 'repositories' discourse which sees faiths as 'gateways to access the tremendous reserves of energy and commitment of their members, which can be of great importance to the development of civil society' (ibid., p. 7), as we have seen. They volunteer, they associate, they vote, they campaign and participate in governance, they provide services, they network and they contribute social capital. And the intersection between faith and these public activities is seen as the 'faith community'. This is where government thinks the resources lie, and faith communities are understood as the repositories of which they talk.

Yet, ideas of community are not clear. For many people of faith, being 'in community' means living with others of faith, for example in monasteries and priories. Christian theologians talk about the 'communities' of Matthew, Mark, Luke and John as the sources of gospel authorship. Some Eastern traditions talk about the community of all things. Islam refers to the 'ummah'.

And, in any case, 'community' is not always and automatically the 'cosy' repository that is hoped for. 'Communities' may sometimes want to challenge things as they are. Often this is moderate, as in the case of local campaigns against a new super store or road crossing. Sometimes they are more radical. In the case of faith communities, there is evidence of an awareness of this in the UK government's 'prevention of extremism' rhetoric, to which we will return in Chapter 5 (see Preventing Extremism Together, 2005). In the US it is located in the language of the 'war on terror'. These 'radical' notions of community must be taken into account in the construction of 'community' as a policy panacea.

They are conceptually associated with the work of Paolo Freire who outlines a (non-violent) radical political consciousness which seeks to challenge what he calls 'the oppression of the poor' (Freire, 1985, p. 1). This is a thoroughly structural conception which is located within radical, rather than consensual, analyses. He suggests that 'praxis' is key to community life that is connected with the state. Within this he emphasises the role of education, which he sees as not 'a commodity to be banked' (ibid., p. 93) in order to achieve positions of power but for purposes of liberation from the oppression of poverty. This is to be found in processes of dialogue and is aimed at challenging conventional explanations of everyday life while at the same time considering the action necessary for the transformation of oppressive conditions. Thus Freire talks about the 'conscientisation' of ability, talent and perspective in communities. It is a process of 'codifying total reality into symbols which can generate critical consciousness' (Freire and Shor, 1987, p. 167). At the same time as producing consciousness of the political contexts of oppression, people are also made conscious of their capacity for addressing problems and the solutions they wish to apply to them. They are empowered by their dialogue in community life. This is a very human-centric notion of 'community' which resonates with those found in faith traditions. This highlights a likely tension between the 'repositories' idea of the faith community and the 'human-centric' emphasis to be found within them.

This also illuminates a fault line between the radical and consensual that raises an important question: should 'community' be about improving conditions within the status quo, or should it challenge the status quo as the source of poor conditions? Producers of 'community' face a difficult practical dilemma, then, between seeking the empowerment of groups and individuals within a pre-existing space delineated by a politics of consensus on the one hand, and stimulating the latent capacities in groups and individuals to take power for themselves upon their own terms and without reference to a consensus which they may have done little to build on the other. This is a crucial dimension of the extension of policy towards 'faith communities'. What sort of 'faith community' will be 'produced' at the public table?

Political considerations are one dimension, therefore. The forces around which communities coalesce are another. Phillips offers a useful account of such understandings of community, drawing on four key communitarian thinkers, MacIntyre, Sandel, Taylor and Bellah (Phillips, 1993). Communitarian notions are pertinent because it is from the communitarian literature that both UK and US policies for community have been drawn since the early 1990s. Here 'communitarianism' is conceived of as the basis for the consolidation of communities leading to the strengthening of civil society in order to 'overcome the social disintegration brought about by the dominance of the market' (Giddens, 2000, p. 17) throughout the 1980s and the period of 'Reagonomics' in the US and 'Thatcherism' in the UK. Though there are different 'communitarianisms', it is Etzioni's which has most influenced UK and US politics (Etzioni, 1993). It is seen as the basis of the transformation of society as a 'community of communities' (ibid., p. 160) in which strong civil responsibility generates robust communities wherein people work hard and play hard, thereby sustaining a thriving economy alongside engaging community. The strong community is regarded as the bedrock of economic success while economic success is seen as the necessary condition of the strong community.

A closer analysis of Etzioni's exposition of communitarianism in *The Spirit of Community* (ibid.) demonstrates an essentially conservative foundation which contrasts with the social democratic governments which have based their 'community' policies on it. Etzioni places his view of the demise of the family at the heart of the problem of Western democracy, suggesting that '... the millions of latchkey kids ... are but the most visible result of the parenting deficit' (Etzioni, 1993, p. 56) and concluding that '... what matters most is the two-parent mode' (Etzioni, 1993, p. 61). He links this to education by arguing that children learn best when both parents have solidarity of purpose – what he calls 'the mutually supportive educational condition' (ibid., p. 71). Further, this 'condition' is threatened, not only by divorce but also by the exigencies of the dual-income family. Pahl points out from a feminist perspective the conservatism of this position (Pahl, 1995) with its implication that one parent should stay at home (presumably the mother, though this is not stated). Etzioni's pragmatic answer is that schools should take on the roles which in 'the ideal state of affairs' would be carried by parents (Etzioni, 1993, p. 89). The main importance of doing so, he argues, is that the 'parenting deficit' threatens the building of 'psychological muscles that allow a person to control impulses and defer gratification which is essential for achievement, performance and moral conduct' (ibid., p. 91). This in turn results in the failure to establish 'core values ... which need to be transmitted from one generation to the next ... that hard work pays ...; treat others as you wish to be treated' (ibid., p. 91). Etzioni goes on to advocate the reintroduction of national service in order to build character (ibid., p. 113).

In these ways, Etzioni argues that necessary functions traditionally located in the family have been displaced by social change and the fragmentation of the family and that the wider community must therefore take on those functions in order to sustain 'core values'. This is an essentially moral (or at least moralising) agenda. Governments in the UK have come to regard faith communities as key actors in the extension of this more widely responsible civil society since 1997 and this has been echoed, though not explicitly stated, in the US where faith-based public services are encouraged, or at least 'allowed', to promote a 'moral' dimension. This contrasts with Canada where 'the citizenship regime has not been purposively reformed in ways that enable voluntary organisations and citizens to participate more fully...' (Phillips, 2006, p. 3), although 'the notion that the philosophy of governing in Canada has shifted from one of new public management to one of shared governance is now widely accepted' (ibid., p. 3). So here is one key dimension of the idea of the 'faith community' – they are sites of societies' missing morality.

Demaine and Entwistle dismiss *The Spirit of Community* as 'the thoughts of an embittered man sinking in a sea of crazy American teenagers, his life flashing before him, reflected in the rose-tinted glasses of his own youth' (Demaine and Entwistle, 1996, p. 26). At the same time, Pahl suggests that the Third Way which encapsulates approaches to community in public policy in the US and the UK is a muddled retreat to a 'middle way between the public and the private' (Pahl, 1995, p. 15). Debates about whether faith is a private or a public affair are caught up in this and the muddle does not bode well for a clear understanding of the 'faith community' either.

But let us try to unravel some further strands. Communitarianism organises 'community' around four main ideas: geographical location; a common history and shared values; common activities and political participation; and moral solidarity. Together these constitute the normative ideals of community which are common to these communitarian thinkers. Can they be applied in relation to faith communities?

Community as location

The first, community of location, is based on the idea that a common locale helps assure that the various shared aspects of community arise from that form of life in which 'members find themselves...to begin with' (Sandel, 1982, p. 152). Here, affiliations are regarded as neither entirely voluntary nor broken at will. Community is understood as an extension of self and a constituent formative part of being. Rawls says of this 'Only in social union is the individual complete...for it is here that we cease to be mere fragments' (Rawls, 1980, p. 529). It is a rich texture of involuntary interconnections which precede social interaction and are unconscious of it. It is in this sense that people 'find themselves to begin with' (Sandel, 1982, p. 152) in a matrix which they have not chosen and which they cannot choose to reject. Though people may leave the geographical location, the psychological and cultural resonances of membership continue to resonate even where the local is 'stretched' physically or geographically. In this way, such interconnections are local first, and national or international after. They find expression in everyday encounters within a fundamentally familiar set of terms of reference in the social environment around and between individuals. This is community which is 'in the bones'.

For MacIntyre, whose interest is Platonic, communities of locality are well expressed in the idea of the 'city state' in which people know each other as community members, not necessarily individually and personally, but by association. But MacIntyre argues that the territorial dimension of people's relationships is not sufficient to make 'community'. 'Relational' factors are also crucial and, though association with others is unlikely to be personal except with a small number of 'loved' individuals, alongside the territorial dimension relational factors are a crucial part of turning a population into a community. In contemporary policy parlance, perhaps the 'neighbourhood' is the closest proxy to the 'city state' in which such relationalism can take place. This is often used interchangeably with 'community' to denote a geographically deline-ated space (or place) in which people have relationality as a result of the sheer intimacy of that space. Thus the smallness of a neighbourhood both supplements 'community', which may be comparatively larger, and substitutes for it, thereby seeking to circumvent or settle familiar debates about what a community is. In reality it can only interrupt or postpone those debates. But perhaps the idea of the neighbourhood is particularly resonant for faiths whose interest in the 'neighbour' is common to all the traditions.

In relation to faith communities, the idea of the unchosen matrix may apply better to some traditions than to others. The UK census may be a good example. We know that more than 72 per cent of people identify themselves as Christian while only one million (out of an esti-mated population of 60 million) attend churches regularly. This is not to assume that 'attendance' is the only indicator of 'having faith' but it does suggest that there is a feeling of belonging to some 'community' even without actively choosing it or translating that into what might be called chosen participation. Is this community 'located' in the psycho-social resonances of the unchosen matrix in which we 'find ourselves to begin with'? Even where this starts off as geographical location, the 'umbilical cord' of that location may be stretched across time and space so that we remain bound in even when our journeys seem to have taken us far away – a sort of 'stretched localism'.

MacIntyre's 'relationalism' may be closer to the experience of other traditions, or traditions within traditions, wherein people of faith do indeed start with where 'they find themselves to begin with' (ibid., p. 152) but move on from there to 'chosen' association within the wider community. One clear theological expression of this is the Eucharistic Feast, or 'communion' in Christianity. Another is the sharing of hospitality in the Langar Room in Sikhism. These are geo-relational comings-together of people who already share a psychosocial religious 'location' and express it through a geographical sharing.

The faith community as 'territorial + relational location' may fit some faiths better than others therefore. It also raises the question of how that territorialism expresses itself and what form relationalism takes within it. In our study of faith as social capital, we found that faith buildings can be highly effective foci of relationships which underpin useful work and presence in the wider community (Furbey et al., 2006). This relationship between the place of the faith community and the interactions within it may be one central dimension, therefore. But this, in turn, raises questions about who is in the place, who knows whom within it and how these associations relate to wider civil society. It is not as simple as assuming that people of faith go to locations of faith and associate with others of faith in ways which produce goods for wider society. People will attend, interact and offer themselves in different ways and to differing degrees and in ways which differ from one day to another. The equation cannot simply be 'place = people = relationships = faith community', no matter how much that might be helpful from a policy perspective.

The idea of community of location is taken up by Tonnies (see Tonnies, trans. Loomis, 2002) in another way. He describes communities based on 'affection and kinship' which he calls 'gemeinschaft'. These are communities based on similarity and are resonant of 'relationalism'. But Tonnies is preoccupied with a fundamental shift away from this 'affection and kinship' model, the causes of which he finds in industrialisation, huge shifts in labour markets and the rise of capitalism. This finds expression, he argues, in a new kind of community of location based, not on affection and kinship, clustering around families and very small and local groupings of people, but on the division of labour and 'contractual' or 'agreed' relationships which occur after those which arise because of where people 'find themselves to begin with' (ibid.). This he calls 'gesellschaft'. This is community based on interdependence of capital and exchange. In one respect this is associated with a shift in the spirit of community from mutual altruism based on familiarity and shared goals to one in which individuals consult only their self-interest arising out of the competition of capitalism (see ibid., pp. 64–6).

Could it be that Tonnies' 'gesellschaft' reflects the direction in which faith communities are being asked to go in terms of entering into public sector agreements and contracts for service delivery – the 'faith community', not as place and relation but as service and contract? This may well be the emphasis of the faith-based initiative in the US. And it is resonant, too, of the service-focus on faiths' engagement in Canada. In the UK, the service dimension is accompanied by a focus on the less tangible social goods of community cohesion which it is harder to 'contract' for (and to which we return in Chapter 5). This may mitigate the strongest effects of a shift from person to contract.

Nevertheless, the strategic and governance level engagements which faiths are increasingly making in these directions (see Dinham, 2007) do seem to recast the 'faith community' towards this contractual relationship of interdependence and exchange, for example through publicly funded infrastructure bodies such as FaithNetEast and FaithNetSouthWest.[1]

So in relation to the 'faith community', location may appear to play an important part, especially given that worshipping communities are often very identified with their buildings and places. But three factors mitigate this. First, many worshipping communities only have their building or place in common and in fact share very little else of the wider 'community' location. Theologians talk about the 'gathered church' in this regard – where groups 'congregate' because of convenience or liturgical taste for example. For government the challenge here may be how to knit those 'communities' into their wider contexts.

It should be noted, too, that in some cases the faith building, far from bringing the 'community' together, is a source of tension, perhaps being dated, inappropriate space, a drain on resources and, where they are heritage buildings, as in the case of a great many Norman and mediaeval Anglican churches, a financial liability to the 'faith community' which is responsible for it.

Second, worshipping communities may form only one part of a faith community and there are debates about who and what else is included. Candidates include neighbourhood projects arising out of a worshipping community but distinct from it, social enterprise 'arms', leaders and representatives who sit on panels or boards for neighbourhood initiatives, and those who use the building or place occasionally for specific purposes such as rites of passage (e.g., weddings and funerals). Such 'community' cannot be seen as one 'thing' therefore, so much as a cluster of mobile parts.

Third, in direct contradiction of a place or location focus, theological and particularly eschatological perspectives amongst some faith traditions may emphasise the 'transcendent' and 'beyond' over the 'here and now'.

Community as 'history and values'

The second strand, that community requires a common history and shared values, helps assure consensus about where people come from and who they are. In *After Virtue*, MacIntyre expresses this in characteristically moral terms, suggesting that community coheres by envisaging its life as directed towards a 'shared good' (MacIntyre, 1981). Sandel shares this view that community exists around 'a common vocabulary of discourse and a background of implicit practices and understandings' (Sandel, 1982, p. 172). It includes traditions, practices, common understandings and 'conceptions of the common good' (MacIntyre, 1981). In other words, community is understood to be an expression of a basic social framework for individuals to understand and relate to one another. As with territorial and relational aspects of community of location, these 'shared values' are understood in part in psychological terms and members accept and internalise the community's shared values and standards (Tonnies, trans. Loomis, 2002). They are an aspect of the narrative of the community which people believe and perpetuate.

This 'history and values' understanding of community is an apt model for faith communities because it resonates with notions of morality, social good, practices and traditions. The aim of a life as directed towards a 'shared good' surely reflects the experiences of all sorts of communities of faith. That faith communities might also coalesce around common vocabularies, practices and understandings may also be the case, though, as we have seen, their sheer diversity must also be taken into account.

But while a 'history and values' understanding sees faith communities as a social framework for individuals to understand and relate to each other (see Sandel, 1982), theologians and people of faith themselves would probably emphasise the liturgical and community belief aspects of their interrelations as well. People of faith themselves might want to add that they are also about understanding and relating to God or the transcendent 'other' as both source and member of the community (though this applies more in the theist traditions than in the non-theistic faiths). Indeed, it is the very fact of 'faith' itself which may differentiate and ultimately define what makes a community a 'faith community'.

Yet 'faith' or 'belief' itself is often the forgotten dimension when policy-makers think about 'faith communities'. It is also the case that faiths are highly differentiated in terms of the practices and traditions upon which they draw. At one extreme this has resulted in the major schisms of history, for example between Protestant, Orthodox and Catholic in Christianity, Sunni and Shia in Islam, Progressive and Orthodox in Judaism and in a plethora of traditions too broad to catalogue here in Hinduism and Buddhism. In some cases this has resulted in forms of liturgy and other formal practices which are unrecognisable to members of different traditions within the same faith. At times it has led to violence and dissent.

Community and common activities

The third strand in communitarian understandings of community is that it resides in common activities and political participation. This rests on the assumption that communities consist of members' participation in common activities which give rise to and arise out of common discourses and consensus about the most desirable form of collective life. In the everyday, this might be expressed in residents' associations, community education and community action wherein local people learn about and actualise their positions, often political, in relation to local issues such as environmental concerns or public services. This draws people into a greater community by means of a 'collective participatory dialectic' (Barber, 1984, p. 36). Here, 'community grows out of participation and at the same time makes participation possible' (ibid., p. 13). Community thus requires that people be actively involved in common talk, common decision-making and common action (see Phillips, 1993). In addition, as with shared location, common history and shared values, the practice of 'common activities' involves an intimacy of sorts, not based on close caring relationships but on shared participation in consensually agreed action.

Certainly all of the major faiths in Britain have a long tradition of engaging in the sorts of 'common activities' envisaged and this is increasingly the case in the US and Canada too. This has sometimes extended into political participation too. The Church of England's *Faith in the City* report is one such example of a faith tradition offering a robust critique of policy and practice in what it saw as a time of great need in urban areas (ACUPA, 1985). The UK's Christian-based Campaign against Poverty (CAP) is another. Such common activities tend to be directed towards social goods and find their energy directly in the gathering of individuals in groups.

In turn, the 'collective participatory dialectic' in this model of community may find expression in a variety of forms in faith traditions. On the one hand, it might be located in democratic forms of faith group governance, for example in elections to certain posts or offices. It could also be found in informal systems of relationships and networks from which action arises. There might be shared decision-making about finances, community activities or acts of worship. On the other hand, some faith traditions tend more towards hierarchy, and 'participatory dialectic' might be strong in itself but not be aligned with power. In other words, there might be lots of *talk* but little opportunity to *decide*. In some cases it may not take place at all.

'Common activities' understandings of community also raise the question of whether faiths are always good at 'collective participatory dialectic' in the first place. Certainly doctrinal and literalist approaches to faith may require a signing up to an established catechism of belief rather than an exploration or discussion of faithfulness which finds its way towards something meaningful. This may produce a community of 'members' but how far does that result in a deeply relational community of brothers and sisters in faith?

Community and solidarity

The fourth characteristic of community identified is a high degree of solidarity. This draws together the idea of 'interdependence' found in each of the other strands but suggests that this is insufficient in itself to constitute 'community'. This arises out of two problems: first, that not all people have the same significance to the self. Rather, this changes and intensifies according to proximity in time, space and biological relationality. Put more simply, we love some people more than others. Differing degrees of interdependence cannot be sufficient of themselves as foundations for 'community' therefore; second, that psychosocial understandings of interdependence suggest that social interdependence is a feature of every individual existence regardless of the idea of community. For example, the idea of transaction in child development provides that human growth depends on the transaction of messages about needs and the meeting of those needs (Winnicott, 1971), usually between mother and child but later burgeoning outwards to a lifelong interdependence in the family, the neighbourhood, the workplace and beyond. Phillips suggests that it is thus 'a sociological truism that we cannot even conceive of a person separate and absolutely alone in the world, independent of other people' (Phillips, 1993, p. 72). Therefore this interdependence cannot of itself be sufficient to constitute 'community'.

The idea of solidarity is introduced, therefore, to describe a general and diffuse sense of community with everyone else in it. It depends upon shared locality, common history and shared activities but recognises that they are not enough on their own to constitute 'community'. Solidarity adds fraternal sentiments and fellow feeling (see Sandel, 1982) and a 'we-sense' (see Bellah et al., 1991) characterised by special concerns and moral obligations which exist 'from the beginning' and which do not exist in relationships with people outside the community. This communitarian conception of community is thus highly moral and focused on the idea of 'the social good'. This seems like a resonant description for a putative 'faith community'. Everybody is interdependent already – but faith communities choose a further fraternity which constitutes this 'we-sense'.

In relation to faiths, this 'solidarity' understanding of community may well be conceived of positively as the distinctive feature of the faith dimension – that elusive 'thing' which 'bonds'[2] a faith community together. But what then of the 'bridging and linking' that governments hope will follow? Could faith communities be so tightly bonded within themselves that they forget to engage outside themselves as actors in civil society? Might they sometimes become actively 'uncivil' or 'anti-social' in their solidarity as a group? We return to these questions in Chapter 5.

Faiths, community work and ideas of community

As well as these communitarian notions of community, the practical activities of community work also operate within a typology of 'community' which takes in the ideas of 'locality' and 'shared interests'. An examination of the 'faith community' through this lens is less focused on the philosophical notions underpinning them than on the practical dilemmas they raise. This is also pertinent to faith communities whose work so often takes place through the processes of community work, as we shall see in Chapter 6.

While accepting the idea of locality-based community, described in community work discourse as 'community of place' (Thomas, 1983), it has been suggested that this risks being romanticised in terms of 'traditional communities of the past' which can be seen as 'cultural artefacts expressive of a fictional golden age' (Anderson, 1991, p. 19). It is possible that romantic notions of the English parish, the village clergyman cycling to mass and the God-fearing collection of interconnected families redolent of some Victorian literature, may be an expression of this 'traditional communities' notion. Yet we know that the sheer diversity of faiths belies such a picture. We know, too, that the history of public faith is as likely to leave many people uncomfortable as to produce warm nostalgia for a lost age.

It has also been argued that the idea of community of place can be potentially exclusive 'reinforcing the unity of sameness by marginal-ising difference' (Mayo, 2000, p. 39). In this way, locality-based com-munity can defend space or privilege and, at its extreme, may lead 'from "nimby-ism" to racism' (ibid., p. 40), excluding newcomers and constraining diversity. We may translate the language to 'faith-ism', as Cantle has suggested, but the meaning is the same. This pertains par-ticularly to debates about faith and civil society at a time when the multicultural settlement is in question and the relationship between faiths, and between faiths and wider society, is highly negotiated (we return to these questions in Chapter 5).

Williams also offers a particular feminist critique of the idea of com-munity of location, suggesting that women risk being trapped within space constructed by romantic notions of a male past, 'consisting of pubs, football pitches and other male haunts' (Williams, 1989, p. 17). Are there such 'male' places in 'faith communities of location'? The answer is almost inescapably yes.

There are also criticisms from community work of the idea of commu-nity based on a common history, shared values and common activities, expressed in community work as 'communities of interest' (Anderson, 1983). Initially this concept was understood as 'a way out for problems for community of place' (Henderson and Thomas, 2001, p. 22). However, it too is fraught with difficulties. First there is a problem with the idea of shared meanings. It is likely that the construction of meanings can no more be shared around a 'community of interest' than round one of locality. If anything, it is even harder in reference to 'interests' which of themselves require a degree of voluntary consensus about meanings pertaining to the point of interest in question. Where faiths are so situ-ated and contingent, and where they deal specifically in the first place with ontological categories, the prospects for reaching shared under-standings may be bleak. Second, as Mayo points out (Mayo, 2000), notions of self-agency have been questioned in relation to arriving at shared meanings. She asks 'How far does the ghetto mother have the ability to self-construct her own life-narratives?' (Lash, 1994 in Mayo, 2000, p. 44). In relation to faiths we might also ask, to what extent do people of faith choose the character of that to which they belong? The answer may seem easy from a Western European and North American perspective where relativism, postmodernism and criticism prevail. But from the point of view of many other places and spaces, belonging to a 'community of interests' may not be a clear matter of the exercise of choice and in this sense cannot always be said to be 'a good'.

The idea of 'community' is exercised, too, through the practices of community work. This constitutes community as an organising principle for public activities and, as such, provides another lens for understanding the idea of the 'faith community'. There are a number of organising narratives in community work and – guess what – they too are contested. I tend to use the following five as a benchmark but I recognise that there are others (see Thomas, 1983, e.g.): 'community care', 'community organising', 'community development', 'community planning' and 'community action'. Faiths have a long tradition of activity in all five of these areas, as we shall see in Chapter 6. In the meantime, they are useful 'windows' on the orientations of 'faith communities' towards public action.

Community care

Community care was originally conceived of as provision of services for need at local levels with a key focus on self-help. It is predominantly understood in terms of the mixed economies of welfare which are (differentially) common to the UK, US and Canada as 'the process of the cultivation of networks and voluntary services concerned with the welfare of residents, particularly vulnerable residents such as older people, people with disabilities and children under five years old' (Twelvetrees, 2001, p. 42). It has become associated across the West with formal policy-led shifts away from big institutional care provided in expensive and unwieldy settings such as hospitals and residential homes to much smaller arrangements for care 'in the community', where people who had previously lived in 'institutions' would instead live independently or semi-independently with differing degrees of support being provided locally to them through small responsive services. Many of these services have been provided by faith-based initiatives. This is not new. Faiths have a long tradition of such service. But the formalisation of their participation in contracts for public service is new and is redolent of Tonnies's 'service and contract' gesellschaft, as we saw above.

This idea of community care has also been understood as 'colonising radical language' (Clarke and Newman, 1997, p. 26) and for occupying the values-ground on which faiths have already long stood. From this perspective it has been highly criticised for three main reasons: first, it has been understood as a politically driven device for the justification of reductions in public spending. The question is asked, should faiths be substituting resources? Second, it has been noted that the use of the word 'community' in the policy is amorphous and that its deployment in this context has more to do with the positive connotations of the term than with any clear understanding of the terms in which 'community' would actually consist (Demaine and Entwistle, 1996). Can there be clarity about who a faith community is and therefore what it seeks to offer? And third, it is argued that community care has shifted the burden of care from the state to the voluntary and community sectors, faith providers and the family (and other personal networks) all of which have been inadequately supported and insufficiently recognised in social policy and practice. The 'contractualising' of faiths in these ways may compromise their role as 'critics' or 'critical friends' of government and policy and theologians might suggest that it neutralises their 'prophetic' dimensions.

Community organising – organising for 'partnership'

The second of these 'practices of community' is community organising. This is understood in the UK primarily as 'the co-ordination of welfare agencies across specific areas' (Trevillion, 1999). This contrasts starkly with the US understanding which derives from Alinsky's view that communities should be organised for participatory democracy (Alinsky, 1971). That enjoins a more radical and empowering notion of the community which might resonate more fully with faiths whose interest is at least in part in exercising a 'prophetic voice' in support of social justice. In the UK, a preoccupation with community organising as a mechanism for extending the mixed economy of welfare has resulted in a dependency upon the idea of 'partnership' between providers and users in which each joins a 'community' of care in the service of needs which it identifies (with the user if possible) to organise and deliver the most appropriate 'package of care' possible from across the skills and services available within that 'community'. Trevillion discusses the relationship between partnership and community in these terms (Trevillion, 1999), suggesting that 'partnership could be said to be only the latest stage in the process of re-inventing welfare as a community process' (ibid., p. 52). Might this result too, in the reinvention of faiths as arms of public service? In this context, then, community organisation through 'partnership has been seized upon by politicians as another in a long line of ideas for saving the welfare state' (ibid., p. 132).

Partnership also has a specific meaning in effective area regeneration since the 1980s where it has been suggested that it depends on 'organisations collaborating and working to shared objectives' (Meryll and Jones, 2001, p. 9). They argue that 'properly understood and managed, partnership working between statutory, voluntary and community organisations can result in enormous benefits for communities' (ibid., 2001, p. 12). This has led in the UK to the development of Local Strategic Partnerships (LSPs) which are required under the Local Government Act 1999 to pull together all welfare actors in an area to contribute in dialogue to the making of strategic 'community plans'. In these ways, an extended mixed economy of welfare has led to extended partnership demands and a concurrent drawing in of hitherto independent actors, including faiths, to new systems of management. This places new demands on faiths and may be understood, once again, as an aspect of that 'contractualisation' which Tonnies first observed in relation to community. In particular it requires that faiths constitute themselves such that they can respond to the new structures with which they are asked to engage. They find themselves in need of health and safety policies, child protection statements, systems for ensuring representation and leadership in new public bodies and on partnerships.

At the same time, community organising is also associated with three added benefits: first, that community organising, based on partnership, is important in order to avoid the unproductive duplication of services; second, that it serves the purpose of 'adding value' to existing services through the identification and dissemination of good practice and other learning around the community of providers; and third, that services are made more efficient and effective for users through the setting up of systems of information and referral. Effectiveness in these ways requires faiths to engage openly, deliberatively and generously with each other and with others at the public table. Some will. Others will not. Many will struggle, not just within faiths but all round the table.

At the same time, such community organising is often taken up by relatively large umbrella organisations such as Councils of Voluntary Service (CVS), though it can also be carried out by local individuals or groups through effective networking (though this is often less systematic). The inclusion of faiths in CVS structures has not been strong, perhaps because of suspicion of faiths amongst other community actors. Others have speculated that faiths do not see themselves as part of the CVS and therefore those systems of support are not available to them (Finneron, 2008: personal correspondence). But there have emerged some umbrella faith-based organisations of this kind in the UK, notably the Church Urban Fund and the Faith Based Regeneration Network which seek to use a national overview to support local activities. Some traditions also operate within quite highly developed organisational structures, such as the Anglican and Catholic dioceses, which can support this kind of organising. But at the same time, radical arguments might see community organising as the exploitation of the voluntary sector and faiths by a government which has only the interests of cost cutting in mind. It has even been suggested that community organizing is carried out by 'professionals whose job it is to offer advice to working class people in an attempt to stifle anger and frustration' (Dearlove, 1979, p. 37).

Community development

A third 'community practice' is community development, at the heart of which is a commitment to the twin ideas of participation and empowerment. These are regarded as expressions of the equal value of all individuals and communities and are familiar themes for faiths. However, the possibilities for the implementation of participatory and empowerment practice are debated and it has been suggested that 'the idealistic commitment to participatory democracy which has characterised many community work ventures of recent years represents the triumph of theory over common sense' (Griffiths in Mean, 1988, p. 43). Thus in practice, Alinsky, though emphasising the importance of participation, considered that levels of between 5 and 7 per cent would be high (Alinsky, 1971) and Arnstein identifies 12 levels of participation on her 'ladder of participation' (Arnstein, 1971) before the highest 'rung' of 'exercising independent control' is reached. In her analysis, the lowest 'rungs' are the most populated. Burns, Hambleton and Hoggart (1994) add that the gap between 'rungs' increases the higher up the ladder you go. There is, then, a major tension at the heart of community development arising out of analyses of power which have been characterised in terms of the polarisation of radical versus pluralist perspectives.

While these themes of participation and empowerment may be highly familiar to faiths, therefore, at the same time they are also very difficult to achieve. In particular, the idea of empowerment has been criticised as 'a construct of high social desirability' (Smith and Fawcett, 1991, p. 5) which is little understood by practitioners (Baistow, 1995). Though Baistow agrees with Adams that 'empowerment has come of age' (Adams, 1990, p. 17) as a professional task for the relinquishing and sharing of power, 'the technologies for turning it into action are unspecific' (Baistow, 1995, p. 43). The leap from intent to achievement may be too significant to make, she suggests. She also asks 'What of those who do not wish to be empowered? Or those who wish to empower themselves? Or to be differently empowered?' (ibid., p. 45).

Nevertheless, the Federation of Community Work Training Groups (FCWTG, now the Federation for Community Development Learning or FCDL) proposes three key principles for doing so: that community development should have a focus on identifying and working together to challenge the relations between people and those institutions which shape their everyday lives; there should be acknowledgement of the particular experiences of black and minority ethnic people and women; and there should be a preoccupation with issues of power and powerlessness in the context of the promotion of participative democracy (FCWTG, 1989).

While faiths are closely associated with the social justice themes inherent in these agenda, their practices have also been criticised in all three of these areas. Popular critiques frequently align faiths with poor relationships between structures and people, and religious organisations are sometimes seen as guilty of perpetuating the wrongs of structures over beings. Faiths are also frequently places of institutionalised inequality towards women and other minorities. And they also stand accused of being preoccupied, not with the redistribution of power but with holding on to it. At the same time, there are examples of faiths working in just these ways, for example in the publication and subsequent activities of the Faith in the City commission in the 1980s when the power and agency of the then conservative government was publicly and roundly challenged by the Church of England.

One understanding of faith and community development is that it seeks to empower individuals and communities to engage but can do so only within the limited terms of what is offered in social policy. In terms of faiths this translates into the 'repositories' discourse around which government wishes to see change. A radical approach, on the other hand, understands power as a contested resource ripe for redistribution along social justice lines. Thus it is one of the tasks of community development, and the faith traditions which do it, to challenge power over aspects of community life. Thus, Thomas suggests that community development is first characterised by work at the neighbourhood level wherein community groups are encouraged to articulate their problems and needs in the expectation that this will lead to collective action in response. At the same time, community development may be seen, second, as the activity of professionals interested in reforming the system through social engineering in partnership with local people. It has also been argued, thirdly, that 'community development seeks to find the common ground with social policy and to maximise its positive potential' (Thomas, 1983, p. 63). In these ways community development has been thought of variously as a community and person-focused activity led by local people (pluralist or radical), a reforming activity supported by professionals (radical) and a process of engagement with government policies as a 'critical friend' of government (pluralist).

Faiths may be understood as already very practiced in all of these terms. They have a long and established tradition of neighbourhood level work, often aligned with the values of personal worth and fulfilment associated with Freireian 'conscientisation'. They have also been effective in bringing together coalitions to challenge structural problems, for example in the Campaign against Poverty and in Faith in the City. Increasingly they have been working to find the 'common ground' with social policy, too. Membership of the Faith Communities Consultative Council in central government in the UK is one such example of the effort to work with what there is. But at the same time, there are some who may worry about a dark side to these activities, too. What are faiths seeking to 'conscientise' people to, and for what purpose? What right do faiths have to 'challenge structures'? After all, theirs is not a democratic mandate. And why should faiths have the privilege of a presence at the public table at all? Might they abuse this privilege by pushing their own evangelical and moral agenda, perhaps even covertly? Faith communities seen through the ideas of community development are, then, especially illuminating of the sorts of concerns raised by their coming to the public table. But this is because community development is concerned precisely with the same issues of power, fairness and human value with which faiths are interested.

Community or social planning

A fourth 'community practice' is community planning. While community development is concerned with engaging with or challenging individual and structural disadvantage in the context of an analysis of power, it is an approach which has also been linked with community or social planning. This may be seen as giving strategic direction to the tasks and outcomes of community development. In this analysis, community development is regarded as inadequate in itself to the task of community change, though this arises out of a context in which it is at least partly dependant on government and other powerful agencies for funding, and not from any inherent theoretical defect in itself. Thomas describes community planning as

> the analysis of social conditions, social policies and agency services; the setting of goals and priorities; the design of service programmes and the mobilisation of appropriate resources; and the implementation and evaluation of services and programmes. (ibid., p. 109)

In these ways it is concerned with liaising and working directly with policy-makers and service providers to improve services or alter policies. Indeed, it is argued that if community work is to achieve anything more than marginal change, it needs to find common ground with government, even if their ideologies are at variance. In this way it ought to be possible to incorporate the demand for open, democratic planning into 'political struggles for social justice' (Marris, 1987, p. 32). The alternative to cooperating influentially in this way is understood to be competition for power and this is seen as inadequate to the key community work task of protecting and empowering disadvantaged people. For faiths, too, the preferred approach is likely to be one of constructive partnership rather than oppositional struggle and contest.

Community action

The fifth 'community practice' is community action. This tends to occupy the most radical position on any postulated welfare continuum and occurs when people organise around a specific and well-defined issue or collection of issues. The tactics employed by community action are characterised in terms of campaigns directed towards those who hold power to effect change in the issue in question. It has been argued that community action involves 'the support of disadvantaged groups in conflict with authority and an accompanying populist, reformist Marxist or social anarchist perspective in society' (Baldock, 1974, p. 54). Faiths have sometimes been effective in terms of community action, most notably in the UK in terms of Faith in the City. In the US this has been associated, not so much with critiques of poverty as with approaches to race. It is in the black-majority churches that much of the impetus of the race relations movement began.

It is likely, however, that community action in the twenty-first century, though continuing to be expressed in terms of campaigns and protests, is located less in political Marxism and radical structural challenges than in issue-based politics through 'New Social Movements' (NSMs) (Touraine, 1981). New Social Movements are curiously resonant of faiths and it is to this idea that we turn now.

New Social Movements

New Social Movement theorists stress a focus on issues and identities rather than the language of power. This depends upon a postmodernist interpretation of the social which rejects meta-narrative, ideology and 'truth' in favour of perspective, choice and construction. In one sense this is at variance with faiths. But in another it echoes with the idea of 'believing without belonging' (see Davie, 1999) which is seen as characterising so much of faith in Western Europe and North America. It may be that the idea of the 'faith community' shares much in common with the new social movements which are, too, communities of sorts.

New Social Movement (NSM) theorists suggest that 'it is important to understand movements seeking social change which have emerged in the post-industrial period as different in important respects from those which have formed around class interests in an earlier period' (Barnes, 1997, p. 47). Because of the rejection of grand narratives, NSMs tend to be arranged around identity, community and culture rather than around power. They are focused on the experiences of being, not on explanatory frameworks for experience, which are understood as delusions. This is associated with a wider shift from 'grand narrative' accounts of history and philosophy to an emphasis on difference and diversity. Mayo has called this 'space and place versus time and development' (Mayo, 2000, p. 6). For faiths this can be detected in something of a detachment from the organised forms of 'belonging' and a reorientation towards a more nebulous sort of 'believing'.

Mayo asks in such a context, 'What relationship have cultural issues to political realities?' (ibid., p. 5) in the absence of a grand narrative which mediates such personal experience through political categories such as 'left' and 'right'? Similarly we might ask, to what do faiths attach their experiences in the absence of 'belonging'?

Mayo argues that policy has appealed to the idea of community to mediate this for many years and that 'community' agendas have long been focused on participants' underlying perspectives as to 'who was who, what was what and what was to be done' (ibid., p. 5). In a sense this is precisely what Freire advocates in his process of 'conscientisation': the development of self-understanding and group knowledge and the emergence, thereon, of a strategy for addressing the issues which are raised. Thus, the idea of 'community' suggests that such a process need not be mediated through organisational systems at all. At the same time, whilst being reluctant to become associated with any one political party or religious doctrine, the idea of community also recognises the need to engage with some system of belonging. The idea of the 'faith community' is, then, suitably amorphous so as to be capable of a general inclusiveness of anyone who wishes to belong at the same time as making sufficiently few demands as to *ex*clude. And yet it remains a 'category' which can be 'used' in policy and in the construction of civil society. It has been suggested that this risks turning inwards, 'undermining the commonality needed to challenge power and oppression'

(Calhoun, 1994, p. 47). This returns us to our earlier discussion of communitarian understandings of the faith community. In NSM terms, then, it is suggested that 'solidarity is as crucial as difference' (Lash et al., 1996, p. 321).

Crossley thus offers a three part typology of 'new social movements', each drawing on the idea of a shared 'family resemblance' (Crossley, 2002, p. 2): first, he suggests that social movements may be understood as 'collective enterprises' (ibid., p. 3) arising out of unrest and dissatisfaction on the one hand plus wishes and hopes on the other. Might this 'unrest and dissatisfaction' aptly describe the widespread and noted appetite which is apparent for spiritual nourishment despite a decline in levels of formal belonging? And are those mirrored in the 'wishes and hopes' which faiths harbour? Second, similarly, social movements may be understood as 'temporary public spaces' and 'moments of collective creation' (ibid., p. 4). In this view social movements coalesce around public and shared issues and arise out of the creative responses of people, though are not necessarily responses either to dissatisfaction or wishes. Crossley ascribes this view to Eyerman and Jamieson (1991) and notes that it is somewhat undermined by the longevity of some such movements. Might we draw parallels here with the strange persistence of faith despite all the assumptions and assertions of secularists in the preceding few hundred years? And third, he suggests that NSMs may be understood in terms of 'sustained interaction with opponents' so that 'ordinary people, often in league with more influential citizens, join forces in confrontation with elites, authorities and opponents' (Crossley, 2002, p. 4). Perhaps this is the least recognisable in relation to faith communities, though could it be suggested that aligning with some of the new age and spiritualist religious movements is precisely about 'joining forces' to 'confront' the over-assertion of capitalism against the human?

An alternative is proposed by Della-Porta and Diani (1999) who suggest a useful typology of NSMs, suggesting that there are four key themes which can be identified: first, social movements as 'informal interaction networks'. These are groupings of people whose relationships emerge 'organically' and whose organisation as a 'movement' is informal so that action arises in semiconscious ways as responses to issues and needs identified in the context of everyday life and without necessarily recognising either issues or action in these terms. They give identity to members through the mutual recognition of shared approaches and understandings and provide solidarity through friendship and companionship. This may be reflected in a steady rise in the number of informal 'house churches' in the US. In least formal terms, such groups may be friends or colleagues whose interaction is coincidental to the solidarity which they feel within it. In more formal terms, they may consist of social clubs such as book groups or coffee mornings wherein people consciously decide to 'attend' but subsequently unconsciously find solidarity in subsets within the group with whom they 'identify'.

Second, social movements may be based on 'shared beliefs and solidarity'. Such movements are characterised in similar terms to those arranged around 'informal interaction networks' but with the important distinction that they are self-conscious of themselves as 'movements' (though not necessarily in this language). In this sense, they identify with and commit to a system of shared beliefs (though it may not necessarily be systematised) in which they find solidarity as a group. Again, are these resonant of informal faith-based gatherings, such as fellowship groups or community support initiatives?

Third, social movements may be based on 'collective action focusing on conflicts'. These are movements which are highly conscious of their beliefs, aims and strategies and which tend to exist solely and explicitly for the pursuit of those aims. They tend to come together around specific issues which are seen in some way to threaten an aspect of the 'identities' of participants. An example is the UK's Countryside Alliance protests, including court cases, against the ban on hunting with dogs. In the US we might cite campaigns against the 2003 war in Iraq.

Fourth, there are social movements which enjoin 'the use of protest'. These are movements which tend to be (though are not necessarily) politicised and which organise around a specific issue to which they object. Traditionally these have been very focused social movements, such as Green Peace or the Campaign for Nuclear Disarmament (CND) which have large memberships and highly developed constitutional aims, objectives and strategies. There are surely many examples of such movements springing from faiths.

Though the rise of NSMs may indicate a trend away from narrative and towards 'issues' and 'identity', it is also pointed out that organised forms, including organised forms of faith, continue to exist. But, though such 'local communities, constructed through collective action and preserved through collective memory, are specific sources of identity' (Castells, 1997a, p. 231), it is suggested that they tend to be reactions against organisation and are thus 'havens, not heavens' (ibid., p. 241). This suggests that, in looking for faith communities, policy must search in the informal spaces as well as the formal. And that what is found in each will be distinctive and differentiated.

Participation and empowerment:
More policy discourses of community!

What has also emerged is a strong use of the ideas of participation and empowerment in talk of community. This has been around since the beginning of the New Labour governments in 1997 and these notions were central in the early flagship policy 'New Deal for Communities' (see Dinham, 2005a) which sought to hand over decision-making for local services and initiatives to 'partnership boards' at least 50 per cent of which were to be local residents. They have re-emerged in relation to faiths in a government White Paper called *Communities in Control: Real People, Real Power* (CLG, 2008) in which empowerment at the local level is emphasised. A section called 'The role of faith groups' refers to 'the importance placed on charitable acts, social action and civic duty in all religions practised in the UK' (ibid., p. 43). It sees this as an aspect of the empowerment and participation which is sought. Nevertheless, it should be noted that this once again returns us to a somewhat instrumentalist view of the contribution of faiths which constructs them in terms of what they bring to civil society. This may not be a surprising aspect of government policy which, after all, seeks to set the parameters for civic space. But an effective and sustainable engagement with faiths will set it within the context of their own experiences and wishes too, if empowerment and longer-term participation are to be achieved.

A government 'framework for partnership in our multi-faith society' (ibid.) also emphasises the importance of working with what is already locally and regionally the case rather than imposing policy edifices from the top down. A £7.5 million fund to support community-led initiatives for multi-faith working aims to extend the participation and empowerment which are valued. A new £7.5 million funding stream, 'Faith in Action', is intended to support this. This follows on the heels of the Faith Communities Capacity Building Fund and on an interim funding programme for the regional faith forums in England. I return to these themes in Chapter 7.

A recipe for compounding controversy?

So both 'faith' and 'community' are highly contested ideas and the notion of the 'faith community' is extremely vexed. As we saw in Chapter 3, faith might be an epistemological category, it can be thought of in terms of its phenomenological manifestations, and it can be understood empirically in terms of what it does. Community, too, is a slippery concept which, though 'cosy' and 'comforting' eludes a clear definition from which we could point and say 'there goes community'.

The idea of the 'faith community' therefore magnifies these complexities and presents compounded versions of the debates. Is a faith community defined by its geographical location? If so, is this based on a building, a neighbourhood, a city or some other boundary of place? How does this relate to national and transnational locations, for example through international movements and traditions such as the Catholic church or the European Convocation of Baha'i?

Alternatively, is a faith community constituted by shared history and values? Then what do we make of differing theological emphases within traditions and even within congregations, for example on questions of mission and evangelism?

Could a faith community really be about its common activities? Or are they too diffuse and varied to coalesce in this way? Or is it more generally defined by its sense of solidarity, drawing on aspects of all of these dimensions in a range of shifting combinations? If so, what then of bridging and linking in those activities which are of such value to civil society?

In addition, the attempt to pin down the idea of the faith community, and its relationship to public policy and civil society, raises a whole other set of questions about participation, representation and leadership. Who is in a faith community? Who is not? On what basis? How are members bought in and, for that matter, sent out? Where does the faith community begin and end? Is the worshipping community a source of wider social activities or separate from it? In turn, who speaks for the faith community? With what authority? How are its members represented? In what places? How do faith-based services reflect upon the rest of the faith community? What do they say about values, beliefs and mission? And who are the leaders, and why? What about dissent and disagreement? I return to many of these questions in Chapter 7.

These questions are provocative, but experience shows that they should be. In particular, women and young people frequently find themselves 'spoken for' in their faith communities (Furbey et al., 2006). What does that say about commonality, let alone the solidarity of which Bellah speaks? And it is known that young people, especially second-generation immigrants whose faith traditions are often newer to the UK, the US and Canada, experience their faiths differently to their parents, often with a greater emphasis on identity than on belief (Furbey et al., 2006; Gale and O'Toole in Dinham et al., 2008).

There are also important differences in the capacity of faiths to articulate themselves as 'communities', especially as they try to relate to systems of government and public space. The Church of England, for example, is highly organised and extremely well-resourced, while the Zoroastrians rely upon a single European structure to communicate strategically across that entire geographical space. While inclusiveness and equitability therefore require the participation of all the faiths, reality often precludes or disadvantages involvement in that construction of public policy which extended civil society promises, because 'community' is often undeliverable in practice. Of this, policy must beware.

5
Faiths, Social Capital and Community Cohesion

We have seen, then, that 'community' is a much favoured word in policy. It pops up all over the place, not least because it is both cosy and convenient. It is also particularly resonant amongst people of faith, though their understandings of it can differ markedly from those used in policy. As a religious category, it echoes with ideas of the good neighbour, shared forms of 'community' living and a universal 'community' of faith. For some it denotes aesthetic monasticism and withdrawal from the world. But while for people of faith, 'community' conjures up notions of relationship and care, the 'repositories' rhetoric of policy is highly focused on the resources faiths contain within them. The potential for talking at cross purposes is distinct. Yet policy is also interested in these relationships of care which are understood, too, as part of the resource. From this perspective faiths are seen as containing within them the essential ingredients which can hold communities together. They are seen as 'good at community'. There is, therefore, a great interest in 'faith communities' as containers of community cohesion.

And alongside the idea of community cohesion is the notion that it depends upon the presence of 'social capital'. Like financial capital, social capital is seen as a 'thing', not just a metaphor – it can be accrued, saved and invested. It is the 'currency' people use in their relationships and resides in and is 'spent' in the exchanges they make amongst themselves. This exchange renders it public because it is happening in public space and it is because of this that it is understood as the foundation for community and for community cohesion. But beware: whereas social capital may be in currency, it does not necessarily follow that it will result in the cohesion which is sought. Social capital can be 'spent' on other things too.

This chapter considers community cohesion as another of the enormously contested ideas in policies directed towards faiths at the public table. It explores ways in which faiths are regarded as repositories of the social capital which is seen as the precondition for community cohesion. Yet the assumptions behind both notions almost certainly do not reflect the full extent of the dilemmas involved, as we shall see.

Community cohesion

It has been noted that 'community cohesion' is a narrative which, on the one hand, 'denies the conceptual complexities' of community (Robinson, 2005, p. 1412) and, on the other, overstates the case that communities are fragmenting. It has also been criticised on the grounds that it 'is unwarranted in maintaining that the problem is with minority ethnic communities' (ibid., p. 1412). Yet Cantle locates the drivers of the community cohesion agenda precisely in immigration resulting, he says, from persecution and war, from the search by many nations for labour forces beyond their borders, from tourism and from what he calls 'tourism into residency' (Cantle, 2005, p. 3). He identifies a range of pressures which contribute to the breakdown of community cohesion in this context of immigration: the role of 'modern communications allowing trans-national identities to be much more easily supported' (ibid., p. 5), perhaps at the expense of intra-national identification; that as 'home' citizens' rights have expanded, so foreigners have taken note and asserted their own, sometimes against resistance to change; and resentment by established residents of newcomers that can accompany already established disadvantage in housing, education and employment which is seen as exacerbated by the needs of new immigrants and can lead to racism and conflict. All of these aspects have been articulated by the far right British National Party (BNP) which has been skilful in gaining ground in areas where these tensions are already present by emphasising the threat they pose to the stability of the 'native' community. It is suggested that the far right from which they come has contributed to the breakdown of community cohesion by emphasising difference rather than commonality and asserting a hierarchy of citizenship rights which privilege the white and the long-term settled. Thus it has been observed that following mass immigration;

> the pronouncements of far right-wing organizations such as Combat
> 18, the National Front and the British National Party did little to allay
> the unfounded fears of the White majority that public services, jobs

and even the country as a whole were being taken over by undeserving foreigners. (Billings and Holden, 2008, p. 7)

Cantle is clear that this reflects and has resulted in communities fracturing and that 'the immigration problem was now, more evidently than ever before, a matter of "race"' (Cantle, 2005, p. 6). He also notes that, at the same time, 'Many British people, it seems, take the opportunity to live in other countries and see it as their right to do so, whilst their former compatriots often remain hostile to the reverse trend – inward migration' (ibid., p. 3). These are features of Canadian and US attitudes to immigration, too. The debates can be tense and emotional.

But in the evolution of the agenda for community cohesion, the swiftness with which the fracturing of local communities was transformed from a 'race' issue to a 'faith' issue is striking. It has been observed that 'ethnic and faith divisions have now begun to replace those based upon ideas about "race"' (ibid., p. 12). But this was the case by the end of 2001 when strife was already seen, not as being between 'Asians and whites' but between 'Muslims and Christians'. Under the impetus of growing concerns about Islam following the events of 9/11 in the US, the angry young Asians of that summer were already popularly cast as 'Islamic militants' by the end of the year (see Amin, 2002, p. 964).

There was also observed a process of 'self-segregation' into what came to be described as 'parallel lives' (see Independent Review Team, 2001, p. 9). The line of division was associated with ethnicity. But it was also to do with faith. The community cohesion agenda is the UK government's response, therefore, to a perceived 'retreating into "comfort zones" made up of people like themselves' (Ousely, 2001, p. 3) wherein different identities break off from one another to their places of safety.

In the US there are similar initiatives and interests though these are more explicitly housed in the context of counter-terrorism rather than community cohesion more generally. The 'Partnering for Prevention and Community Safety Initiative' (PfP) at NorthEastern University, Boston, is a particular example. It:

> seeks to identify and help implement promising practices for building relationships between federal, state, and local law enforcement and American Muslim, Arab, and Sikh communities. Such partnerships enhance counterterrorism initiatives, protect communities from hate crimes and hate incidents, and help preserve American civil liberties. (PfP Programme NorthEastern University, Boston, US www.spcs.neu.edu/pfp/about/index.php)

But it is also noted that 'community cohesion has no place in the lexicon of urban theory or public policy prior to the street confrontations of summer 2001' (Robinson, 2005, p. 1415) and to that extent has been plucked out of the air from nowhere. At the same time it can be seen as an almost inevitable extension of the over-dependence on 'community' which had taken hold since the mid-1990s. If community is the 'cosy' and desirable ideal, then strife must surely be a sign that community has failed. The argument is circular. Community is a social good. Therefore social 'bad' must be because of an absence of community. And yet there is no real analysis in policy of whether 'community' is a social 'good', nor of what it means, how it plays out in relation to faiths and with what impacts, as we have seen. This results in rather muddled policy solutions which sit somewhat uneasily and can contradict themselves, as we shall see.

Approaches to immigration and the perception of a breakdown of cohesive communities were initially associated with anti-discrimination measures on the one hand (see Race Relations Acts, 1965, 1968) and 'limited attempts to "promote good race relations" by working with the white community to improve their understanding of the black and minority ethnic communities' (Cantle, 2005, p. 6) on the other. In the US this had been anticipated in the anti-discriminatory measures of the 1940s and 1950s and by 'affirmative action' in the 1960s, 'culminating in the monumental piece of legislation – the Civil Rights Act of 1964' (ibid., p. 7). But the links to poverty and disadvantage were not widely accepted until the Scarman Report in the UK in 1981 which associated racial tension with structural disadvantages holding back immigrants from the sorts of educational opportunities and employment seen as the key to the success of others, and which led to resentment and conflict. Another significant moment was the Macpherson Report in 1999 which identified 'institutional racism' in the London Metropolitan Police Force – the sort of racism that is built into the structures and processes of policing, as well as in the personal racisms of individual officers. The idea of 'institutional racism' has been influential much more widely in other settings, too.

Yet, as Cantle notes, approaches to the anti-cohesive forces of division along racial lines continue to be 'based on controlling behaviour and making good the deficits' (ibid., p. 8). This, in turn, has frequently led to claims of preferential treatment of black and minority ethnic people. In Canada this has been a source of bubbling resentment amongst white Canadians against 'First Nation' compatriots since law and policy started to differentiate between the two in the 1970s. At the same time, such approaches are also criticised for 'problematising' minorities on the one hand and for ignoring 'the white community who were experiencing as much, if not more, difficulty in coming to terms with the change' (ibid., p. 9), on the other.

What 'prevention and promotion' strategies seem most to have achieved, Cantle argues, therefore, is a sense of 'separateness'. It is feared that in some cases, this separateness may result in the building of 'a common bond of disaffection, both within nation states and across national borders, embracing a transnational identity, rather than with their fellow citizens' (ibid., p. 10). It is this which is seen primarily as the threat to cohesion.

And yet these are the very approaches which have been emerging in relation to faiths. The UK government's approach has emerged under the banner 'Preventing Extremism Together' which starts with the premise that

> Addressing the problem of extremist activity within communities in the UK has never been more important. Whether it is people planning terrorist attacks or attempting to subvert British values of democracy, tolerance and free speech, the Government is committed to tackling extremism head on. (Home Office, 2005, p. 1)

The language is strong and government claims that it has been asked 'to deal firmly with those prepared to engage in ... extremism; and most particularly those who incite or proselytise it' (ibid., p. 1). There is reference to 'the problems of radicalisation and extremism in their midst' (ibid., p. 1).

At the same time the rhetoric attempts to avoid the separation out of Muslims, for example in the statement that the 'Muslim community in the UK is a responsible and respected part of our multi-cultural and multi-faith society and, in particular, has insisted on taking action against extremism, lest the activities of extremists in recent months taint the good reputation of the mainstream Muslim community' (ibid., 2005, p. 1). And yet, in doing so, it singles Islam out as a special case. Despite reference too to 'other faith communities' (ibid., p. 1), the singling out of Muslims as a special issue is clear in regards to extremism, even where they are not named. In particular it is noted that

> there have been a number of high profile cases where extremist preachers, clerics or teachers have taken over, or have encouraged supporters to take over, places of worship and use them to disseminate

extremist views and practices. This has included fomenting extremism in others, inciting others to terrorist acts, and, even occasionally, aiding or inspiring the planning of such acts. (ibid., p. 2)

And within this, the problem of radicalisation is seen as a particular issue 'for young men' (ibid., p. 2).

The approach is strong then, at least in the language. It is consolidated in the UK government's strategy 'Preventing Violent Extremism: winning hearts and minds' (Home Office, 2007) which emphasises four approaches: 'promoting shared values'; 'supporting local solutions'; 'building civic capacity and leadership' and 'strengthening the role of faith institutions and leaders'. The overall aim is 'to build resilient communities able to challenge robustly the ideas of those violent extremists who seek to undermine our way of life' (ibid.). The stated goal is a situation

> whereby all communities, and particularly British Muslim communities identify themselves, and are accepted, as part of a wider British society reject and actively condemn violent extremism, develop community capacity to deal with problems where they arise and support counter terrorism work by the police and security services. (ibid.)

This approach claims to have been a 'fundamental rebalancing' (ibid.) of government's engagement to focus on organisations 'that are taking a proactive leadership role in tackling extremism and defending our shared values' (ibid.). This can be achieved, the policy has it, through the broadening of provision of citizenship education in supplementary schools and madrassahs and ensuring the most effective use of the mainstream education system in promoting faith understanding.

The new approach drew in part on poll-based research in 2007 that showed that London Muslims were as likely as the general public to condemn terrorist attacks on civilians (88 per cent vs 92 per cent), more likely than the general public to find no moral justification for using violence for a 'noble cause' (81 per cent vs 72 per cent), and that, despite widespread anti-US sentiment within the global Muslim population, only a small minority sympathised with the 9/11 attacks. No correlation was found between religiosity and violent extremism (see Gallop World Poll, 2007). Yet this is part of a flurry of similar research polls in the same period exploring Islam in the West, some of which says different. Other research found that 51 per cent of 18 to 24-year-old UK Muslims believed that 9/11 was a conspiracy by US and Israel (Channel Four TV, UK, 2006).

Fifty-six per cent of UK Muslims believed that the 'War on Terror' is a war on Islam (Populus June, 2006); 20 per cent of UK Muslims felt some 'sympathy' with the motives of the 7/7 bombers (ICM, February 2006); 79 per cent of UK Muslims felt that hostility towards Muslim communities was increasing (Populus June, 2006); 46 per cent of UK Muslims believed that Muslims have become more radical in their views towards British society (ICM, February 2006). It is striking that the questions asked, and therefore the answers given, emphasise Islam as a problem. Nevertheless, there is a clear implication that Muslims themselves are concerned about their singling out as 'problem' – conspired against, the focus of a global 'war' and subject to increasing hostility. This suggests that, despite government's best intentions for a re-balancing of policy towards the inclusion of all within resilient communities, Muslims' own everyday experience is of 'othering'.

The 'prevention and promotion' approach of the UK government, then, has four strands. First, it focuses on helping faith institutions and leaders to engage effectively with all members of Muslim communities. Second, there is an emphasis on working with the regulatory body for the voluntary sector, the Charity Commission, to raise standards of governance in faith institutions. Thus it states, 'Any links between charities and terrorist activity are totally unacceptable... The Charity Commission will deal with any allegation of links between a charity and terrorist activity as an immediate priority.' (Home Office, 2005, p. 3). Third, there have been efforts to establish a framework of minimum requirements for all imams engaged by the state. Fourth, there is envisaged a fully accredited Continuous Professional Development programme for faith leaders. This emphasis on governance and education is striking. It is supplemented by a programme of 'roadshows', for example on 'Tackling Violent Extremism' and the 'Radical Middle Way'.

The UK government has also extended legislative powers so as to be able to 'prosecute those who foment extremism at or near places of worship with the current offences of incitement and the... offences of encouragement to terrorism and dissemination of terrorist publications.' (ibid., p. 3). Extension of the parameters of threat to include 'speech crimes' as well as action are illustrated in new laws against 'incitement to religious hatred'.

But it is also notable that, as policy has emerged, though the prevention dimensions have not diminished, and the singling out of Muslims is still seen as an issue, the language has in places been balanced away from a focus on Muslims and faiths and towards the broader terms of 'protection of the public'. In its 2007 document, '*Working Together to*

Protect the Public: The Home Office Strategy 2008–2011', the UK government says that

> Working together to protect the public is our new statement of purpose for the Home Office. We want that to be the guiding principle for our policies to counter terrorism, cut crime, provide effective policing, secure our borders and protect personal identity. But public protection is only a means to an end. We want the framework of public protection which the state provides to reinforce and strengthen the freedoms and values which are fundamental to being a British citizen. We want people to feel safe and confident in their homes and neighbourhoods, so they can live freely, contribute, and prosper in their daily lives. (Home Office, 2007: foreword)

This rhetoric does not refer to faiths or to Muslims. Rather it says that 'we need to work better with all our partners, including the police, intelligence agencies, local authorities, voluntary bodies, other departments and other governments. Most important of all, we must work with the public' (ibid., p. 2). Now government will 'counter radicalisation by making communities stronger, through support for local organisations and partnerships' (ibid., p. 5) and seek to ensure 'preventing radicalisation in the cause of violent extremism' (ibid., p. 13). This includes 'challenging the ideology of violent extremism; addressing radicalisation in prisons; working with educational institutions to counter extremism; and tackling the use of the internet to radicalise and groom young people'. (ibid., p. 13). But this is not put forward with reference to faiths. Indeed it is striking that in the entire document 'faith' is not referred to once. This compares with its appearance eleven times in the earlier 2005 Home Office document in the 'working together' set.

What is also striking is the relocation of the debate within the terms of a recast citizenship, based not in the unfettered multiculturalism of the period prior to this, but in a more boundaried Britishness in which one's nationhood may take precedence over one's faith or other dimensions of identity.

This reflects the idea that community has come to be seen as 'a realm of governance through which to counter the apparent crisis in social cohesion' which was shown up in the disturbances in the UK in 2001 (Robinson, 2005, p. 1412). But it also casts that 'cohesion' within the terms of a new kind of multicultural settlement, the parameters of which are not made clear. This reflects Cantle's observation that we are in a 'moment of transition' (see Dinham et al., 2009).

The emphasis in 'community' is on the immediate, local and associational. The concern is about the strength of communities in locations – communities of geography – where difference is lived and played out. But at the same time it is also about communities of identity which can take the form of 'stretched localisms', as we have seen above. These might be widely geographically dispersed and maintain connection through telecommunications, especially the internet. Such forms of community in particular are of concern to governments who specifically seek 'community' based in the idea of the nation first and of ethnicity and, now faith, afterwards. Connections across space and beyond borders may threaten this. In this sense, such transnational community may serve to maintain the hearts and minds of people in one place whilst their bodies are physically in another. This is certainly a popular concern about Islam which is frequently characterised in terms of divided loyalties and a betrayal of Britain in favour of the supranational Islamic nation. For community cohesion this means that policy wants to work with difference 'not only to agree upon the areas which should be rigorously defended, but also where the bond of nationality requires a greater sense of commonality' (Cantle, 2005, p. 12). In practice this has resulted in citizenship education in schools, a citizenship 'test' and a citizenship 'ceremony', not only for immigrants but also for school leavers in general. These are expressive of that 'moment of transition' in which the parameters and hierarchy of identity are not yet settled.

But there is a tension between 'difference' and 'commonality' and it is here that the debate is at its most difficult. Difference, as we have seen, is simply the case. As it relates to faiths, we know that there are significant mixes of Christians, Muslims and others in all of the metropolitan areas, as well as in 'pockets' in less urbanised places too (see Chapter 2). This means that people of different faiths are exposed to each other in very many places across the UK, Canada and the US. Where this is going well, the mix can be enriching. But where those 'lines of exposure' arise in the context of overstretched services, poor housing, high unemployment and crime, as is often the case, the 'other' is often experienced as 'threat', and conflict can arise.

It is also clear that faith is a highly situated phenomenon, with differences being embedded within faith traditions – even within traditions in different parts of the same towns and cities – as well as between them. This contingency means that relations might be excellent in one context while in another, even one which appears to be identical or similar, they might be quite tense. In such a context there is no 'recipe' for community cohesion.

And it is also true that traditions often cluster together in shared geographical places. Faiths are concentrated in certain areas, for example Southall in London, Leicester in the English midlands or Toronto in Canada. Such concentrations can present challenges, for example to the ways in which services are delivered in those areas, or to practices of local governance which are altered in accordance with sensitivity to holy days, dietary requirements or liturgical and theological practices. Such differences can be experienced by others outside of those areas as 'preferential treatment' and this, too, can give rise to tension.

As this relates to 'commonality', the challenges are stark. Where 'difference' is celebrated as one basis of community cohesion, how then is 'sameness' incorporated as another? Is it possible to be both different in faith and the same in citizenship? What, then, is the relationship between the person of faith and the person in society? Many people of faith would reject the distinction on every level. Others have tried to resolve this by distinguishing between the private and the public person. But this is only helpful, in policy terms, if we assume that in the person, private faith 'ends' in a place conveniently coterminous with where public 'nationality' begins. Yet the two are much more likely either to coexist or, in a minority of cases, to clash. This precisely is one of the concerns of community cohesion.

Yet the language of 'cohesion' has been evolving and, since its early days, there has been ambivalence in the distinction between 'social cohesion', which characterises the experience *within* spatial areas, and 'community cohesion' which describes the cohesion that is essential *across and between* spatial areas if society is to remain whole. Social cohesion has also been defined as 'the reduction of disparities, inequalities and social exclusion' and 'the strengthening of social relations, interactions and ties' (Berger-Schmitt, 2000, p. 28) and is distinguished from community cohesion on the basis that it thus circumvents the necessity to accept the construct of community in any analysis of it. It has been noted elsewhere, too, that the success of interior cohesion may guarantee good inward relationships among the people in a potential 'community'. But it is unlikely to lead to the sorts of exterior or outward focused relationships associated with community cohesion – that is, cohesion between otherwise 'parallel' groups (see Furbey et al., 2006).

Social capital

These tensions can be explored within the language of social capital. Community cohesion is closely related to this idea which embodies an important proposition – that people are enriched not only by their financial and material assets or by the 'human capital' stemming from their skills and qualifications, but also by their social relationships. Thus, social capital is seen as contributing to better educational attainment, lower crime levels, improved health, more active citizenship, better functioning labour markets and higher economic growth (Performance and Innovation Unit, 2002). This positive view has been consolidated by research that has identified social capital as a key consideration in the search for sustainable neighbourhoods (see, e.g., Green et al., 2005). Communities cohere, it is suggested, where there is ample social capital holding them together. And social capital resides in abundance, it is thought, in faith communities. This has been explored in a Joseph Rowntree Foundation study, *Faith and Social Capital: Connecting or Dividing?* in which I was involved (see Furbey et al., 2006) and we will consider the data coming from that later in this chapter. But what is social capital and how does it relate to community cohesion?

Social capital is defined as consisting of 'trust, networks of co-operation and reciprocity, civic engagement and strong community identity' (Gillies, 1998, pp. 99–120). It has been criticised as an 'elusive concept that is currently poorly specified...and that the use of the term is inherently problematic' (Morrow, 1999, p. 12). Nevertheless, as Fine suggests, 'What is striking about social capital is not only the extent of its influence, and the speed with which this has been achieved, but also its ready acceptance as both analytical and policy panacea' (Fine, 1999, p. 3).

Despite criticisms of its amorphousness, social capital has been identified as a concept which, like 'community', has 'immediate intuitive appeal' (Baron et al., 2000, p. 1). There are two pivotal thinkers in the development of the concept – Bourdieu and Putnam. Their ideas are complemented in the concepts of trust and networks, as outlined in Fukuyama's *Trust: The Social Virtues and the Creation of Prosperity* (1995) and Castells's discussion of networks in *Network Society* (Castells, 1997b).

Pierre Bourdieu

Bourdieu is first to take the term and incorporate it into a much wider and more developed framework. Here the concept of social capital gradually emerges from his interest in social space as a feature or prerequisite of a culturally dynamic and creative society. Bourdieu's is a class and power analysis which is preoccupied with the idea of social capital as a means whereby elites reproduce their privilege through the transformation of interior individualism into collective expressions of perspectives which have hegemony as a result of being most strongly voiced. The strongest network effectively get themselves heard. Indeed, they become the very people who also do the hearing.

The idea of social capital begins, then, as a metaphor whose correlative is economic capital. Like money, social capital can be accumulated, saved, cashed in and spent in exchange for particular social commodities. It is linked with a range of other metaphorical forms of capital which are held together in the concept of 'habitus' – 'a system of more or less well assimilated or more or less transposable schemes of thought' (Bourdieu, 1991, p. 5). This is intended as a means of linking subjectivity (personal and individual experience) with structure (culture, society or community) without reducing either one to the other. 'Habitus' is thus understood as an entity, and not merely a concept, whose form derives from the sum of individual experience expressed in a collective social outcome. In Bourdieu's view 'habitus' is practically a physical reality in the sense that otherwise amorphous and interior individualisms take on external expression in the social world which they add up to form. It is in this idea of 'habitus' that we see the beginnings of social capital, therefore, as something like the invisible yet tangible threads of commonality between individuals which, in abundance, produce community, society or culture. It is clear from this understanding how faiths might be assumed to be sites of social capital, therefore.

Bourdieu's *Reproduction* (Bourdieu and Passeron, 1970) develops this by introducing the category of 'cultural capital'. Cultural capital can exist in various forms: it may be institutional cultural capital, such as academic qualifications; it may be embodied cultural capital, which are particular styles and modes of presentation such as etiquette or self-assurance; it may be objectified cultural capital including material goods and often associated with an aesthetic sensibility expressed through activities such as art collecting or an interest in antiques. Bourdieu is interested in how economic capital, which he regards as the source of all other forms of capital, interacts with wider social structures and processes and is thereby converted into cultural and social capital in ways which reproduce inequality. In this sense, cultural capital is identified as the site of the making of judgements, the dominant group of which presents its conclusions as universal, thereby legitimising them. Cultural capital is a vehicle for achieving social capital. Economic capital is the currency (literally) in which it deals. Social capital is a necessary concomitant – but it is there to help ensure the continued success of economic capitalisation.

Thus individual experience, finding almost physical form and expression in a 'habitus' deriving from the collectivity of that experience, evolves a complex personality which is expressed as culture, the dominant voice of which is able to claim hegemony and therefore to perpetuate itself. It is in this sense that Bourdieu understands cultural capital as judgemental for culture is understood as the cohering of facets of habitus into a hegemonic expression of those which are strongest. In this act a judgement is (inadvertently) made about which facets are (most) legitimate and inequalities are therefore established and sustained. 'Capital', then, is measured in terms of how much money one has, how one spends it on cultural outlets, such as opera tickets, exclusive restaurants and collections of art, and who one knows. Bourdieu's concern, then, is in how 'capital' of various forms is accrued and spent to perpetuate power.

Though Bourdieu is silent on the specific matter of faith and social capital, it could be inferred that, as purported repositories of social capital, faiths would wish to assert their own 'habitus' in this 'judgemental' way – to seek to make hegemonic the cohering facets of their communities. This would, surely, be of concern to others in public space who may already be suspicious of a faith 'agenda' at the public table. And yet, in the instrumentalist rush to embrace the concept, this is one concern that has not been raised.

Though Bourdieu exploits the idea of capital in an extending range of metaphors, including cultural, economic, symbolic, academic and a 'capital of services', the idea takes a more focused form in the early 1980s when 'social capital' is given an irreducible and far more prominent position in his thinking which has influenced the use of the concept fundamentally. In *The Forms of Capital* (Bourdieu, 1997 [1983] in Halsey, 1997, pp. 46–58) Bourdieu acknowledges his earlier tendencies to prioritise economic capital, followed by cultural capital with social capital as a distant third. Here, he shifts this position by positing the idea of a 'unitary capital' which 'can present itself in three fundamental guises' (ibid., p. 47): economic, cultural and social. In this matrix, social capital is defined as

> the aggregate of the actual or potential resources which are linked to possession of a durable network of more or less institutionalised relationships of mutual acquaintance and recognition ... which provides each of its members with the backing of collectively-owned capital. (ibid., p. 51)

It should be noted that in this schema the 'collectivity' consists only of powerful 'capitalists'. Thus social capital is seen as one of three necessary aspects of 'capital' which may manifest economically, culturally or socially and which in its social form is that part of the whole which produces relationships of acquaintance and recognition. These, in turn, contribute to the unitary whole as factors producing the conditions within which culture may make its judgements and economics may make its money. In this sense, it is economic and cultural capital which both produce and depend upon social capital, though each in addition has a life independent of the others. Social capital thus acts as a multiplier for the other two forms while being created and maintained by the conversion of economic and cultural capital in 'the unceasing effort of sociability' (ibid., p. 51).

These class-critiques are generally unfamiliar territory for later devotees of social capital theory, many of whom, especially in public policy settings, tend to assume that the rather comfortable cosiness with which they associate the notion has always been the case. But social capital began life as a striking critique of the production of power before settling down into this somewhat un-contentious 'good'. But how did the idea segue from political radicalism to policy panacea?

Robert Putnam

It is in Putnam's work that the concept of social capital is really popularised. His study on the subject of regional government in Italy explores differences between regional administrations in the North and the South of the country to identify 'civic community' as an explanatory variable in 'institutional performance' (Putnam, 1993). Transporting his model to the US, Putnam moves on to explore decline in civic engagement there. Using the example of a decline in the highly associational social activity of bowling, Putnam seeks to demonstrate that civic America is in serious decline (Putnam, 1995, pp. 65–78). This is developed in Putnam's criticism of television as a major factor in the decline of social capital which he defines as 'features of social life – networks, norms and trust – that enable participants to act together more effectively to pursue shared objectives' (Putnam, 1996, p. 56). So social capital is conceived of as networks, norms and trusts and aligned with shared objectives.

In this way, Putnam takes the class analysis out of the idea and relocates social capital within communitarianism. This recasts social capital in its more familiar guise – as a tool for building strong communities. At the same time, Putnam does regard social capital as a force for egalitarianism, stressing the twin ideas of 'bridging' and 'bonding' forms of social capital. Here, bridging is seen as the building of connections between heterogeneous groups whereas bonding is understood as the links between like-minded people which reinforce homogeneity. Thus, Putnam's bonding argument suggests that strong social bonds and effective organisation within communities provide the foundation on which poor people can develop the capacity to address the problems of poverty, rebuild their communities and achieve measure and control over their lives. It may be characterised in one sense as strength in numbers. Ethnographic studies have suggested that in this way poor communities 'depend upon social capital as their bottom line' (Edin and Levin, 1997, p. 37). Putnam argues, though, that poor communities need to move from surviving at bottom lines to a social capital which has positive effects. Saegert et al. describe this as moving from 'social capital which helps them "get by" to social capital which helps them "get ahead"' (Saegert, Phillip, Thompson and Warren, 2001, p. 15). Nevertheless, Putnam regards bonding capital as a crucial precondition to any effort to engaging people to improve their communities. Bridging capital, on the other hand, describes ties which can help bring greater resources and opportunities into poor communities. Putnam argues that it is a necessary correlative of bonding capital because it challenges the homogeneity of bonded social capital through the processes of bridging with others.

Four types of bridging are identified: first is bridging across different types of social capital within communities; second is bridging between different communities of similar profile; third is bridging between the poor and the more affluent, producing a common identity, commitment and increased power from association with more affluent communities; and fourth is bridging between people and communities nationally in pursuit of effective strategic work.

A third overarching type of social capital is 'linking' social capital and this is the relationships and networks formed between bonded and bridged communities and those outside of them. It is based on the idea of linking out to unknown 'others'.

Put another way, Gilchrist expresses social capital in terms of three types: bonding, bridging and linking. She describes them as follows:

- Bonding based on enduring, multi-faceted relationships between similar people with strong mutual commitments such as among friends, family and other close-knit groups.
- Bridging formed from the connections between people who have less in common, but may have overlapping interests, for example,

between neighbours, colleagues, or between different groups within a community.

- Linking derived from the links between people or organisations beyond peer boundaries, cutting across status and similarity and enabling people to exert influence and reach resources outside their normal circles. (Gilchrist, 2004, p. 6)

Gilchrist argues that *all* these types of social capital are needed to produce the well-connected community.

Trust and networks

Another dimension is the role of trust. Francis Fukuyama has a very particular understanding of social capital which is expressed in these terms. By this device, he is seminal in placing the idea of social capital at the centre of notions of strong civil society. He does so in the context of what he calls 'the end of history' (Fukuyama, 1992) wherein capitalism is understood to have won the argument against socialism in the context of the fall of Soviet communism across Eastern Europe. It has been argued elsewhere that this notion has formed the conceptual basis for the rise of Third Way thinking in the UK and Canada (though this does not account for its significance in the USA in the 30 years previously) and provided the platform for New Left interpretations of social justice within a thriving economic market. Fukuyama argues that where there is no longer a contest between contrasting macro-economic systems, liberal democracy is the only remaining legitimate ideology. From this basis, he suggests that 'liberal political and economic institutions depend upon a healthy and dynamic civil society for their vitality' (Fukuyama, 1995, p. 4). That health and dynamism in civil society is derived from interpersonal trust wherein social capital is regarded as its 'crucible'. And as we have been seeing, policy-makers think faith communities make excellent crucibles.

In this way Fukuyama sees social capital as the crucial factor in sustaining healthy liberal democracy. Thus '... a nation's well-being, as well as its ability to compete, is conditioned by a single, pervasive, cultural characteristic: the level of trust inherent in society' (ibid., pp. 7, 33). Fukuyama distinguishes between 'high' and 'low' trust societies. High trust societies are identified as Japan, Germany and the US and are characterised by an extension of trust from families to corporate businesses. Low trust societies are identified as China, Italy and France which restrict trust to the family alone.

Manuel Castells also contributes to discourse about social capital through the concept of networks, which he understands as 'a set of interconnected modes...open structures, able to expand without limits, integrating new modes as long as they share the same communication codes' (Castells, 2000, p. 14). The idea arises out of social network analysis which stresses the relationships among social entities and the patterns and implications of these relationships (Scott, 1991). The key assumption is that actors and actions are understood as interdependent and that 'relational ties between actors are channels for the transfer of material and non-material resources' (Baron et al., 2000, p. 26). These are understood as 'the contacts, ties, connections and group attachments which relate one agent to another and so cannot be reduced to the properties of the individual agents themselves' (Castells, 1991, p. 3).

Criticisms of the idea of social capital

For faiths, the idea of social capital is resonant, and it is this which policy-makers have been noticing. Faiths are assumed to be well bonded – the preconditions for social capital are automatically there since faith communities are something like families. Faiths are also understood to be interested in bridging, whether for purposes of evangelism, or because of the invocation to be good neighbours or to embrace the unity of things. And they are regarded as keen on 'linking' for much the same reasons. Spreading the word, doing good, propagating God's 'kingdom' and so on are all important spurs to linking out to others. There may be some truth to these perceptions. But we should be cautious in our embrace of them, as we shall see, below.

The trouble with social capital is that it is 'a nebulous concept that can include anything from how parents interact with their children to how people feel about where they live, to whom they know, how much they use their "networks" and how much they trust their politicians' (Morrow, 1999, p. 749). Morrow argues, thus, that 'it is gender blind, ethnocentric and arguably a concept imported from the US without due attention to cross and inter-cultural differences' (ibid., p. 749). It has been suggested that social capital has come to have significant political currency because 'a small number of influential people at the heart of politics recognise the tenets of social capital in their own circumstances, for example in declining voter turn outs' (Lemann, 1996, p. 4). Lemann argues, too, that the fall of communism in the former Soviet countries of Eastern Europe has given renewed impetus to debates about citizenship and the state. Against this backdrop, he suggests that the idea of social capital is fashionable as a response to individualism – 'the revalorisation of social relationships in political discourse after a period of harsh dismissal of them in the face of globalised market relationships' (ibid., p. 13) so that in such a context ideas of social capital 'offer a purchase on such interaction' (ibid., p. 14). In all of these senses, social capital has been criticised for being an 'ideological tramline' (Furbey et al., 2006, p. 6) outside of which it can become difficult to think. In Putnam, it is also perhaps overly associated with voluntary and community forms of social capital at the expense of thinking about how it might operate in those already powerful settings such as government and in the civil service. It is also suggested that it is in some ways a disturbing language which draws upon 'the instrumental economic language of capital in the context of (often informal) social networks' (ibid., p. 5).

In his article, 'It Ain't Social and It Ain't Capital' (Fine, 1999), Fine proposes several further criticisms of the idea. First, he asserts that it is hard to define. Moreover, 'the notion of social capital is chaotic as is...reflected in frequent suggestions that it is merely a metaphor or a heuristic device' (Fine in Morrow, 2001, p. 17). As a result, he suggests, it is also difficult to measure (though tools and scales have been designed which are criticised for oversimplification and cultural specificity). Second, Fine suggests that 'social capital has a gargantuan appetite' (in Morrow, 2001, p. 12). In this sense it has been used to explain 'everything from individuals to societies' (ibid., p. 12) and may be deployed in any aspect of social, cultural and economic performance. At the same time, he argues, it has been used across theories and methodologies. Third, it is suggested that, 'although social capital is unlimited in principle in terms of what it can incorporate and address, and how it does so, the evolution of literature in practice is far from neutral in terms of its content and direction' (ibid., p. 12). At the same time, most of the literature has tended to focus on associational forms of civil society but, as Fine points out, does so 'in isolation from...serious consideration of economy, formal politics, the role of the nation state, the exercise of power, and the divisions and conflicts that are endemic to capitalist society' (ibid., p. 13). In this sense, ideas of social capital have been treated in terms of their own interior local contexts without regard for the wider influences which help determine the shape of that 'capital'. This fits with the 'repositories' understanding of faiths and social capital. Fourth, Fine suggests that the complex and critical aspects of social capital identified in Bourdieu have been effectively superseded by the 'tamer versions' of Putnam (ibid., p. 13).

Like 'community' and 'faith community' then, the primary criticism of the idea of social capital derives from its definitional diversity. There are a wide range of understandings deriving from a breadth of disciplines and conceptual positions. Thus, sociologically it may be understood as an explanatory device for understanding civil society. Here the focus is on that part of life which exists between and in addition to individuals. At the same time, sociological perspectives may embrace social capital only reluctantly as an heuristic device with interpretative resonance. Economically, on the other hand, social capital has been seen both as a metaphor for describing relationships as a social resource and as a precondition for successful economic interactions to which social capital can also add value. On the other hand, it has been suggested that 'the theory of social capital is, at heart, most straightforward. Its central thesis can be summed up in two words: relationships matter' (Field, 2003, p. 1).

But whether complex or simple, we should recognise the danger that dominant strands in social capital theory and research could lead us into a narrow and simplistic understanding of faith communities and their members as 'social capital'. The notion that they might operate as a sort of 'social glue' is implicit in Coleman's conservative stress on the functional importance of religion as an agent promoting 'closure' across institutions and generations and thus promoting social capital. Putnam recognises the decline in church membership. Yet he also sees religious organisations as important pillars of civil society and positive influences in building community and governability. As we have seen, this binding civic role of 'faith' is what the UK government has also sought to enlist. However, social capital need not take this 'legitimate', officially approved form and the complexity of religious faith and the diversity of social ideologies is not captured in a phrase like 'social glue' (Farnell et al., 2003). It is important to look beyond 'legitimate' religious social capital and to recognise that faiths may also present in the form of retreat, resistance and critique (Furbey and Macey, 2005).

Faiths and social capital: Connecting or dividing?

In Chapter 2 I argued that faiths must be understood in all their diversity and approached with a localism which embraces this. But in relation to faith and social capital, it can also be argued that all the major faith traditions share some similarity of core principles that can motivate bridging and linking through the acceptance of others and through 'community service, co-operation, peace-making and the pursuit of social justice' (Furbey et al., 2006, p. 8). But the same words do not guarantee the same meanings, as we have been seeing with the notions of 'faith' and 'community' already. Oliver McTernan concludes, nevertheless, that, despite their obvious differences in thought and practice, there are 'important resemblances in belief that exist between the mainstream world religions' (McTernan, 2003, p. 148). All have 'commitments to peace, justice, honesty, service, personal responsibility and forgiveness which can contribute to the development of networks and the trusting relationships which characterise positive social capital' (Furbey et al., 2006, p. 10). In particular, all faith traditions involve a tolerance, respect and an obligation to 'the other' which suggests an innate predilection for 'bridging' and 'bonding'.

Yet, all this must be in the recognition that religion can be a powerful source of division as well as connection. Thus McTernan also recognises that 'competing claims on the exclusivity or superiority of one interpretation of truth over the other have often lead to abandonment or outright violation of these ["connecting"] principles' (McTernan, 2003, p. 148). Put more starkly, 'There is brutal, callous, intolerant religion and there is compassionate, kind and tolerant religion' (Ward, 2004, p. 121).

At its worst, the disconnection between faiths has been given expression in physical violence and terrorism. But faiths can demonstrate disconnection in other less dramatic ways too. Some groups are motivated to engage outside themselves whilst others feel that they must effect a degree of segregation from other faiths and from wider society. Perhaps they regard the 'other' as a threat to their integrity, their capacity or even their purity. In some cases, theology may seem to require a clear boundary with the rest of 'the world' and this might lead to retreat or defensiveness. Ruthven contrasts introverted and isolationist sects with more challenging religious movements that are more prone to 'fight back' against the pluralist secular world. Thus, 'For the active fundamentalist (as distinct from the passive traditionalist) the quest for salvation cannot be realised by withdrawing into a cultural enclave' (Ruthven, 2004, p. 57).

We must also acknowledge that, although all faiths aspire to peace, they have all at various times also sanctioned intolerance, segregation and violence. The role of faiths in social capital must be set within this context, too. Far from bonding, bridging and linking, faiths have shown themselves to be more than capable of dissent, disagreement and violence; within, between and beyond themselves. And it has been noted that in the post-9/11 world, and in the context of global and instantaneous telecommunications, 'the secular and the religious encounter one another with a new sharpness, while religions that had lived at a distance from one another are often together on the same street or looking at each other over the same wall' (Furbey et al., 2006, p. 11). In this context of what he calls an increasingly 'liquid' world, Zygmunt Bauman thus identifies 'a constant threat to social integration – and also to the feeling of individual security and self-assurance' (Bauman, 2004, p. 82). This, he notes, can result in the search for a 'haven' or retreat. As we assess the potential for faith communities as a source of social capital, therefore, we must recognise that faiths are operating in a context of anxiety and uncertainty.

This is unsettling for those who hope that faiths are unequivocally repositories of social capital as a basis for community cohesion. And it is strange to observe that the same policy agenda which sees faiths as such a repository is also in large part motivated by the very fractures to which faiths are also seen as contributing. The disturbances in English towns in 2001 were rapidly recast as 'faith' based as much as 'race' based, and their context has since been ever broadening in the terms of a 'war on terror'. This has repeatedly been associated with an attack by faith fundamentalists on an otherwise enlightened (Western) way of life. Faiths are seen, thus, as both heroes and villains: sources of bonding, bridging and linking at the same time as its usurpers. This paradox may be one that faiths themselves find difficult to accept.

At the same time, there is an implicit suggestion that there are two kinds of faiths: moderate faiths who are friends of the state – repositories of resources which can help it to function; and immoderate faiths who are its enemies. This may seem fair enough at first glance. And yet we must ask who are the moderates and the immoderates? Who decides which is which? And where do we draw the line? In the popular imagination, immoderation is likely to be associated with Islam while moderation includes everybody else. This is a blunt analysis and one which is likely to be both inaccurate and ultimately ineffective in policy terms. Fundamentalism and even fanaticism are likely to be found in all the faiths, just as is moderation. The singling out of Islam as a special focus of policy attention, even with the best of intentions, is likely to extend rather than resolve fracture. Muslims are unlikely to feel welcomed to the public table if at the same time they are also characterised as villains.

What the data show

In our Joseph Rowntree Foundation study (Furbey et al., 2006), we explored the social capital constituted by faiths in specific initiatives, informal meeting places and particular 'episodes' that illustrate or embody connecting social capital and, or, exemplify the obstacles to it. The research included episodes stemming from Christian (including black-majority), Hindu, Jewish, Muslim and Sikh organisations.

Our guiding research question was 'how far can faith organisations and their members contribute to social capital that not only bonds people together, but also enables them to cross boundaries and build bridges and links with others in civil society?' The data are complex and the area is conceptually contested (and sometimes even emotive), as we have seen. Nevertheless, the evidence does provide some answers.

Frameworks and networks

First, the study noted that growing numbers of people live in areas where faiths are highly diverse. In some places there is evidence of neighbourhood being somewhat segregated so that 'parallel' lives are being lived which may be strongly bonded within their own 'communities' but with limited bridging and linking to the 'other'. The study found, nevertheless, that frameworks for reaching out have been emerging which might compensate, though these are not always visible or recognised. In the UK, at the national level, there are both multilateral and bilateral structures. For example, the Inter Faith Network for the United Kingdom has built up a membership with representational and consultative structures. The Faith-based Regeneration Network UK (FbRN UK) has also been formed to work with nine faith traditions engaged in regeneration practices and community practices in general. There is also a growing range of bilateral organisations. At the national level in the UK, the Council of Christians and Jews was the first such organisation, formed in 1942. This has now been joined by a national Christian Muslim Forum. There is also a range of discussion groups for Muslims and Jews, Hindus and Muslims, Christians and Hindus and others. These include organisations such as the Three Faiths Forum, which brings together the three 'Abrahamic' Faiths. And at the regional and local levels there are representational structures linking faiths to government. We shall return to these issues in Chapter 7). At the local level there has been enormous growth in faith forums and councils of which there are at least 185 in the UK, many of which have come into being since 9/11.

As well as these formal structures for bridging and linking, there are also all sorts of informal engagements between faith community leaders at local and national levels. Because they are based in informal relationships they tend to underpin the 'trust' dimension of social capital of which Castells talks. This is reflected at the micro level where there is a dense (and largely unmeasureable) network of relationships across faith communities with a fundamentally important impact on the effectiveness of faiths as agents of social capital.

Buildings and places

Second, the study found that faith buildings very often act as physical markers of presence and diversity with the effect that the very visibility of the building can stimulate social capital. This happens in two main ways: first, the provision of public services, such as child care, cafés and car schemes, can bring people across the group into closer contact and increase mutual understanding and trust. This is the bonding form of social capital; and second, the provision of services and facilities to the wider community outside of the faith group can bring faiths and the wider community together more generally, too. In turn, this often brings individuals, both of faith and outside of it, into association with wider forums or activity which they had hitherto not engaged with.

Certainly, premises can become the focus of community activity and this very often leads to opportunities for bridging and linking within, across and beyond faiths to the wider community. On the other hand, we observed that, as sacred spaces, faith buildings can sometimes be containers of histories and relationships that can militate against the production of social capital. This can be because of a strongly proprietorial sense of the sacred space as inviolable by others. Or it may be because of a strong internal 'bonded-ness' which retreats from the bridging and linking which are valuable to civil society. This is sometimes reflected in formal restrictions on their use or on who may use them. Nevertheless, many faith settings have buildings or rooms in addition to their worship spaces, or they are permitted by tradition to make varying use of their premises. This physical capital of faiths can often be of significant value in the development of social capital as people find within them places where they can 'transgress' the boundaries within which they normally operate and make new relationships and networks. These new contacts, both formal and informal, often lead to new bridges and links. In particular, accounts of coincidental or serendipitous bridging through visits to faith buildings are sufficiently widespread as to suggest that at least some of this is the aim of the 'visit' or 'episode of exposure'. And certainly, the informal activity that takes place around the margins of more formal events in faith buildings is substantial. In these ways, the buildings can facilitate a coming together of people who would otherwise not know each other.

Associational 'spaces'

But people associate, not only in physical places, but also through the 'spaces' of their shared interests and motivations. Often this gets 'organised' in groups or structures and consolidated through the trust that grows therein. Faiths are adept at this 'organisation' of people's associations with each other through the sorts of activities and events they run and the organisational structures which inhere. They have the potential to bring people together in relationships, often within the framework of an overarching structure or organisation, sometimes at international, national or regional levels, as in the case of the Christian Church of England, the Lutheran Church in Canada and the Council of Muslims in the US. Thus many faiths tend to be organised in ways that bring people of faith into connection on a relatively large scale. 'Community' of this kind constitutes a rather stretched form of social capital that may bear little tension or pressure. It is a weak form of social capital which is broad but shallow. Its strength lies in its capacity for taking a rather thin general bonded-ness within which many people identify themselves with a 'tradition' and acting to bridge and link, often strategically.

But there are also examples of smaller, more robust, forms of strategic association. For example, the UK's Churches' Regional Commission for Yorkshire and the Humber (CRCYH) was formed in 1998 in response to the recognition that a new national government presented an opportunity to engage with a new policy agenda. CRCYH was set up as a mechanism to equip people for engagement. Beyond this, our study found three further consequences of the commission's formation. First, CRCYH could command attention because of its strong reputation derived, in part, from the other organisations out of which it emerged. Second, it has its own additional resources for supporting networking. Third, CRCYH can take an overview across the region in a way that its more local counterparts cannot. Thus it is in a position to search for, identify and share episodes of activity in such a way as to make bridges and links between otherwise separate groups and organisations. A practical example is the commission's hosting of a 'financial exclusion breakfast' attended by local people, representatives from credit unions and financial organisations, local authority officers and councillors and faith groups. This began a conversation and relationships resulting in other initiatives for addressing debt in the area. At the same time, CRCYH acknowledges that the social capital that is built depends to some extent on '...a couple of individuals in the right group at the right time' (ibid., p. 27). Yet CRCYH is able to identify the conditions that might support the growth and deployment of social capital and harness them. It can do this sensitively because it has real relationships in the first place and can mediate them up and down the ladders of power. In this way it develops bonds within and among faiths but also bridges and links more widely across the whole region.

A second example is Church Action on Poverty (CAP), whose 'poverty hearings', between 1993 and 1999 brought people together from across sectors and faith groups to explore issues and solutions to poverty in local areas. This very practical approach to understanding poverty is all the more distinctive for its emphasis on including people who themselves are living in poverty. The hearings still take place at the instigation of local people from time to time, with or without CAP's formal involvement. One example of a concrete outcome from such a hearing was seen when a local church joined in partnership with its local authority and set up a credit union. This arose directly out of the generation of social capital between two organisational partners brought into dialogue as a result of this third.

Faith 'spaces' can also be supportive contexts for social capital through the capacity they have for inspiring trust and confidence. Established figures, such as a Bishop or well-known Imam, and organisations, for example the Church Urban Fund or Jewish Care, can lend great credibility to initiatives which might otherwise do less well. And in some cases they can command influence and power in places which could otherwise not be reached, for example where a clergy leader is on a school's board of governors. This can afford opportunities for association across power differentials. Similarly they can bring people together in associations that are developmental and strategic, for example in committees or forums which are funded, staffed and supported.

However, our study also noted that there are gender and generational differences that can inhibit this, as we have noted elsewhere. Faiths' organisations and networks are often shaped by theological understandings that motivate and direct particular approaches to questions of social justice and human dignity. Paralleling many secular organisations, faiths can be bad at listening to their women and young people. Where social capital depends upon relationships, as it does, and where many of these are informal and 'soft', as we have observed, forms of sexism and ageism can be rapidly institutionalised at the same time as being obscured by an assumption that they are not happening. Yet we know that the skills required to build social capital tend to be associated with the sorts of networking which accrues to older people and to men. This can be a problem because often the views and experiences of one generation are starkly different to those of another as faiths struggle to relate to their new contexts over time. And many women also have distinctive experiences of bridging and linking. Our study observed that they are frequently associated with informal roles with less visibility. In both cases, there are distinctive stories and lessons to be heard. It is likely that the experience of social capital building is differentiated for other minority and oppressed groups too, including lesbian, gay, bisexual and transgender people, and people with disabilities. Though this is true of wider society, perhaps it is more pronounced in some faith communities where particular values, traditions and theologies are part of what determines their character.

Our study also noted a significant social capital contribution in local governance, to which we shall return in Chapter 7, and in 'a less regulated public domain' (ibid., p. 42), by which we mean 'an open-ended and negotiated "associational" politics rather than as providers of government-approved "social glue"' (ibid., p. 42). Again I return to these themes in a discussion of deliberation in Chapter 7.

Faith communities contribute to social capital through their very presence in the public domain, therefore. However, as is often the case in non-faith contexts, external networking and action is usually undertaken by a relatively small number of faith group members. This is an aspect of how stressful the 'bridging' demands can be, particularly where there is linguistic and cultural diversity as is often the case. Most faiths also bring together people of different ages and socio-economic situations in mixes not found in wider society. Relations between an externally networking minority and their 'home' communities can vary. Sometimes the activism of the 'bridger' or 'linker' clashes with the internal preoccupations of the 'home community', producing a weakening of 'bonds'. In other cases, the starting 'base' may remain a strong resource and, at the same time, draw others into bridge building and linking activities.

Faiths also contribute substantial and distinctive social capital through being present together, especially in urban areas. The very fact of being there, perhaps on the same street or in the same neighbourhood, seems to produce a bridging and linking between faiths and traditions. They are also good at bridging and linking through their 'connecting frameworks' – the structures and mechanisms they set up to relate with one another, for example interfaith and multi-faith networks. And it is significant that faith buildings demonstrate a presence to which people of other faiths and none respond. Often they are used for things other than worship and this has the effect of bridging and linking where people from all sorts of backgrounds share the use of the building. This frequently extends into the associational networks which coming together in faith buildings can result in. People come into contact with one another who otherwise would have no reason to do so. Their shared but differentiated use of the same buildings can produce new relationships and social capital in abundance. Faiths are also effective in their engagement in governance and in their work across boundaries with others in the public domain. We shall explore each of these claims more fully below.

Nevertheless, our study suggests that faiths could be more effective producers of social capital if they did not face various obstacles. Some are associated with misunderstandings and suspicions of others outside of faiths. Others are concerned with financial barriers associated with, for example, prejudicial funding regimes, a suspicion of the use of public money by faiths and certain theological obstacles such as prohibitions on gambling which inhibits access to lottery funds. There are also questions about the burden of inappropriate buildings which require adaptation before being put to wider community use, and about intensive managerialism and regulation, for example in the monitoring of grants and projects.

Finally, the study found that changes and developments are needed within faith communities themselves. Although practice varies considerably, bridging and linking is very often undertaken by a small minority of members of a 'faith community'. In turn, their potential skills and contributions may go unrecognised, or be constrained within certain organisational or bureaucratic structures. And the particular qualities required for wider associational deliberation and participation in the activities of social capital are often not a subject of explicit reflection and development.

Social capital as community cohesion?

It can be demonstrated, then, that faiths are active within the terms of bonding, bridging and linking social capital, notwithstanding debates and contests about the concepts. Setting aside those debates for now, let us assume that social capital exists and that faiths are agents of it. What, then, is its relationship to the community cohesion which it is hoped will result?

We have observed that in some faith communities strong 'bonding' forms of social capital can result in resistance to outside influences and relationships and a closing of ranks against the exterior 'other' (see ibid.). Cheesman and Khanum suggest that this is a particular feature of emerging perceptions of Islam as an homogeneously radical and dangerous 'community' which seeks to cut itself off from the mainstream of society. This is hardly conducive to community cohesion. And yet policies for the prevention of extremism and legislation in the UK, the US and Canada seem to go along with that by locating the problem in one particular faith group rather than, say, in an ethnicity, or recast completely as a geopolitical issue about the global distribution of power or wealth. Does policy thereby collude with what Cheesman and Khanum have observed as a sort of recasting of Muslims in terms similar to the medieval English 'othering' of Catholics? They suggest that this contributes to what they call a 'soft segregation' – of hearts and minds rather than streets and houses – which is both cause and result of suspicions of Islam. At the same time, they want to show how Muslims are in fact in many ways at the centre of British life, as in the flip but instructive example of the prevalence of curry restaurants in the UK (Cheesman and Khanum in Dinham et al., 2009).

Weller focuses more on the bridging and linking dimensions. In terms of the faiths which are newer to Britain, as well as those which are longer established, he identifies a trajectory which results in a focus on identity, not only in terms of ethnicity but also faith (in ibid.). He suggests that this is part of a multiculturalism in which faiths have had to develop modes of mutuality which have been given impetus by a whole range of newly extended forms of participatory governance, which seek to include the representation of faiths. What is of great value is the role interfaith and multi-faith endeavours can play in building social capital as a basis for community cohesion. Where faiths are exposed to one another in such settings, their bridging out to one another can set them in good stead for then linking into the governance settings beyond them. Weller suggests that this is to the good. Indeed, he wonders whether these sorts of inter and multi-faith working might add up to a new 'socio-religious contract' (Weller in ibid.) in which faiths – and others – work together constructively and with empathy.

In keeping with these fundamental themes, Maqsood Ahmed, Ted Cantle and Dilwar Hussein have debated whether faith displaces or extends multiculturalism's focus on ethnicity to take account of faith as an increasingly acknowledged marker of identity (see Lowndes in ibid.). They are clear that this is not so much a signal of the end of multiculturalism as 'a moment of transition', still unresolved. While 'community cohesion' might yet prove to be a useful idea in addressing those 'parallel lives' which Cantle has observed, they say it must emphasise commonalities as well as recognise difference. Might positive forms of bridging and linking social capital, such as those envisaged in Weller's account of inter and multi-faith work, support this balance between commonalities and difference? Or is the diversity which we have observed such that the differences prove to be overpowering?

So policy regards social capital as the bedrock of community cohesion and faiths as its effective agents. But social capital is insufficient in itself to ensure that communities cohere. There is a job to be done, then, in directing social capital towards certain commonalities upon which we can all agree. The implication is that only this will ensure our peaceful and productive coexistence. Community cohesion is, then, a balancing act between commonality and difference. What differences do we celebrate and when must sameness take priority? Within that, how can bridging and linking be ensured, even where bonding may provide a feeling of safety and retreat? It is also about balancing the local and the global. The links which are made between local community life and the 'global identities [faith] can represent through diaspora communities' (Lowndes in ibid.) demonstrate the significance of strong relations between faiths, not only in local terms but also as a world issue. And at the same time it is about the personal and the private. Where does my faithful self begin and end, and where, in turn, the social?

6
Faiths and the Provision of Services

In the previous chapters we have seen how faiths have come to be regarded by governments, especially in the UK and US, as repositories of resources of potential value to wider society. But that value does not relate only to the rather amorphous and subtle notions of community and community cohesion. As I have argued, it relates to two other main areas as well: the provision of services; and governance. Quite in which order to address these aspects is, itself, vexing, since the relationships between them are complex and the overlaps are frequent. This is indicative of the problems themselves. One approach is to see governance as a natural extension of the community and cohesion dimensions because these are all associated with the ways in which governments try to set, or at least to influence, the parameters of civil society by legislating here and there, promoting this or working with that. But where, then, would we deal with faiths as service providers? After all, this is numerically the biggest and most visible aspect of their activities in public space and it seems glib to 'tack it on' at the end. Happily, from the author's point of view, the biggest contribution of faiths in service provision is through community projects and a great deal of this work can be understood from a community development perspective therefore. So there, like a good news anchor, we have a useful link: faiths are 'communities', they contribute to 'community cohesion' and they are big in 'community development'. Sorry if you thought you had got away from 'community' once more. As has been observed 'it is an idea which refuses to lie down' (Pahl, 1995).

However, this is not the only dimension to faiths as service providers. Alongside the idea that services can be delivered via community development initiatives, there are also faiths delivering specific social services, such as accommodation for young homeless people (e.g., the

YMCA), on a large scale through public sector contracts. We will consider examples, and some of the problems for faiths doing this.

Another arena for thinking about faiths as providers is found in the new policy imperatives being placed upon service providers, including faiths, through aspirations to financial self-sufficiency and stability of services through social enterprise. How does this affect faiths and with what responses?

Education has also been a significant area of faith provision for many years. But faith schools have more recently become a hot topic politically in the UK where Christian schools have been commonplace for many years but where schools run by other faiths are increasingly proposed. We will consider some of the key debates this has raised. What will also help is an example from Ontario, Canada, where some of the fundamental questions about the relationship between faiths and public space are being highly debated because of a provincial election campaign in which one candidate promoted the public role of faiths in education. This has thrown open the doors on wider debates about the legitimacy of public faith at all.

So, though one would be forgiven for thinking that service provision should be a simple matter – finding out what faith-based services are providing, and what form they take, maybe giving a useful example or two, before moving on to more contentious ground with meatier 'policy' ideas about governance and citizenship – such simplicity eludes us once more, for 'faiths and service provision' is not a straightforward matter after all. For a start, the perceived 'value' of faith-based service provision derives from two perspectives: an instrumentalist one which looks at faiths in terms of how they are practically 'useful' directly in the business of providing services; and an idealist one which views them in terms of the moral or ethical ethos it is hoped they will bring into public space. This is often housed in the language of 'community', as we have seen, and draws on those comfortable notions of neighbourhood, 'spirit' and togetherness. The 'mix' of instrumentalism and idealism varies where there is an interest in faiths and civil society, and the variance is starkly illuminated in the case of services.

Then there are important debates about the modes of provision with which faiths can engage. We will see that the dominant mode in both the UK and the US is funding for usually relatively local projects with reference to wider governmental strategic objectives. In the US, these are associated specifically with ensuring that a sufficient level of services is provided to meet need across the piece. Faiths are one part of the jigsaw in this provision. In the UK, there is a similar association with meeting needs, though there is more of an emphasis on neighbourhood level initiatives aimed at rebuilding 'community' in areas of particular disadvantage.

In addition, there are contests about whether and how faiths should provide public services at all. These are often associated with concerns about the relationship between provision and evangelical mission. Should services be open to all? Should there be 'strings' attached – either for providers or for users of services? This, in turn, raises questions about what makes a service 'faith-based'. What is the relationship between the service and the worshipping community? How is faith expressed in that service?

As has been clear from the outset, the involvement of faiths in service provision, as in other areas of public life, is a highly political affair both in the sense that policy helps set the parameters of civil society and that the presence of faiths at the public table can shake things up. In the end it raises the fundamental question, where does faith sit at the public table? Does it have a legitimate role? If so, where and how? Are faith-based services to be considered part of the voluntary sector? Or does this compromise their independence and 'critical' or 'prophetic' voice?

A long tradition of faith-based service

Certainly faiths have a long tradition of working with people, particularly in disadvantaged areas, to achieve change and development. It has been argued that this arises out of 'an holistic, faith based view of communities which values and dignifies all people' (Finneron et al., 2002, p. 12). This tradition is, in one sense, timeless. Indeed, all of the Abrahamic faiths invoke their followers to give service to one another in community. Thus it is that John Wesley, the eighteenth-century revivalist, proclaimed that believers should not only 'earn all you can' and 'save all you can' but also 'give all you can' (Wesley, 1771, vol. 1, pp. 705–12).

In another sense, religious or faith-based service provision is in many ways rooted in Victorian philanthropy, when society 'boasted millions of religious associations providing essential services and a moral training for citizenry...' (Prochaska, 2006, p. 2).[1] The Victorians, in this view, 'believed that religion and the public good were inextricably linked' (ibid., p. 3) and that 'charity could only be effectively exercised under the influence of sacred principle' (ibid., p. 3). Indeed, in his review of Prochaska's book, Bowpitt comments that

What Prochaska describes is nothing less than a welfare society in Britain before there was ever a welfare state, but a welfare society thoroughly permeated by a religious quest that justified and directed all philanthropic effort, to cure souls as well as bodies. (Bowpitt, 2007, p. 1)

This describes a 'services' ethos which is highly idealistic, deriving from the values and mission of the Christian churches at the time. Christian philanthropy extended especially into education and health, too, so that

> Long before the first Board Schools, charity schools, Sunday schools and Lord Shaftesbury's 'ragged schools' taught children to read to give them access to the Bible and Christian literature, and an elementary education grew from this. While Florence Nightingale walked with her lamp in the hospitals of the Crimea, Ellen Ranyard's Bible nurses tramped the streets of London, giving comfort and medical help to the sick and dying in their own homes, inspired by the longing that none should leave this world without being prepared for the next. (ibid., p. 2)

Bowpitt also notes that 'other areas of Christian philanthropy reflected the character of Victorian society and appear anachronistic to us now' (ibid., p. 2). He refers to Prochaska's account of the practice of 'district visiting' to all the inhabitants of a neighbourhood, the point of which was to show that no one was beyond the love of Christ. Bowpitt concludes in his critique that 'Prochaska presents Victorian philanthropy as little less than a golden age of Christian social service that yielded benefits far beyond the provision of welfare services' (ibid., p. 3). Thus Prochaska argues that it lays the very foundation of civil society by setting a higher moral tone, promoting community cohesion and skilling disadvantaged groups. But at the same time, he observes that the welfare state, when it did come, inherited much of that Christian spirit and does not merely or necessarily represent a secular take over of services which had been provided by faiths. This view of the welfare state as a secularisation of religious provision has been challenged in other ways, too. Indeed, Bowpitt notes, for example, that 'Social work as a secular humanist alternative was emerging from an ideological struggle for the heart of social welfare long before the advent of the welfare state' (Bowpitt, 1998).

In many ways the Victorian period has been seen as a golden age for faith-based social action when faiths (or rather, Christian traditions) were not just active, but were leaders in providing services in response to need. This was a time when there were '2,349 subsidiary associations to dispense the Bible' (Prochaska, 2006, p. 17) and the 'myriad parish societies... had membership numbers that varied from under ten to hundreds' (ibid., pp. 17–18). At the same time, though there was debate about religion and faith more widely, this was not the white-hot period of the Enlightenment when the nature, existence and purposes of God were widely and heatedly disputed in ways which affected the very political foundations of society. Rather, this was a time when the idea of God was relatively settled, in England at least: God was Christian, male and an Englishman. The role of the churches in social action was, in this context, seen as both legitimate and necessary. From a missiological point of view it was, too, seen as no less than the duty of people of faith to provide for need. Thus for Toqueville, Christianity was 'not an opiate, nor a morality of slaves but a religion of self-discipline and personal service that answered social and political needs' (in ibid., p. 26) and in his 'memoir' on pauperism written in 1835 after a visit to England, he writes that one of the merits of Christianity is that it makes charity a divine virtue.

The rise of welfarism – faiths as well-meaning amateurs

The twin pressures of the extension of the franchise and a growing awareness of the persistence of poverty and want led in the 1940s to the emergence of a radically different context in which faith-based services, along with other non-government provision, were absorbed into the activities of central government. This was crystallised in the UK in the establishment of universal welfare after the Second World War. Though it had started earlier, with the exponential professionalisation of social services, the idealism of universal welfare was too strong an influence for a disparate non-governmental matrix of service provision to elude. Practically every aspect of social service, from health, to the family and community development came under the auspices of central government in the period after 1948. This was a period of high idealism whose effect, despite all good intentions, was to recast the widespread, experienced and highly effective network of non-government providers, many of which were faith-based, as outside the strategic idealism of government. The needs of post-war Britain were seen as too important to be left to the well-meaning amateurs. This also had an instant effect on their funding since the welfare state encouraged the expectation that needs would be met without resort to charity, and giving and philanthropy suffered accordingly.

Thus the philanthropic approach was largely rejected after 1948 when the Labour Party's critique of philanthropy and the introduction of state welfare led to optimism that the state would eradicate social ills. Despite this, the optimism of the years immediately following the Second World War , aligned with the emergence of the new Keynesian economics, gave way to what has been called 'the rediscovery of community and the development of community-based policies in the 1960's and early 1970's' (Mayo et al., 2003, p. 24).

Welfare as the problem, not the solution – a new space for faiths?

Thus the realisation that the post-war welfare consensus had not resulted in the eradication of society's 'five great evils' led to renewed enthusiasm for community-based policies rooted in neighbourhood and self-help – precisely the sorts of work faith-based providers had been so good at. In particular it was apparent that architectural renewal was insufficient to the building of communities and by the end of the 1950s, community work had come to be seen as 'a third method of social work intervention' (Younghusband, 1959, p. 24) alongside group work and case work. Much of this new community work was conducted in neighbourhood level projects and many of those were initiated by faiths. This was in part a result of the Church of England's parish system which ensured that there were staff, buildings and resources in every area of the country, even where other agencies had withdrawn. At the same time, the Gulbenkian Report (Younghusband, 1968) envisaged work in communities which is 'concerned with affecting the course of social change through the two processes of analysing social situations and forming relationships with different groups to bring about desirable change' (ibid., p. 22). It identified a set of values which reflect those of many faith-based endeavours. First, people matter and policies and public administration should be judged by their effects on people. Second, participation in every aspect of life is of fundamental importance. Third, work in communities should be concerned with the distribution of resources towards people who are socially disadvantaged. This represented a new context in which non-government actors could engage, with government support, in public space to address need. And it was a context with which faiths could identify in terms of its insistence on human worth and value and on structural critiques of society which refused to locate the causes of poverty and disadvantage within the people who suffered from its consequences. Faiths were prolific in providing interventions in communities at this time in ways which could reflect this political ethos and were able to thrive in a context which was friendly to them.

However, by 1979, when the first Thatcher government achieved power in the UK, these approaches, and welfarism in general, had come to be seen, by her party at least, as part of the problem, not the solution. There was a shift to 'market led approaches in the 1980's and early 1990's' (Mayo et al., 2003, p. 28) characterised by a focus on the economic, as opposed to community, development of local areas and the 'trickle down' approach to wealth for which Galbraith used 'the less than elegant metaphor that if one feeds the horse enough oats, some will pass through to the road for the sparrow' (Galbraith, 1992, p. 108). It has been argued that at that time, in so far as there was any emphasis on participation, it 'became a strategy for sustaining administrative stability and subduing potentially troublesome elements' (Stewart and Taylor, 1995, p. 14). On the other hand, it also marked a conscious shift towards provision of all sorts of services, not by government, but by voluntary sector agencies. Though this proved ultimately helpful to faiths as providers, this was a difficult period in which potential providers were required to compete with each other to win contracts.

So the role of the state was minimised throughout the 1980s in favour of the handing over of service provision to non-government providers whose expertise and experience would better place them to deliver appropriate and timely services which addressed needs that they were also better placed to understand. This was part of a move away from the state-dependant welfarism of the earlier period and towards a more mixed economy of welfare, as Table 8 shows. Well, that was the theory. It has been hugely and consistently criticised from two main angles: first, that the hoped-for reduction of the role of the state in practice led to an enormous increase in regulation of non-government services which placed a massive bureaucratic strain, both on providers who had

Table 8   A chronology of phases of service provision in the UK

Nineteenth century	Post-Second World War	1980 onwards	1997 onwards
Faiths	Government	Government and the voluntary sector	Government, voluntary sector and faiths
Philanthropy	Welfarism	Mixed economy of welfare	Extended mixed economy of welfare

to demonstrate their effectiveness and efficiency at every turn, and on the civil service which had to monitor these aspects; and second, the whole process of becoming a provider was based on contracts which were awarded on a competitive basis. This meant that the winner was often the cheapest bidder, which impacted on the quality of services. For faiths, it also often cut across the values of human being and collective community endeavour which infused them. A third critique concerns a Thatcherite emasculation of local government in this period, where the Labour party remained strong in the 1980s. Some local councils responded to Thatcher with a particular radicalism which incensed her. She saw socialism at large in many local authorities and their powers were systematically reduced as a result.

These shifts affected big public services, such as refuse collection, hospital cleaning and school meals in very obvious ways which were quickly felt by large numbers of people. There was great unhappiness among users of services, who felt that their quality was diminishing fast, and among staff working in those services, many of whom were forced to reapply for their own jobs, often to find that they were 're-employed' at a reduced wage. It was one of the first acts of the new Labour government after 1997 to abolish compulsory competitive tendering for public services in favour of what it called 'Best Value' – a formula in which providers would need to demonstrate the value of their services in relation to cost and effectiveness. This, it was hoped, would mean that the best, not the cheapest, would win contracts.

At the same time, it introduced the 'Voluntary Sector Compact' which it claimed would guarantee that government would consider the impact of every policy on the voluntary sector and work to ensure that the effects would not be perverse. This was a recognition of how far the mixed economy of welfare had been extended to include the voluntary sector, and of just how enormous the contribution of that sector has become. Thus the UK Voluntary Sector Almanac 2006 showed in key statistics 2003/04 that the sector has an income of £26.3 billion, derives only 38 per cent of its income from statutory sources, has an operating expenditure of £24.9 billion, has total assets of £66.8 billion and has a paid workforce of at least 608,000 (Lowndes and Smith, 2006).

At the same time, behind the formal figures lies a huge amount of informal service provision in the shape of care which would otherwise be provided by the state. Thus the Family Policy Studies Centre has estimated that the value of 'informal care' is between £15 – 24 billion per year (Millar, 1989) estimated on an hourly rate to carers of £4, which is below the value at which the minimum wage was originally set in 2000.

It is also pointed out that this figure does not take into account the costs of travel, adaptations, forgone careers and incomes and the cost of childcare. In contrast, government spending on social services in the year of the study was £3.4 billion.

In a mixed economy context, then, there remain residual government provided services, even after a journey towards greater reliance on services provided outside the State. These are fewer and further between as time goes by and government has been attempting to provide less itself and to facilitate other providers more. This has found expression in an extended mixed economy of welfare which includes faith providers alongside many others. Next, there are voluntary sector providers of services which are mostly located in projects in neighbourhoods, though some are delivered by and through large organisations via public sector contracts. The voluntary sector compact is an expression of government's commitment to these actors. These projects receive funding from local, regional or national government to provide their services in the understanding that they will identify local need better, be more responsive to it and have greater capacity for adapting to change because of their specificity of knowledge. There are also some larger 'umbrella' strategic partners in the voluntary sector who provide certain networking services in collaboration with government. Such partners are almost always national agencies whose skills and networks place them as useful conduits for helping to deliver government policies through strategic services such as capacity building with neighbourhood level projects and networking of small local services to improve efficiency, avoid duplication and build models of good practice.

This is part of an overall trend towards the greater self-sufficiency of service providers and an eventual reduction of reliance on funding from government. This is reflected in an agenda for social enterprise which encourages voluntary sector providers, including faiths, to develop income-generating streams which can be ploughed back into social service without the need for government funding. These will be considered, below. This trajectory towards the greater self-sufficiency of service providers is illustrated in three domains in Figure 3.

These three domains translate in practice into four spheres of activity. First, they provide services through community development projects. These services are very local and respond to locally identified need, often with locally resident staff and volunteers. Second, they provide them on a larger scale through public sector tendering. Third, they also provide strategic services as partners and networks for smaller

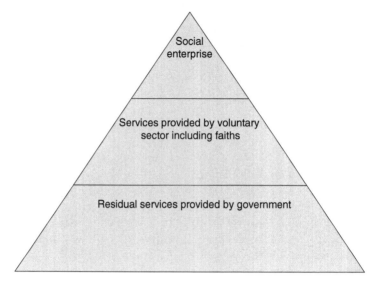

Figure 3   Triangle of trajectory towards self-sufficiency of service provision in the UK

organisations and endeavours. Fourth, they are increasingly providing them as social enterprises.

Faiths and services as community development

There is a thriving grey literature on faiths and community develop-ment activities and this reflects the significance and value of these activ-ities in wider society. Thus, *Flourishing Communities* (Musgrave, 1999) examines the potential for and actual engagement of churches with the government's New Deal for Communities (NDC). In doing so it makes recommendations both to Churches and government about the practice of mutual engagement. *Challenging Communities* (Finneron et al., 2001) presents an analysis with practical examples of church-related commu-nity development, including new opportunities and methods. *Faiths, Hope and Participation* (Lewis, 2001) investigates the contribution made by faith groups to neighbourhood renewal, identifying their holisticism of view, their theological and practical motivations for change, their hopefulness and their wide reach as crucial factors in such work. *Building on Faith* (Finneron and Dinham, 2002) examines the ways in which each of the major faiths in Britain have engaged with agenda for social justice and urban disadvantage, particularly through their use of faith buildings and material resources. *A Toolkit for Faith-Based Regeneration Practitioners* (Ahmed et al., 2004) analyses the methods and thinking behind effect-ive faith-based regeneration practice and is intended for practitioners and theorists as they increasingly grapple with work of this kind in concert with a generally supportive government which recognises the potential and achievements of faith groups. Resources published by others include *Neighbourhood Renewal in London: The Role of Faith Communities* (GLE/LCG, 2002), *Faith and Community: A Good Practice Guide for Local Authoritie*s (LGA Publications, 2002), *Faith Makes Communities Work* (Smith and Randolph-Horne, 2000) and *Angels and Advocates: Church Social Action in Yorkshire and the Humber* (CRCYH, 2002).

A national review of the literature on faiths' activities in communities in the UK was conducted in 2007 (Dinham, 2007). This demonstrates the breadth and scale of what faiths are doing in communities in England. In the South-East, *Beyond Belief* (March 2004) claims that there at least two community action projects for each faith centre in the region. In the East, *Faith in the East of England* (July 2005) identifies 180,000 beneficiar-ies of faith-based community development. In London, *Neighbourhood Renewal in London: The Role of Faith Communities* (May 2002) identifies 7,000 projects and 2,200 faith buildings. In the West Midlands, *Believing in the Region* (May 2006) reports that 80 per cent of faith groups deliver some kind of service to the wider community. In the North-West, *Faith in England's North West* (November 2003) shows that faith communi-ties are running more than 5,000 social action projects and that faith communities are generating income of £69–£94 million per annum. In Yorkshire and the Humber, *Count Us in* (2000) shows that in Hull 90 per cent of churches are involved in social action and *Angels and Advocates* (November 2002) reports that there are 6,500 social action projects in churches. In the South-West, *Faith in Action* (June 2006) demonstrates that 165,000 people are supported by faith groups in the region by 4,762 activities. In the East Midlands, *Faith in Derbyshire* (May 2006) claims that, on average, churches run nine community activities.

Though the regions differ considerably, one thing is clear: the types of activities which faith communities are engaged in is broad and can be organised into at least 48 categories,[2] as shown in Table 9.

The review also shows that the majority of faith-based community activity takes place through projects and associations, as demonstrated in the pie charts at Figure 4.

A snapshot of the data demonstrates certain trends. Thus the pro-portions in London indicate a predominance of children and youth-orientated projects in the London region (31 per cent). The only other

Table 9   Categories of faith-based engagement in England

Advice and counselling	Health
Alcohol abuse	Health and Fitness
Anti-racism	Health and sport
Arts and Music	Homelessness and deprivation
Cafes and drop-ins	Housing
Campaigning	Local forums of faith
Child related	Local issues
Children, young people and families	Lunch clubs and coffee mornings
Community support (credit unions, drop-ins, counselling, education, drugs, homelessness, crime prevention, ex-offenders)	Meeting places
	Neighbourhood projects
	Older people
	Partnerships (services)
Crime prevention	Partnerships (strategic)
Disability	Refugees
Drug abuse	Religious-based groups
Economics/shops/sales	Social activities
Education and training	Social capital
Employment and training	Social enterprise
Employment/social enterprise	Substance abuse
Enterprise	Support groups (prison/ hospital)
Environment	
Faith buildings	Support network
Family support	Uniformed
Finance, debt counselling	Vulnerable groups
Governance	Women
Hard to reach groups	Young people

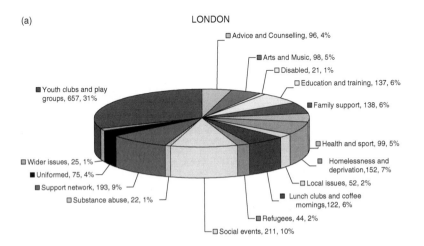

(a)   LONDON

(b)

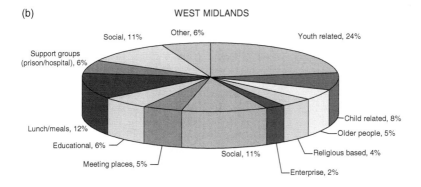

WEST MIDLANDS

Social, 11% — Other, 6% — Youth related, 24% — Support groups (prison/hospital), 6% — Child related, 8% — Older people, 5% — Religious based, 4% — Enterprise, 2% — Social, 11% — Meeting places, 5% — Educational, 6% — Lunch/meals, 12%

(c)

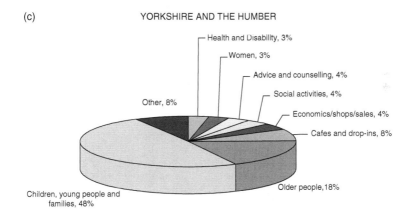

YORKSHIRE AND THE HUMBER

Health and Disability, 3% — Women, 3% — Advice and counselling, 4% — Social activities, 4% — Economics/shops/sales, 4% — Cafes and drop-ins, 8% — Older people, 18% — Children, young people and families, 48% — Other, 8%

(d)

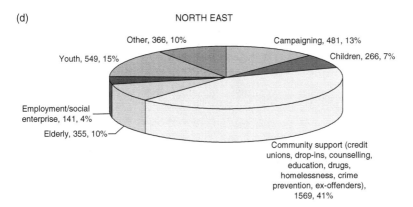

NORTH EAST

Other, 366, 10% — Campaigning, 481, 13% — Children, 266, 7% — Youth, 549, 15% — Employment/social enterprise, 141, 4% — Elderly, 355, 10% — Community support (credit unions, drop-ins, counselling, education, drugs, homelessness, crime prevention, ex-offenders), 1569, 41%

Continued

(e)

EAST OF ENGLAND

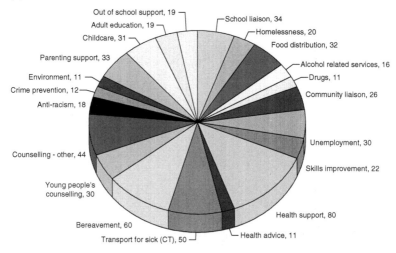

(f)

EAST MIDLANDS (Derbyshire)

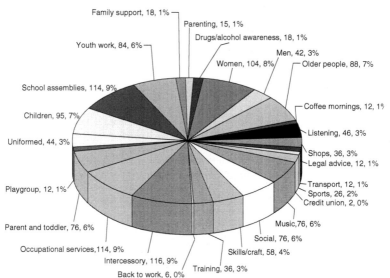

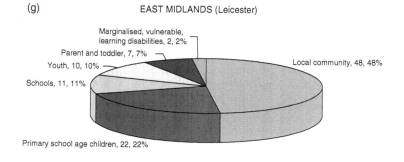

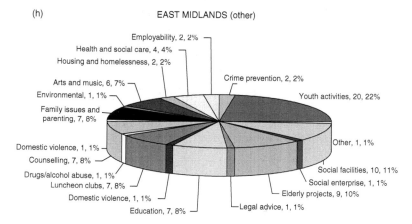

Figure 4   Charts of categories of faith-based community activities in England, 2007

category of more than 10 per cent is 'social events', which, as a very general category, is likely to refer to a relatively wide range of activities including lunch clubs, befriending schemes and cultural events. The rest is spread amongst a wide range of other projects. At the same time, the overall range of projects falls predominantly into 'project' type activities as opposed to larger organisations and concentrations of activity at the supra-neighbourhood level. Similarly in the West Midlands, there appears to be a preponderance of youth-related work and this is augmented by a similarly wide range of other 'project' focused activities. In the North-West, the two largest categories of activity are 'education' projects and 'arts and music' projects. This indicates more of an emphasis on community education and arts (as opposed to community action, community development and community organising, on Popple's typology of community activity[3]). In Yorkshire and the Humber, we return to a very strong focus on projects to work with children, young people and families,[4] as in London and the West Midlands. In the North-East there appears to be a very strong preponderance of 'community support' projects.[5] Again, 'community support' is a very general category and includes a wide range of activities within it, as demonstrated in the lengthy list of examples given alongside. Nevertheless, this is indicative of the 'project' type focus which is present in the other regions. This is reflected too, in the East of England, though it should be noted that the data there are even more complicated than most.[6] They were gathered as percentages of numbers of projects reporting doing work in a number of pre-set categories. Many respondents indicated positively to more than one category for the same work and this has resulted in a percentage total of many more than 100. Nevertheless, it indicates a strong presence of project-level work in the area of health support. There is also a significant amount of child and young-people focused project work, as in many of the other regions. In the South-West, there is a strong focus on education, housing and homelessness and environmental work, all at the project level.[7] Finally, sources[8] in Leicester show that youth activities, education and work with the elderly are predominant activities, again at project level.

I rehearse these data here because of what they say about comparability and usefulness of existing sources. A key message from this review, and particularly from the example of the East Midlands, where there are three sources, is that data are gathered and presented in highly differentiated ways from place to place. This distorts comparison. More importantly, it raises a crucial point about the ability of faiths nationally and, for that matter, internationally, to identify, demonstrate, discuss and develop the services they provide and the community activities they deliver in a coherent and widely communicable way. Because the categories and words used to grapple with this differ so much from place to place, it is unlikely that research means the same things from one conversation to another. This is symptomatic of the debates explored in the previous chapters about meanings and understandings. Yet, in a context where so many non-faith actors want increasingly to work with faiths, and where people in one tradition want to work with people in another, it is important that a language is used which can cross the divides, and is understood and shared as widely as possible. This is a major challenge for faiths and those with whom they work.

What is also clear about faiths and social action in community projects is that faiths are particularly well placed to engage in such ways. Many traditions have organisational structures which respond to the local, for example in the diocesan structures of the Anglican and Catholic churches. These often mean that they maintain a long-term and very rooted presence in every area, even where many other agencies may have withdrawn. Others draw on their long histories as providers of community support through established charitable organisations.

Faiths, services and public sector tendering

Another way in which faiths are engaging in service provision is through the more formal processes of public sector tendering. This is a mechanism by which the mixed economy of welfare can identify providers who are best placed to deliver specific services, as identified by local, regional or national government. They are services which are required by government to be delivered but which are felt to be better delivered outside of government on its behalf. This contrasts starkly with the community projects which faiths have proven themselves so good at within neighbourhoods which tend to spring up in response to needs identified locally. There are also differences in the capacity required of faiths wishing to deliver via public sector contracts. Often the services are on a larger scale and over longer time periods, and any group wishing to tender for such contracts must demonstrate that it has the staff, resources and experience to deliver. This relates also to questions of professionalism, associated both with the larger scales and with the contractual obligations of public sector tendering. Do faiths have the human resources, the organisational flexibility or the business orientations required of public sector partners? While the evidence suggests that faiths may be skilled and experienced at providing community-level project-type interventions, the skills and capacities required to deliver larger scale services, as laid out in public sector contracts, are of a different order. A UK faith-based body called FaithAction, which supports faith organisations in public sector contracting, has conducted research in each of the nine English regions to explore faith-based public sector contracting. The evidence indicates that some, but by no means many, are well placed to do so. For example, in the study of faiths delivering public sector contracts in the East of England (Dinham, 2007) of 2,347 questionnaires sent out, just 228 were returned (a rate of 9.7 per cent). This is relatively low and probably reflects the limited capacity of many faith groups in the region in terms of staff, resources and time. An evaluation of the research process also indicated that it may also be an issue of capacity (finding the time to respond), language (faiths not perceiving themselves as engaging in public sector contracting), self-perception (projects not regarding themselves as sufficiently significant) and readiness (some projects being interested for the future, but not seeing themselves as candidates yet).

At least in part for these reasons, when the questionnaire asked faith groups to indicate whether they are engaged in public sector tendering, or whether they would like to be, only three groups responded positively. At the same time, the larger organised faith traditions, especially the Roman Catholic, Anglican, Methodist and Baptist churches say they are engaging broadly and actively in public sector tendering. Yet in the Eastern region study, repeated and extensive attempts to make contact with these proved very difficult. Reflections on why this should be observed that those organisations which are running contracts experience themselves as quite separate from the faith groups from which they might have sprung. In other words, it seems that some of the larger public sector deliverers have professionalised themselves into separate space. This has meant that it is difficult to access one from the other. They are no longer closely associated.

Indeed, in many cases this means that faith-based organisations are recognisable 'brands' in their own rights and are no longer understood primarily or popularly as 'faith based'. Examples are of contracts run by the larger organisations, such as the YMCA whose 'social action' programs are large but have become dissociated from the faith base from which they started. Certainly their relationship with worshipping and fellowship communities is distended.

Another example of large faith-based public sector tendering is in the housing sector. Housing associations are frequently faith-based, as in the example of the English Churches Housing Group (now part of the Riverside Group) which is one of the countries largest housing associations providing homes for over 26,000 people. They manage over 11,000 homes, operate in over 176 local authorities and employ over 1,200 people. Their services also include affordable high-quality accommodation including flats and family houses, sheltered housing, personal care services, supported housing services supporting over 9,000 individuals, outreach workers to assist rough sleepers, drug and alcohol management programs, and a 24-hour, 365-days-a-year customer service centre dealing with over 80,000 calls. This is big business – and a faith group is the operator.

However, an interesting dimension of the study from which these data come, was how difficult it proved to *find* faith-based public sector contractors in the first place. They are often not described or understood as 'faith-based' by their partners. It is also difficult to *reach* faith-based public sector contractors, even where it is known where they are because the way in which their details are recorded frequently defies their categorisation as 'faith-based'.

There are other obstacles too. Some respondents said that they felt that governments' pledges to work with faith communities may amount to little more than lip service and that there is a long way to go before faith groups really are part of 'joined-up' provision in communities. An important obstacle is the mistrust of faith-based providers among funding bodies and a lack of knowledge and expertise on the parts of both the public sector and faiths at the local level. In this study, in the case of one hospice, for example, there was some tension over how 'Christian' the organisation should or can be. For example, it started to 'de-Christianise' remembrance services to encourage wider participation. This echoes the wider challenge faced by faith groups in accessing public funds and the concern that public funds will be used to evangelise.

There is a lesson here for both faith groups and the public bodies. For the former, as one responder put it, 'if people are converted by your actions in the community, then fine, but public money should not be used to evangelise'. For the public sector the lesson is one of recognising that faith groups have religious starting points and positions and sometimes their work in public spaces comes from that motivation. In other cases, faiths are motivated simply by a commitment to social justice and human fulfilment. In either case, the line between the social provision and the faith-based motivation for engagement may not be clear. This is the practical outworking of the division between the public and the private.

Conversely, some faith groups feel that public bodies are reluctant to allow autonomy and once funding is awarded, 'still want to pull all the strings'. The experience of one provider in the study illustrates this. They described running a homelessness project, which they had set up. When they won a contract from a public body for their services, they began to experience problems. They felt that there was extensive interference with monthly visits requiring changes costing them £8,000–10,000 a month. They found this impossible to maintain and eventually the public body took over the project. While the faith group tried to remain in partnership, the public body were not supportive of this and partnership in the end proved impossible. The project was eventually subcontracted to another group, though it continued to be run from the faith group's premises. Overall, the experience of this group was one of negative interference and control rather than support.

Table 10   Faiths and the public sector study: Reported difficulties in engaging with public sector tenders, Dinham 2007

If one group predominates within a partnership this may lead to fracture

Faiths should get involved in procurement because they need to have their vision and mission there in public space – this is seen by many as an opportunity for faiths to bring specific values to the public arena, for example, tackling some of the values of corporations, such as supermarkets, by doing things differently through service delivery in the public arena

There is an important question nevertheless about the relationship between the worshipping community and that part of it which engages in public sector contracts. In particular the role of evangelism is a key concern in relation to this – should faiths be providing services with values conditions, either explicitly or implicitly?

At the same time, it may be that openness about starting points, intent and purpose, may be sufficient, just as 'mission statements' are for other non faith-based organisations

There may be opportunities for faith traditions to come together in consortia to deliver services, with some potentially very interesting ramifications, including possible valuable synergies?

Might some also want proudly to remain single faith?

Policy-makers and procurers may not see the relevance of issues of faith and belief in the first place and such debates may be seen as wasteful and redundant

There is a very important difference between 'making money out of doing good' and 'making money anywhere in order to do good' – it matters what kind of service is contracted for

There is a big difference between faith-based social enterprises and faith-based public sector tendering because in public sector tendering there is very little spare capital and therefore limitations to what can be reinvested into other activities

Equalities legislation is likely to bite in new ways for faith groups wanting to engage in public sector contracts as faith groups engage as employers and contracting authorities grapple with sometimes cross-cutting values within faith groups

Whatever happens, faith-based public sector tendering is new territory and it is important to remember that 'too fast might be too frightening' and that learning about financial and legal responsibilities in particular, as well as about the functions and mechanisms of project managing contracts is key

Faiths need to think carefully about the relationship they want with government – do they want to be its agents, critical friends or independent critics? Or something else? Or a combination?

Another provider reported similar challenges in their running of a contract for working with children and families. The main difficulty was in matching the expectations and objectives of the church with those of the funding body. With the public body setting the boundaries and the objectives to be met, there was little room for the more relational and long-term approach to support that had characterised the church's approach. In this sense, the church had become frustrated by having to change their ideas to fit the targets and boundaries set externally. In this particular example, a change in the management of the public body one year into the project also meant a further change in objectives, which did not suit the church, but which they felt powerless to influence.

A recurring theme in the relationship between faiths and the public sector bodies with which they contract is how to develop knowledge and expertise of public sector services and funding at the local level and in both directions – from faith communities to public sector partners and from public sector partners to faith communities. Success can often depend on a 'clued up' individual who knows about public monies and how to access them, and vice versa.

As part of the 'faiths and the public sector' study, a small event was held to bring together faith groups with the intention of providing an opportunity to exchange experiences and views of faith-based public sector contracting. The event identified a number of difficulties for faiths engaging in public sector tendering. Responses are reported in Table 10.

Faiths and social enterprise

Just as the mixed economy of welfare is motivated by a desire to share the burdens and responsibilities of care with a wider civil society, which is perceived as best placed to provide it, so public sector tendering is one mechanism by which that 'extension' can be effected. For faiths as they increasingly appear at the public table, this presents important challenges, as we have seen. Though some larger faith-based organisations have been delivering public sector contracts for some time, their relationship to the faith community from which they spring may be stretched – perhaps broken – and it seems clear that they are, in any case, in the significant minority.

At the same time, governments are keen to encourage all the actors in the extended mixed economy, including faiths, to develop financial self-sufficiency. Not only should the activities of welfare be taken on by organisations in civil society. So too should the costs. Social enterprise is a key mechanism by which governments in the UK and US would like to achieve this.

It is arguable that many non-government actors, including faith groups, have been doing social enterprise for decades or even longer. An example is the Oxfam shops whose income supports wider community work in the developing world. But, while many organisations might be doing social enterprise, according to some of the definitions of it, many more do not think of themselves in that way.

Nevertheless, the UK government is enthusiastic about social enterprise as an approach to developing the self-sufficiency and sustainability of the voluntary and community sector in particular, where organisations almost always depend upon relatively limited amounts of funding, competitively sought and usually time limited (to one, or more recently, three-year cycles).

The UK Labour government launched its Social Enterprise Strategy in 2002. This envisaged a dynamic and sustainable social enterprise sector as a key part both of welfare delivery and of strengthened economy. The strategy set out a three-year plan to promote and sustain social enterprise and was accompanied by the setting up of a Social Enterprise Unit (now based within the Small Business Service in the Department of Trade and Industry). Its primary purposes are to act as a focal point and coordinator for policy-making affecting social enterprise, promote and champion social enterprise, take action needed to address barriers to growth of social enterprises and identify and spread good practice.

Social enterprise may be thought of in at least two key ways. The first relates to structure. The second is associated with ethos. Thus, social enterprise can be a definition of a kind of organisational structure or a certain mind set, attitude or approach – its values. Government and business-support frameworks focus strongly on the organisational dimensions of social enterprise and thereby tend to characterise them in this way. The UK's Department for Trade and Industry therefore defines a social enterprise as

> ...a business with primarily social objectives whose surpluses are principally reinvested for that purpose in the business or in the community, rather than being driven by the need to maximise profit for shareholders and owners. (Cabinet Office, 2004)

Other perspectives might focus more on the 'values' dimensions and less on structure. For example, the Social Enterprise Coalition focuses on three key characteristics or 'ethos dimensions' of social enterprises: an *enterprise orientation* – they are directly involved in producing goods or providing services to a market; a *social aims orientation* – they have explicit social and/or environmental aims such as job creation, training or the provision of local services; and a *social ownership orientation* – governance and ownership structures are based on participation by stakeholder groups (e.g., employees, users, clients, local community groups and social investors).

Any combination of these characteristics may give an organisation a social enterprise perspective or ethos. Some of the most well-known examples include Café-direct, The Big Issue, The Co-operative Group, Welsh Water (Glas Cymru), the Eden Project and Jamie Oliver's 'Fifteen', each of which is organisationally quite different from the others. In addition, there are many thousands of smaller, less well-known, social enterprises. The Department of Trade and Industry supported research which shows that there are approximately 15,000 social enterprises in the UK with a combined turnover of £18 billion (REF). This represents a contribution to GDP (gross domestic product) of over £5 billion per annum.

A number of factors have coincided to drive an interest in social enterprise. Local authorities and other public sector bodies have passed on to new or pre-existing organisations areas of work they used to run themselves, like social housing, leisure or social care. Charities, including faith-based organisations, have to keep financially sustainable while many traditional sources of funding such as membership fees and institutional grants become harder to access. More recently, individuals and groups thinking of meeting local needs have perceived a business or commercial approach as a more flexible and sustainable route to delivering multiple social benefits – members, staff and customers can all be beneficiaries in different ways.

Much of the focus of published material and policy in relation to social enterprise is on what particular sectors can do to get involved. Whilst that is important and useful, it is also instructive to reverse the question. Providers of the sorts of services and initiatives which are the target of government policy for social enterprise are often working with vulnerable and challenging groups, and are financially stressed, thus may be struggling to keep staff and resources going in a climate of short-term funding and constantly and rapidly changing political contexts. This is as true for many faith-based organisations as for others in similar sectors. Many may feel that before they start to think about what they can offer to social enterprise, they want to see what social enterprise can offer them.

Social enterprise models are of interest to several government departments as they offer the possibilities of meeting targets in several policy areas. The Department for Trade and Industry (DTI) is primarily interested in increasing levels of economic activity and employment. One key target is to increase economic activity amongst those perceived as excluded from the mainstream economy – those on very low incomes, disabled people, ethnic minorities, refugees, older people and others. Social enterprise claims to offer an accessible model which the DTI is promoting. They say that

> By using business solutions to achieve public good, the Government believes that social enterprises have a distinct and valuable role to play in helping create a strong, sustainable and socially inclusive economy. (DTI, 2005)

In addition, the nine English regions through the regional development agencies all have strategies for increasing economic participation, which include social enterprises. The Department for Environment, Food and Rural Affairs also sees social enterprises as a key partner. The Charity Commission has increasingly relaxed its limitations of what constitutes a legitimate activity for voluntary and faith-based organisations. The primary question now, is not whether an organisation meets the historical criteria for charities, but that it passes a wider and all embracing test of 'public benefit'. This means that at certain levels of activity a faith-based organisation can engage in social enterprise without setting up a new company. But even where a separate structure is desirable, the UK government has introduced new forms of legal entities, including the Community Interest Company specifically designed for social enterprises.

But the engagement of faiths in social enterprise comes with its difficulties and challenges. In our study of faith and social enterprise (Dinham, 2007), we found that these are frequently associated with a sense of lacking – in skills, resources, partnership skills and capacity, adaptability, governance know-how and ability, volunteers and staff and time. A second important set of challenges is about a sense of fear – of not knowing how to professionalise, of competition with others, of getting on the wrong side of legal obligations, of risk taking, of a resulting disjunction between business aims and values, of what is known being swamped by what isn't, and ultimately, fear of failure.

Both concerns – 'lacking' and 'fear' – are underpinned by a sense of ignorance about what social enterprise is, how to do it and what effects it could have. Overall, there is enormous anxiety amongst many people of faith that they simply do not know what to do, how to do it or whether they want to. It seems easier to plough on as before than to engage with this complicated and rather frightening new form of organisation. The findings from this study are summarised in Table 11, which presents

Table 11 Faiths and social enterprise in the UK in 2007

Question	Cluster	Theme – what faiths bring/need
What role can faiths play in social enterprise?	Values or attitudes	• Hopefulness • Non-judgmentalism • Caring and compassion • Focus and commitment • Holisticism • Ethos • Distinctiveness of mission • Transformativity • Helping the disadvantaged
	Skills and practice orientations	• Skill and talent • Stability • Continuity • Long-termism • Sustainability • Leading by example • Buildings and resources • Responsiveness and speed • Reaching parts others cannot reach
	Relationships and networks	• Rootedness in communities • Reaching into communities more broadly • Community cohesion/ social capital • Educative and reaching beyond faith groups • Educative about faith in wider contexts • Encouraging of diversity
What do faiths need in order to do social enterprise?	Practical orientation	• Provision of support and leadership • Resources • Skills training and understanding of other faiths • Good communications

Continued

Table 11   Continued

Question	Cluster	Theme – what faiths bring/need
		• Documents in clear English • Research and evidence • Supportive policy and procurement contexts • Templates and models
	Practical actions	• Identifying a clear market • Having a clear product or service
	Supportive general contexts	• Strong community • Strong partnerships • Distinctive idea and creativity • Strong motivational starting points • Living in the real world • Supportive policy and procurement contexts • Good governance
	The role of faith	• Having faith
What opportunities are there for faiths to do social enterprise and with what advantages?	Opportunities	
	Mission	• Serving the community • Drawing people into its benefits • Engaging with partners of other faiths and none
	Image and role of faiths	• Faiths are in fashion • Counters the negative image of faiths
	Human well-being	• Spiritual hunger • Broadening people's experiences • Raising aspirations • Increasing morale • Empowering communities
	Advantages	
	For faith groups themselves	• Identity • They are met at their starting points, not those of others • Sustainability • Access to public sector contracts

Table 11 Continued

Question	Cluster	Theme – what faiths bring/need
	For others	
	(i) A practical dimension	• Buildings and resources • Local trust • Social capital and knowledge • Infrastructure • Skills and talents • Good at risk taking
	(ii) A spiritual dimension	• A 'whole person' view embracing a wider vision
	(iii) An ethos dimension	• Independence
What are the difficulties and challenges for faiths doing social enterprise?	A sense of lacking	• Skills • Resources • Partnership skills and capacity • Adaptability • Governance know-how and ability • Volunteers and staff • Time
	A sense of fear	• Of not knowing how to professionalise • Of competition with others • Of getting on the wrong side of legal obligations • Of risk taking • Of a resulting disjunction between business aims and values • Of what IS known being swamped but what ISN'T • Fear of failure
	A sense of ignorance	• What social enterprise is • How to do it • What effects it could have
What role does government play in supporting faith-based social enterprise?	What government could do	• Extended forms of participation • Facilitation • Trust

Continued

Table 11   Continued

Question	Cluster	Theme – what faiths bring/need
	Government as exploiter	• Not being up to speed, producing 'sticks' • Being bureaucratic • Being inaccessible • Idealising faiths • Setting short deadlines • Saying one thing and doing another • Changing the rules
	Ambiguity	• Sticks might also have carrots • The idealisation of faiths might also validate them • Standardisation might help faiths to be more consistently understood • Talking shops might be better than silence

the question asked, followed by clusters or areas of responses, which are then broken down into specific themes within each area. Aside from the concerns of faiths themselves about social enterprise, and despite a demonstrable willingness to get involved, it is a challenging model for faiths at a number of levels.

First, social enterprise requires a business ethos which may not be home territory for many faith groups, whose interests lie in questions wider than and sometimes somewhat at odds with accepted social hegemonies about capitalism, what makes people happy and how people should interrelate. We should avoid the pitfalls of clichés about business being cut-throat, inhuman and uncaring. But at the same time we should recognise that profit-generation, even where those profits are intended to be used for social 'goods', is a different kind of activity to that more usually engaged in by many faiths groups. At the same time, there are many fine examples of faith-based social enterprise stretching back over a long period when medieval monasteries were selling wine, beer, pots and pans long before anyone coined the phrase 'social enterprise'.

The concern of many faith groups in relation to this is the invasion of their ethos and values with those of a business culture with which they are not familiar. Associated with this too, is anxiety about the potential for separation from a core mission, or set of activities. We have already observed the possible discontinuity within faith communities between worshippers, project workers, leaders, representatives, clergy and others. Where social enterprise activities are introduced, might this further threaten that continuity? In some cases might it even fracture it? And yet this also assumes that discontinuity is always a threat. Could we consider social enterprise rather, as an opportunity for rethinking and recasting aspects of the public activities of faiths, at the same time as re-empowering them in terms of the financial self-sustainability, which can provide the freedom to act independently of government grants or the whims of policy fashions and funding streams?

Another area of concern for faiths in relation to social enterprise is the demands made by the need to 'professionalise'. Many faith-based activities are already working in professional ways and some have a long track record of doing so. But at the same time, the regulatory and monitoring regimes associated both with public sector contracting, and with business in social enterprise can be onerous. The range of employment and health and safety regulations alone is a challenge for compliance. Equalities legislation in relation to age, ethnicity, gender, disability and sexuality also apply to faiths, as they provide services and employ staff and in these areas too. Some traditions or groupings may find that their values and theologies are at odds with the law, an issue we will return to in Chapter 7.

Faiths and education

Another way in which faiths provide services in the UK is through education in faith schools. There are currently 4,700 Church of England, 2,400 Catholic, 37 Jewish, 28 Methodist, 7 Muslim and 1 Seventh Day Adventist state-funded schools in Britain, with the first state-funded Hindu school opening in London in 2008 (Doward, 2006; Meer, 2007; Walford, 2001).

As with other areas of faith and public life, the position of the Church of England as an established church in England and Wales has helped determine the relationship between faith schools and the state (see Chadwick, 2001). During the nineteenth century, Protestant churches provided the majority of education, funded by the state (Grace, 2001). Educational reforms after 1870 resulted in a two-fold system of church and state schools to ensure that education would be available everywhere and for every child, whether it be delivered by the churches or the state. But it was in the 1993 Education Act (superseded by the

Schools Standards and Framework Act 1998) that it became possible for non-state sponsors, including faith-based ones, to apply to establish state-funded schools.

Including independent (private) schools, there are 5,000 Church of England and Church of Wales schools, educating a quarter of primary school pupils and 6 per cent of secondary school pupils. In addition, the Catholic school system serves approximately 10 per cent of the school population in England and Wales (ibid.).

But it is also observed that

> The new government [Labour in the UK in 1997] was clearly aware that a system which gave huge amounts of state funding to thousands of Church of England and Roman Catholic schools but hardly any to schools of other faiths was inherently discriminatory. Anxious to demonstrate its commitment to multiculturalism, it quickly set about addressing the problem. (Gillard, 2001)

Thus, extension of the right to open non-state schools had been established in the Schools Standards and Framework Act 1998 and government guidelines promoted this. In January 1998, Islamia Primary School in Brent, London and Al Furqan Primary School in Sparkhill, Birmingham became the first state-funded Muslim schools in England. Indeed, the UK government's White Paper *Schools Achieving Success*, published on 5 September 1998, contained much about the involvement of the private sector – including the churches – in failing schools, and about independent religious schools being welcomed into the state sector 'with clear local agreement'. Additionally, there are a number of state-funded Jewish schools, mostly located in the major cities, educating approximately 12,000 pupils (Valins, 2003). Flint also observes that

> In addition to state-funded faith schools there are an estimated 160 fee-paying independent Catholic schools; 101 independent Jewish schools educating 11,000 pupils; 115 independent Muslim schools, primarily located in inner-city areas educating 14,000 pupils; and at least 70 independent Evangelical Christian schools (Grace, 2001; Walford, 2001; Valins, 2003; Meer, 2007). (Flint in Dinham et al., 2009)

Significant numbers of Christian, Jewish and Muslim children also receive supplementary religious education in evening or weekend schools.

But, as with their engagement at the public table in other aspects, the involvement of faiths in education has been seen by some as driven by a great deal of self-interest. It has been suggested that 'Few who first meet religion in adulthood are able to take it seriously; priests know that to keep the old faiths alive, they have to get their hands on children' (AC Grayling in *The Guardian*, 24 February 2001). This reflects the fact that faith schools have been one of the most disputed arenas for debates about the public role of faith. Almost all the concerns pertaining to faiths' involvement in other aspects of public life coincide in debates about this one issue. Though they are raised in relation to the provision of services too, when it comes to the education of children, widespread rationalist instincts spring to the fore. The intersection between faith and rationalism is starkly drawn. Questions are asked. Do faiths have an agenda which they wish to pursue? If so, is it sinister, illiberal or morally blinkered? What role does evangelism play in faiths' desire to be at the public table? What partisan values and perspectives will be promoted? Will alternatives, choices and contingency be acknowledged, or will 'certainty' be fostered? How will science and philosophy be conceived of in what is widely perceived to be an essentially irrational setting?

These questions became central in a heated debate in provincial elections in Ontario, Canada, in the autumn of 2007. There the Progressive Conservative candidate for provincial Premier, John Tory, proposed in his manifesto an extension of provincial funding for privately run faith schools. The Toronto Star reported it thus:

> John Tory and the PC Party believe that we need to achieve more effective integration of Ontario's increasingly diverse student population into the mainstream of our province. That's why we are committed to creating an opportunity for non-Catholic, faith-based schools to choose to join our publicly funded education system the same way Catholic schools have already done. (Toronto Star, 30 August 2007)

It was thus presented as an issue of equity and fairness. If one tradition can run schools, then so should all the others. Indeed, the same article quoted a response from the Executive Director of the Ontario Association of Jewish Day Schools (OAJDS) who said 'We welcome John Tory's pledge for equal funding of Ontario's faith-based schools. For too long, the government's discriminatory policy of funding only Roman Catholic schools... has persisted without reform.'

The issue gave rise to widespread anxiety and, for that matter, fury, about the possible impacts on communities in a self-consciously multi-cultural milieu. It led to comments such as this one: 'People come to Canada because they embrace diversity, not so they can be separated from each other' (Education Minister Kathleen Wynne [Ontario Liberal Party] in the National Post, 25 August 2007). She added 'We should ask ourselves if we'd be a stronger province if we separate our kids' (ibid.).

David McGuinty, the sitting provincial Premier, added 'You don't improve a community's schools, you don't build community when you take half a billion (dollars) out of publicly funded schools to fund private religious schools as the Conservatives are promising to do' (Toronto Star, 21 August 2007).

A day later McGuinty added this in a television interview for CTV:

> I don't think that Ontarians believe that improvement or progress is defined as inviting children of different faiths to leave the publicly funded system and go to their own schools. I think that's regressive. I think that takes us backwards. I think our responsibility is to continue to improve the publicly funded system of education ... An important part of our foundation for social cohesion is a publicly funded education system where we invite children of all backgrounds and faiths, economic circumstances, to come together to learn from each other and to grow together. It's one of those issues where I'm hoping to grab Ontarians by the earlobes and say it's not just another election, it's about the kind of Ontario you want. (Premier David McGuinty, CTV, 22 August 2007)

John Tory himself suggested that 'They teach evolution in the Ontario curriculum but they also could teach the facts to the children that there are other theories that people have out there that are part of some Christian beliefs' (Tory, 5 September, Toronto Star). By now the debates had become very muddled and, ineloquent though it is, this statement resonates with what made them so heated: the notion that religion is irrational (preoccupied with ideas about creation and the like) and that it must be evicted from the realm of the rational, which is to do with 'facts'.

Some arguments for and against

From the perspective of the British Humanist Society (BHA), Andrew Copson has rehearsed the arguments for and against faith schools. It is not clear whether he is writing in his capacity of Education and Public Affairs Officer at the BHA or in a personal capacity. Nevertheless, the arguments are illuminating. He sets up ten common assumptions which he proceeds to challenge (Copson, 2006). I rehearse them here because they are illuminating, both of the popular arguments for each case, and of the weakness of the evidence for the arguments which are often bought to bear. This is consolidated by the problem that it is not clear where, or from whom, the 'assertions' he claims to have observed have come from in the first place.

First, he says it is argued that 'faith schools are successful because they are faith schools'. His reply is in three parts: that many are in fact not successful; that where they are, this is because they are selective; and, as an aspect of this, it is because they take fewer children from disadvantaged backgrounds.

Second, he observes the argument that 'Only faith schools can teach spiritual and moral values and religion properly'. Against this he argues that the implied weakness of religious and moral education in other schools will only get worse if 'many of the religious withdraw their children into separate schools' (ibid.). He is also concerned about 'whether this transmission of faith is a suitable object for public funds' (ibid.) and whether such 'transmission' is in fact educationally valuable or appropriate at all in a diverse society.

Third, he rehearses the view that 'We are better off with faith schools in the state system, where they have to teach the National Curriculum' but observes that sex education and religious education are not part of the national curriculum, allowing faith schools to teach what they like in regard to these two areas. The implication is that they will do so according to their own very particular and specious agenda.

Fourth, he introduces the argument that 'everyone wants more faith schools'. He says that the Church of England's example as a provider of education is a 'slippery slope' which calls forth the desire of other traditions to follow. He also cites (unreferenced) survey evidence that 'anything from 64% to 96% of the general population does not want the expansion or even the continuance [*sic*] of faith schools' (ibid.).

The fifth argument he cites is that 'faith schools serve everyone' – a claim he refutes without evidence saying

> actually they really serve only those who belong to faith groups that are well organised, geographically concentrated, and that want to separate themselves from, or convert, the rest of us. (ibid.)

He observes a 'new, more evangelical approach in Church schools' (ibid.) targeted at securing the long-term well-being of the Church of England.

Assertion number six is that 'Faith schools increase choice' to which he replies 'schools are not like jelly beans, where my choice has no effect on yours because there are always plenty more jelly beans' (ibid.). The 'sweet shop' metaphor is used to point out that schools, unlike sweets, are finite in number.

His seventh proposition is that 'Faith groups put substantial amounts of money into their schools' to which he replies that this is in fact no longer the case, since the state provides '100% of the running costs for faith schools and 90% of the capital costs' (ibid.). He adds that nevertheless under the new 'Building Schools for the Future' programme this will become 100 per cent of capital costs too.

He notes an eighth 'assertion' as 'Church schools have a long and noble history of education; we should let them get on with it'. Against this he argues merely that 'we should make today's decisions based on today's facts' (ibid.). It is perhaps unfortunate that he goes on to use facts from the 1870s to shore up his argument by suggesting that the Victorian church worked to prevent the setting up of schools by the state.

Ninth, he cites the argument that 'Parents have the human right to have their children educated in a faith school'. To counter this he says that there is no specific obligation on the state to provide any particular type of education and that in any case 'children have rights too' (ibid.).

Finally, tenth, he rehearses the argument that 'Faith schools are good for social cohesion' which he says is an 'unproven assertion made by minority faith leaders promoting their own state-funded schools' (ibid.), a statement which is in itself 'unproven'. He goes on that it seems 'unwise for the state to be actively encouraging religious divisions by funding single faith schools' (ibid.) and that the interfaith aim of having exchanges between faith schools merely complicates a mutuality which could happen without faith schools anyway. His conclusion is that

> the state should not be funding divisive, unnecessary and discriminatory faith schools. We will regret this counterproductive use of public money in decades to come. Our society is increasingly diverse and the population as a whole is increasingly secular – a progressive change, generation to generation. (ibid.)

In this way, Copson's comments draw together many of the concerns and anxieties which we have been observing in relation to faiths at the public table. They also reflect some of the category errors which inhere in many of the criticisms. As we have seen, secularism is not progressive and the data show a strong persistence in believing, even if not in belonging. Public space is not neutral but in fact highly committed to liberalism and capitalism. And, as we have seen, some traditions and communities may assert an evangelical agenda, but there are many which engage at the public table for a whole range of reasons other than this.

This highlights a number of interesting questions more widely about faith at the public table, and in this sense faith-based education reflects those wider debates. At their root is a concern about the essential and fundamental irrationality of faith as a force which undermines the hard-won freedoms and insights of liberalism and the scientific method. Associated with this is a concern to preserve the neutrality of the public table. But it has been observed that this is itself a mere chimera. Robert Furbey puts it thus: 'the idea of a relatively fixed liberal "neutral" public realm has been challenged. Rather, it is a terrain characterised by inequality of power and increasing social plurality. Historically, the public realm has been shaped by monism, both Christian and classical liberal' (Furbey in Dinham et al., 2009, p. 38).

The stark case of the US faith-based initiative

The debates highlighted in the curious case of the Ontarian faith-schools debacle, above, and in the humanist arguments rehearsed here, resonate too, in the circumstances of the Faith Based Initiative in the US. This is an enormously significant program relating to faiths and the provision of services which has been just about as contentious as policy could be. It is an excellent policy to get our teeth into in relation to the UK because its explicitness highlights distinctions both with the UK and in Canada. This helps us shed light on the UK context, despite the differences, by illuminating further the debates which faith-based service provision can raise.

And that is the first and most obvious thing to say about it, that the Faith Based Initiative stands in contrast to the UK context because it is so starkly explicit, (if not straightforward), about the role of faith at the public table. As far as government is concerned, faiths are there to provide services. Thus the Faith Based Initiative weekly email advertises support in such terms as these:

> This conference is part of a new series of regional conferences in part-nership with states across the country. These events are designed to connect effective social service organizations with resources that can

strengthen and expand the services they offer to the people they serve. (Faith Based Initiative Email Communication, 18 September 2007)

There is no mention of any other role for faiths or of any other dimension to their engagement. This is provocative, to say the least and, at the same time, the policy has raised an enormous amount of debate about faith and the public which is illuminating more widely and which helps inform our own debates about the place of faiths in wider society.

It has been suggested that 'years before George W Bush became President, a network of politicians, policy makers, think-tank representatives and constitutional scholars who advocated more direct interaction between the church and state was coalescing' (Black, Loopman and Ryden, 2004, p. 49). This was driven in part by critiques of the secularisation of social services, which argued that the non-involvement of faiths was perverse given that, as in the UK, religious institutions were historically the most effective vehicles of service and 'compassion' (see Olasky, 1992). In the mid-1990s the influential Centre for Public Justice, a civic education and policy research organisation in the US, stated that it was 'committed to public service that responds to God's call to do justice in local, national and international affairs' (Black, Loopman and Ryden, 2004, p. 46) and that this could be generated by 'creating the proper relationship between government and non-governmental responsibilities and society, upholding equal access for and treatment of all faiths in the public square' (ibid., p. 47).

The faith-based initiative was also preceded by important changes in social services policy contexts. As the role of government grew through the 1940s and after, so the parameters set by policy for service provision became clearer and narrower. The role of faith-based organisations became problematic in this context in two ways. First, just as the professionalisation of public services and their colonisation by government was the ideological story of public services in the new welfare state of the UK after the Second World War, in the US too, policy was moving in the direction of regulation of services, which had the effect of squeezing non-government providers, many of whom had been faith-based. In this sense, they found themselves displaced by government through processes of regulation and professionalisation, many of which they could not keep pace with. Second, alongside this, the federal public funding of non-governmental services became more problematic as attitudes to public faith hardened after the 1960s. This had the effect of sidelining faiths in the realignment of public services since it was assumed that, in deference to the First Amendment, public funding could not easily be used in support of religious bodies. This reflected wider changes in attitudes to faith, which were influenced, as in the UK, by secularisation theorists and declining formal affiliations to faith bodies. By the 1960s therefore, those faith-based services which were seen as legitimate had come to be categorised as 'faith affiliated' social service agencies whose relationship to the faith traditions from which they had sprung was by now largely nominal. Certainly, such services were no longer easily able to present themselves as springing from faith.

Paradoxically, it was the Reagan–Thatcher approach to social services in the 1980s that led to their re-admittance, though this was by no means consciously the intent in either context. In the UK, as we have seen, the contracting out of services competitively in this period allowed for the greater participation of non-governmental providers, and this included faiths. In the US, it marked the beginning of an extension of the already mixed economy of welfare to include as many potential actors as possible and this, by logical extension, included faiths. This wide open market of welfare provision was enshrined in the 1996 Welfare Reform Act in the US, a move encapsulated in the 'charitable choice' policy which meant that service provision could be made by anyone outside of government able to demonstrate their capacity and skill for delivering – anyone, including faiths.

The legislative battle over Charitable Choice was difficult and long. Much of it was fought under Clinton's Presidency and was preoccupied with welfare reform. Under Bush however, it took on a different kind of ideological dimension, drawing on a commitment to the power of evangelical Christianity to reify public space in the direction of Christian conservatism. Opposition to this included the coalition of 'American's United', the American Civil Liberties Union (ACLU) and the Baptist Joint Committee on the grounds that, in extending charitable choice to include faith providers, this breached the constitutional separation of church and state. A former Associate General Counsel of the Baptist Joint Committee warned 'Religion is a prophetic critic of government and if it is subsidised it will be less likely to bite the hand that feeds it' (ibid., p. 57). This was one of the main concerns of opponents of charitable choice and its extension into the faith-based initiative – that its implementation would diminish religions' central roles, both as focus for spiritual engagement and/or as critical prophet in a secular age. It was also feared that the faith-based initiative would 'tame' faiths. These debates came up against others who, conversely, feared what they saw as the destructive power of religion to undermine debate and to threaten democracy itself. Its proponents, however, promote religion as a tool for enhancing pluralism, diversity and tolerance in an otherwise secular public life and believe that faith itself can enhance the quality of public services just as it can enhance the well-being of individuals and groups.

By the time George W. Bush took office in January 2001, there were four charitable choice laws on the statute books. However, in the political mire of Clinton's near-impeachment in the late 1990s and the dying days of his second term in the White House, very little had been done to implement them. At the same time, it has been noted that even before Charitable Choice, in certain states, many intensely religious groups received federal funding anyway via delegation to their State processes and legislatures (see Monsma, 1996). This reflects the constitutional, legislative and administrative ambiguity of the issue which is part of its contentiousness. Nevertheless, in 2001 a report in the Associated Press found that only five states aggressively used federal Charitable Choice provisions to involve faith-based organisations – Arkansas, Indiana, Missouri, Ohio and Texas.

It has been argued that 'Nothing put forth in the first 100 days of his administration has sparked as much passion, discord, and suspicion as President Bush's proposal to make it easier for faith-based groups to get federal dollars to deliver social services to the nation's needy' (Mary Leonard, Boston Globe, 29 April 2001). Yet, as we have seen, this found its origins in bi-partisan policy. During the 2001 Presidential campaign, both Bush and Gore promoted expanding opportunities for faith-based groups to partner with government.

Nevertheless, this belies a shallow consensus and once Bush's faith-based initiative got to the House of Representatives, opposition had grown fierce. For Bush, his support of these policies moved him to the left of traditional Republicans because he embraced the role of both government and community organisations in meeting peoples' needs. At the same time, he did not move left enough for the Democrats who saw this as an inappropriate reaching out to the religious public. Indeed, while it has been argued that 'Most Americans accept religion in the public square even while maintaining stated support for the separation of church and state' (Black, Loopman and Ryden, 2004, p. 82), the support of elites was a different matter. Thus it is argued that 'Just under half the public agrees that government should not help religion, but nearly 70% of the media, 80% of the government and 90% of the academic elites surveyed believed in the "no aid" principle' (Jelen and

Wilcox, 1995). At the same time, there is the perception that Bush personally believes in a role for faith and in faith groups' contributions. Indeed, his promise to rally the 'armies of compassion' was integral to his philosophy of 'compassionate conservatism' (see Soloman and Vlissides Jr, February 2001, p. 1). Thus, while Democratic candidate Al Gore supported expanding service choices to include religious as well as secular ones, Bush's proposal 'signified a paradigm shift in the way we provide social services in this country from a top-down, secular government model to one that is deeply infused by faith commitment' (Black, Loopman and Ryden 2004, p. 94).

Americans remain divided about the mixing of religion and government. Indeed, it is a highly charged issue and one which is replicated in the UK and Canada, though with differences. In the UK this is perhaps in part because an established church has made people feel already familiar with a role for faith in public space. In the US, some argue church-state relations have been damaged by the initiative, likening it to 'poking a stick into a hornet's nest' (ibid., p. 274). Others feel good that there is high-profile debate and increased public awareness of the potential of religious groups in delivering social services.

For all its contentiousness, the faith-based initiative has been observed to have 'failed to prompt a meaningful collective exploration of "religion in the public square", no matter one's particular view of the question' (ibid., p. 277). That said, it may have set the stage for more meaningful discussion later. The question of where future debate should take place is central since the legislative arena has proven too contested in the negotiation of power. Are these matters, not for legislation, then, but for some other forms or contexts of deliberation? There are questions of community, too, which are familiar in the UK context where discussion already includes the role of faiths in strengthening civil society. These broader community dimensions are not yet part of the faith-based matrix in the US and there are few signs that they will head there.

Nevertheless, the Faith Based Initiative has been shown to have made significant differences in the sheer volume of services provided by faiths. Thus it is observed that

> Amy Sherman's 2002 survey cataloguing new publicly funded faith-based programs in fifteen states revealed a sizable upswing in the numbers of faith-based programs operating with government funds. That study revealed more than 700 contracts totalling $125 million. (ibid., p. 276)

Instrumental or ideal?

The role of faiths as providers of services, is clear at one level then. They are significant providers in a mixed economy of welfare in the UK, the US and Canada. They operate predominantly in community and neighbourhood level projects and, despite widespread concerns to the contrary, the great majority offer their services not only to people from their own tradition, but to others outside of it, and of none. They also provide through public sector contracts, though these often stretch the capacity of many neighbourhood level projects and tend to be undertaken instead by larger organisations, many of which have, over time, become less connected to the faith tradition from which they sprang because of the processes associated with the growth required to deliver. The demands of professionalisation required of the larger public sector contracts can lead to changes which can render organisations practically unrecognisable to their original members.

Similarly, faiths operate through social enterprises, many of which offer services and products for profit which is then reinvested into the core 'mission' identified. And faiths are very involved in providing education. This is an arena of especially heated debate – not least because it is concerned with the forming of young minds. Faith and non-belief, religion and science, superstition and rationality are prone to being polarised in an atmosphere of panic and hostility, often driven by the desire to protect children. Where children and young people are concerned, the stakes are very high. And where faiths are involved, the debates are already heated, often emotional and sometimes confused.

What faiths as providers of services share though, is a mix of instrumentalism and idealism in the policies through which they work. This is the case across the policy matrix but in this arena of service provision the mix is starkly illuminated. The provision of services by faiths to a sometimes-sceptical public locates them precisely on the intersection between private and public, rendering them fair game for all sorts of debates which are helpful to our purposes here. How much faith, and of what kind, is it legitimate to bring to the public table? Policy allows for a curious combination in which there are strands which see faiths solely in terms of their usefulness to welfare services and others which idealise them as centres for more nuanced contributions – social capital, community cohesion or some other commodity from a range of amorphous social 'goods' which are thought to be desirable.

In this, comparisons with Canada and the US are helpful in sharpening the distinctions. The US is in one sense the more instrumentalist in that it sees faiths primarily through the lens of what they can provide in the way of public services in an extended mixed economy of welfare. The Faith Based Initiative, and the focus on faiths in public space, is very much on their role as providers. Yet at the same time there is an idealist streak in the permission faith-based services have to bring theological and moral perspectives from their traditions directly into the services they provide, for example by using prayer as part of interventions for drug and alcohol addiction. Such activities have been criticised for constituting services with 'strings attached'. But idealism is also to be found in the suggestion that, by bringing aspects of faith itself into the services they provide, faiths can help bring about a re-moralisation of public space by bringing back to the public table certain principles and values seen as desirable. In the US these have been associated with the evangelical conservative religious values of family, community and duty, which may be desirable to a conservative government with strong links with the evangelical right, but this has proved highly divisive of an America which is also in part characterised by the left-leaning liberalism of the Californian seaboard. In this, faiths are also often, and controversially, aligned with sexism and homophobia.

There is a comparable 'moralisation' strand in the UK context associated, not with the religious right as it is in the US, but rather with a sort of understated Christian social democracy, drawing in large part on communitarianism, as we saw in Chapter 4. This celebrates the idea of community as a riposte to the individualism of the previous conservative (and Republican) governments and sees faiths as sharing a commitment to the ideas associated with that – the value of human beings, the importance of collectivity and sharing, the imperatives of social justice and so on. Faiths in the UK are, then, frequently idealised as sources or sites of the socially desirable goods of social capital, community and community cohesion. But this idealisation does not translate into ideal-*ism*. Faiths are involved at the public table, not because of some political or cultural idealism about faith as such, but because of what they are ideal*ised* as bringing or offering to civil society. In the main, they are understood as sharing somewhat in the political vision which is already there. That vision encompasses idealistic notions about strengthening community (to which we shall return in Chapter 8) as well as instrumentalist ones about extending the mixed economy of welfare. Since faiths are regarded as responding in both these domains, their presence is assured. But symptomatic of the mix is that in the UK there is far less interest in the faith dimension itself within services, and in so far as this has been debated at all, public consensus coheres largely around a general insistence that services must be open to people of other faiths and of none and their public role does not add up to a public domain for discussion *about* faith. This is reflected in the Canadian context too where, with the notable exception of the Ontario faith-schools debate, faith-based providers are a familiar part of the welfare landscape but their theological views are, by general consent, unvoiced. In each case, this contrasts with the US where the faith 'flavour' is permitted in public services. In contrast, in the UK the regulatory body for charitable activities, the Charities Commission, has its own Faiths Unit which works to ensure compliance with the requirement for a general 'public benefit' which does not discriminate on the grounds of religious belief. Faiths may provide so long as they do not use provision as an opportunity to evangelise and so long as they provide to everyone. This has sometimes led to difficulties, as in the case of the refusal of some Catholic adoption agencies to work with gay adopters. It constitutes an instrumentalist emphasis but it is balanced by an associated idealistic strand which values faiths, not as ideals in themselves, but as *ideal sites* of social capital, community and cohesion, as we have seen.

The other big question raised by faiths as providers of services concerns their relationship with other actors in civil society. There is considerable informal debate about whether, when proffering public services, faiths constitute a 'sector' comparable to the private, voluntary, community and public sectors. One suggestion is that they sit within the voluntary and community sector where they are doing similar sorts of work to it, such as in neighbourhood projects (see Dinham and Lowndes, 2008). But others have felt concerned about the impact on faith communities of being constituted as a 'sector' at all. There is an instrumentalism associated with being thought of in this way. It oozes the idea of a mono-directional homogenous whole, into which are subsumed all the diversities which might make faiths special. Might this compromise faiths' independence, their ability to act as critical friends, perhaps even the very diversity which is seen as part of their strength?

And in the end, many of the experiences of faith and service provision which have been reported in the albeit limited data reflect concerns about what Luke Bretherton has called the 'commodification of faith' (Bretherton, 2007). His warning against what he calls three 'temptations' in relation to the public role of the church are salutary. They are equally applicable to all the faith traditions as well as to Christian churches. He suggests caution against the ease with which we might

   ... let the church be constructed by the modern bureaucratic state as either just another interest group seeking a share of public money or just another constituency within civil society who can foster social cohesion and make up the deficiencies of state run welfare programmes. (ibid.)

The distinctiveness of faith itself is lost in such a scenario and that loss will, in turn, result in the collapse of the group which cohered around that faith in the first place. Second, he warns against construction of public faith

in terms of either multiculturalism – the church becoming just another minority identity group demanding recognition for its way of life as equally valid in relation to all others – or the rhetoric of rights – the church decomposing itself into a collective of rights bearing individuals pursuing freedom of religious expression. (ibid.)

Again, he is stressing the centrality and essentialism of faith in the 'faith and civil society' equation. And third, he counsels against public faith being 'constructed by the market as a product to be consumed or commodity to be bought and sold' (Bretherton, 2008).

To these might be added the concern that commodifying market approaches enjoin market methods and faiths risk also being drawn into the sorts of competitive processes which could set them up against one another. Though this may be a legitimate and appropriate aspect of public activities for some, it is also the case that success in competitive processes depends upon the power and capacity of competitors. In the case of faiths, we know these to differ dramatically. So some traditions will certainly fall behind and existing inequality is likely to be extended. At the same time, some of the work between traditions remains somewhat fragile and many have chosen to make themselves vulnerable by daring to open up dialogue. Some of the competitive processes and methods of a commodified civil society might threaten that dialogue by setting people up in competition rather than partnership.

These are salutary reminders of the importance faiths place on faith as the source of their public activities. They raise pertinent questions as the engagement of faiths at the public table unfolds increasingly in the direction of the provision of services. Once again, we see that the public engagement of faiths raises important wider questions about the nature of society and of public space.

7
Faiths, Governance and Democracy

Things are busy for many people of faith. The policy spotlight has been shining in their direction, illuminating them in some revealing ways. As we have seen, faiths are being noticed again for the roles they play in community cohesion and social capital on the one hand, and in community projects, public sector contracting, social enterprise and the provision of services on the other. This often gives rise to controversy and debate about the legitimacy of faiths at all in these public spaces and the spotlight of policy has been brightening some contested corners in its glare.

At the intersection between the provision of services and the building of community cohesion is a realm which affects them both and which is preoccupied with how faiths and others engage in the governance of a recast public space in such a way as to help achieve that recasting effectively. The involvement of faiths in spaces of governance is then, important to an investigation of faiths at the public table. It is interesting to note, en route, that the governance dimension is particular to the UK of our three comparison countries. Neither the US nor Canada extends its interests in faiths sufficiently beyond their role in the provision of services so as to consider them serious mainstream actors in policy-making and decision-taking itself in any formal way, at least by direct dint of their faith, though they do embrace them for the values they are perceived to bring out in public. Thus they are lauded in the US as 'one of the strongest forces holding the values of individual neighborhoods together... often a lone anchor in their blighted neighborhoods' (Goldsmith, 2002, p. 77). In this they are regarded as 'grassroots, value-shaping organisations' (ibid., p. 78) which could 'dream up, organise and implement programs much more effectively than [government] could' (ibid., p. 78). But the focus is on their role in services and, aside from their service providing role and a public 're-moralisation' dimension, faiths are of interest as a public category in the US and Canada primarily in terms of an agenda for the prevention of religious extremism, and not really in terms of governance. There we are in the confused territory of faiths as both heroes (providers) and villains (extremists).

Governance is itself a newly extended domain in the UK since there have been significant policy commitments both to devolving power away from the centre and to increasing and widening participation in governance. These goals have been associated with concerns to 'reactivate' people as 'citizens' in 'communities', as we shall see in Chapter 8. With differing degrees of success, these twin aims have been at the root of attempts to engage local people in the running of things.

In this chapter, we will consider the ways in which faiths are involved in governance in the UK at parliamentary level and in the civil service processes of policy construction, as well as in regional and local government where certain powers are devolved or delegated from central government to local authorities and others. We will also consider ways in which the governance of area-based initiatives for neighbourhood renewal in the most disadvantaged areas in the UK has been extending and taking account of faiths.

But the laying out of policy parameters is only one part of the task – and, in any case, policies change. What is more interesting is to draw out the underlying implications of the participation of faiths in governance. As with their engagement in the provision of services and community cohesion, the involvement of faiths in aspects of governance generates debates and controversies which can be highly illuminating. These are to do with the relationship between person, community and state in regards to faiths but may well be applied more widely to questions about the character of the public table itself. In particular, there are issues about leadership, representation and participation. Among faiths, who takes the lead? With what authority? What constituencies do they represent? How do they cope with dissent? Who takes part? And how are the voices of non-participants brought to the table? And since these are questions about how things are governed, they also enjoin contests about democracy itself. How do faiths engage with democratic processes and principles? Which democratic modes are faiths suited to? This chapter explores these questions, too.

Contexts of extended governance

The phrase 'extended governance' does not promise much in the way of an interesting read. And yet, far from being dry and theoretical, this policy arena has resulted in some substantial shifts in practice. An emphasis on extended forms of participative governance in the UK comes from a shift in thinking since 1997 which is about a renewed focus on communities and social justice. This is a fundamental relocation of the political away from the unfettered free market and towards a more human-focused concept of the social. This is a strong starting point for faiths whose interests are theologically located in the human over and above the economic.

This emphasis is also inextricably bound up with reform of the state as an instrument for promoting the much broader participation of people in decision-making processes. Hitherto 'passive individuals' are transformed as 'active participants' who are both economically active and community-orientated, thus exercising both 'rights and responsibilities' as citizens in communities (Etzioni, 1993). It is such communities which are seen as the bedrock for the successful society. The reliance on notions of community is central, as we have seen, and faiths are regarded as repositories of all sorts of 'capitals' which can be bought to bear in them.

The community nexus is the central theme in what the British Labour Party and the US Democratic Party have called the 'Third Way'. One of its great apologists, Anthony Giddens (now Lord Giddens) identifies seven key planks underlying it: 'reform of the state; fiscal discipline; welfare reform; equality of opportunity, not outcome; firm law and order; commitment to ecological modernisation; and taking globalisation seriously' (Giddens, 2000, p. 12). It is noteworthy that 'reform of the state' takes top billing. Central to the overall agenda is the recasting of the relationship between person and state in the intermediate space of 'the community'. The conceptual and material framework of state is seen as a central precondition for active participation. It is an attempt to stimulate active citizenship (about which more is discussed in Chapter 8) through thriving communities – that word again. This is a governance agenda in which the energies of local people are 'harnessed' in revamped systems of decision-making which *include* them. Hence the importance of faiths, which from a government perspective are understood as excellent sources of community.

It might also be suggested that faiths bring a particular way of thinking to the public table which challenges governance to ask new or unfamiliar questions, many of which are really about the human condition. Who is a neighbour? How do we love one another? What role for forgiveness? Hitherto such questions have been largely relegated from governance discourse and only raised in other contexts, primarily those already sympathetic to them. But where better to ask them than in the politics which set the context in which those lives are lived? By bringing such categories back to the public table in systems of governance, faiths, and a perhaps more human-focused ethos associated with them, have the potential distinctively to inform the parameters, policies and practices of civil society.

Their presence is founded on what faiths are presumed to have to say about community after a long-term dominance of the market under the New Right. It also rests on a presumption that a traditionally socialist response to the resulting social disintegration which was observed is politically and economically impossible and unnecessary. The Third Way instead 'accepts the logic of 1989 and after' (ibid., p. 27) and proposes a post-Soviet reformed alternative of recasting individuals as citizens through active democratic engagement – which is played out here in the extension of new participative forms of governance. I have suggested that faiths may have accepted this too, in particular in relation to the Church of England in its 2006 report 'Faithful Cities' (see Dinham, 2008) but it may be true of other traditions too. Their role in challenging the body politic may be compromised by their enlistment further and further into its realms.

Faiths are participants at the public table because they are regarded as good, already, at the things which make it valuable. The data show that faiths are already particularly effective as 'active citizens' in terms of participation in public activities. The UK Home Office's Citizenship Survey found that 23 per cent of people participate as volunteers in a faith-based setting (Home Office, 2005). Within this, the proportion is higher among women than men and higher among minority ethnic groups than White citizens (63 per cent of Black people and 59 per cent of Asian people) (ibid.). While religious affiliation on its own makes little difference, the data show that those who actively practice their faith are more likely than others to volunteer. A similar pattern can be detected in relation to civic engagement more generally. Rates of participation in consultations and lobbying, and involvement in decision-making bodies (ibid.; National Council for Voluntary Organisations, 2007) are higher for those actively practicing a faith. And, as we have seen, (in Chapter 6), individual rates of participation are reflected in collective engagement too in the range and extent of community-level projects they operate. If faiths are such sites of activity already, how much more can they contribute by their inclusion in and harnessing to formally extended forms of governance?

The extension of governance to include faiths (and others) at the public table is regarded then, as one mechanism for the reactivation of supposedly inactive people and the harnessing of already active ones (we shall return to this theme in Chapter 8). And it has been intended to penetrate all the way through the system (though whether it has done so is a matter of debate – and not our central concern here). Thus the reform of governance begins at national level in the reorganisa- tion of the national Parliament through reform of the Upper House, the House of Lords and devolution to the nations of the UK (Scotland, Northern Ireland and Wales). Hundreds of hereditary peerages were abolished in 1999 in favour of an interim appointed House. Alongside, a 'People's Peers Commission' has appointed a small number of new peers on the basis of popular criteria. There are also important debates about the role of the Lords Spiritual, the 26 Anglican Bishops who have seats in the UK's upper chamber, the House of Lords. There have been a number of discussions in the various reform commissions reflecting a growing preoccupation against single-faith representation in that forum. Suggestions have been made that a reduced number of 'faith' seats, (possibly sixteen), should be redistributed among all the trad- itions, though no solution has been proposed for how those seats would actually be distributed.

At the same time, devolution has resulted in new assemblies for Wales and Northern Ireland, and a Parliament for Scotland, as well as regional assemblies and/or regional development agencies in each of the nine English regions. The attempt is to reconnect people with pol- itics generally. But some of the assemblies and development agencies have reserved a seat or two specifically for faiths. Here too, faiths are required to organise themselves such that a representative or two can be found to act in these capacities. This has also resulted in the set- ting up of regional faiths forums in each of the nine English regions, including London, though these are at differing stages of develop- ment and capacity. These have each set themselves a specific remit to respond to regional governance agenda and they have received fund- ing from central government and from the regional governance bod- ies to do so.

Reform of governance is also extended through reform of local government, the necessary reconstruction of public institutions in order to redress the 'over-sized but under-performing state' (Giddens, 2000, p. 41). Local models of participation in governance involve an emphasis, at least in the rhetoric, on resident-led decision-making and partnership of local people with local agencies, including the Local Authority. An example is the neighbourhood renewal agenda and 'New Deal for Communities' (NDC), which allocated additional funding of

£2 billion over 10 years to 39 of the most disadvantaged areas in the UK. Its distinctive feature is its claim to put local people 'in the driving seat' (SEU, 1999, p. 1). In practice this means that services and community planning are managed by 'partnership boards' at least 50 per cent of which must be local residents. Many of these boards have significant faith representation. A government report into their role suggested that 'faith communities are keen for an active role in working with NDCs and other neighbourhood renewal initiatives on the basis of genuine engagement' (Angoy, 2004, p. 2) and that they have been 'substantially involved in a range of activities consistent with neighbourhood renewal' (ibid.). Farnell has also observed significant activity by faiths in neighbourhood renewal and outlines the importance of a research agenda for understanding it (Farnell, 2001).

In each of these settings, what is envisaged is the reconnection of people with the structures of government. This is also the intention of the introduction of Local Strategic Partnerships (LSPs) in each local authority area. These are boards made up of representatives of each of the main agencies and sectors in every local authority area who come together to pursue processes of community planning designed to take better account of the needs and wishes of local people. Many LSPs reserve a place on the board for a faith representative amongst the range of groups which participate and faiths have been highly active within them. Research about

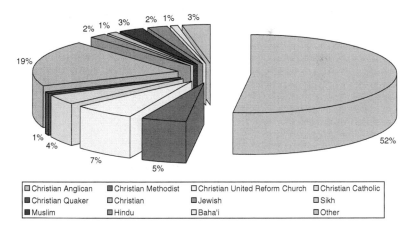

Figure 5 Rates of participation in LSPs by faith tradition

Source: Berkeley, N. and Barnes, S. (Coventry University), Dann, B. and Stockley, N. (CUF) and Finneron, D. (FbRN) (2006), Faithful Representation: faith representatives on Local Public Partnerships, London: CLG/CUF (www.cuf.org.uk).

their participation has suggested that in such settings

> Faith representatives have a unique contribution to bring – as those
> who are usually strongly locally rooted, possibly in touch with and
> trusted by people and groups often suspicious of 'officialdom'. They
> have a good grasp of local issues and priorities. They will be net-
> worked with a range of formal and informal community groups,
> with many of the latter likely to be completely 'off the radar' of the
> local authority, as well as voluntary sector infrastructure organisa-
> tions. Some have strong links into BME communities; some partici-
> pate in inter-faith networks. (Berkeley et al., 2006, p. 3)

In a government national evaluation of LSPs (Berkeley et al. 2006),
71 per cent identified a faith organisation or individual as a member
within the wider membership of the partnership, if not on the board
itself. Another report provides useful data on rates of participation by
faith tradition (see Figure 5).

But it also identifies some of the challenges for faiths working in these
domains of participative governance:

> It can be hard for them to speak for or effectively represent all faith
> groups. Individuals who get involved as faith representatives can be
> in areas where there is a low level of engagement by faith commu-
> nities. Generally, there is insufficient clarity concerning the role of
> faith representatives – consequently how this works out in practice is
> left to individual initiative. Inadequate structures can exist at local
> level for enabling faith communities to develop shared strategies in
> community regeneration and strengthening community cohesion.
> Anecdotal evidence suggests that there are also particular issues
> around building the capacity of members of faith groups in order for
> them to be perceived as being eligible to join local public partner-
> ships, and to enable them to participate fully on these. (ibid., p. 4)

Thus there can be problems in identifying individuals who can legit-
imately represent faiths in the first place. This is associated with difficulties in getting people to give their time to participate. But it has also
to do with lack of clarity, sometimes with weak relationships between
faiths and often a lack of skills for effective engagement on the parts
both of faiths and their potential partners. There are also more conceptual questions about what confers such legitimacy in the first place.
What seems clear is that, given the sheer diversity of faiths noted in
Chapter 2, representation cannot claim alignment with forms of direct

democracy. Rather, representation is delegated or designated by general consensus and it is understood that there is little or no numerical relationship between representatives and the whole constituency of faiths. What representatives do, in these contexts, is give voice to the general issues and perspectives which having a faith might bring. The strong representatives are those trusted across traditions to assert the presence of faiths and ensure that faith is a remembered dimension at the pubic table.

But this is difficult. Similar issues were identified in a study of faiths' participation in neighbourhood renewal which found a number of obstacles including:

> a lack of 'religious literacy' among regeneration professionals; a perception among religious groups that they are discriminated against in the allocation of funding; difficulties in engaging minorities, women and young people; some incompatibility between secular and faith definitions of appropriate gender roles and equal opportunities; and competition and sometimes conflict within, as well as between, faith groups. (Farnell et al., 2003, p. 39)

These issues are replicated in increased participation in the civil service too, where the Inner Cities Religious Council was first set up in 1992 to advise from faiths' perspectives on government policy in inner-city areas. This has since been replaced with the Faith Communities Consultative Council with a wider remit to advise from the perspectives of faiths on a wider range of government policies in communities. The Council is made up of people who in one way or another are regarded as somehow leading or representing a tradition or traditions. Yet the nature of those claims about representation varies significantly. In some cases they are clergy and therefore have some claim to 'lead' their worshipping community. What does this mean for the parts of their 'faith communities' which are outside of the worshipping domain, for example in associated groups, clubs and projects? Others are prominent commentators in their own traditions who are invited because they are well-known. Their claims to represent may be disputed by some while others may legitimate their participation quite happily. In most cases they are delegated, not elected, to give voice to the concerns and interests of the groups they represent. The processes by which they form their messages are in themselves a crucial determinant of the degree to which such 'voicing' can be associated with democracy. In each of these settings the representation of faiths throws up new challenges and questions about how it can be achieved and what it should mean. How are representatives chosen? Who do they represent? What is their legitimacy? The process of addressing these questions is as likely to lead to strife as to participation, as people jostle to become the voices of their tradition while others feel misrepresented, distanced or silenced.

Participation

Participation, then, may be a laudable aim – the 'hurrah' concept to which White and Pettit refer (White and Pettit, 2004) – but it is also a difficult thing to achieve. At the public table to which faiths are invited, places are limited and it requires the finding of representatives to occupy them. This is one of the key challenges of extended forms of governance, which require more and more participation from 'newcomers' to the public table. Inevitably there is jostling amongst people and communities of faith and the number of formal places available for voicing faiths at the public table is limited. In some cases this is negotiated with care and mutual respect, as in the establishment of many of the English regional faith forums. For example, the East of England Faiths Council (EEFC) has come into being over a period of years in which great care has been taken to include as wide a range of traditions as possible, to work with those whose capacity is lowest and to make relationships with others whose interest was not initially there. The creation of the mutuality, reciprocity and trust on which the success of participation depends has been painstaking. At the same time, there have been many debates, some of which continue to happen, about precisely who speaks for whom, both at the council and externally to other bodies on its behalf. And there is ongoing acknowledgement that the faiths council cannot claim to represent the people of faith in its region except in a delegated form. There are certainly some who feel disenfranchised by the systems of participation which have emerged and there are those who are convinced that they are not adequately or appropriately represented. In the simple numerical terms of the ballot box this is certainly the case. In some cases this is associated with disputes with or dissent from 'leaders' in their communities. In others they arise from theological, missiological or values differences which can result in argument. At worst they have resulted in division. It is clear, then, that what form participation takes is an important consideration with regards to new forms of governance. They are associated with modes of democracy, too, since the choice of representatives and their function once chosen, determines its shape fundamentally.

One way of looking at the relationship between participation and democracy is to see participation as a mechanism – 'a process through which stakeholders influence and share control over development initiatives and the decisions and resources which affect them' (World Bank, 1994, p. 12). In governance contexts it is not clear to what extent faiths are able to influence decisions and resources. This returns us to debates about the relationship between instrumentalism and idealism. Is the role of faiths in governance to reform the ideas associated with it and to bring change to the preoccupations of public policy? Or are they there simply to contribute to the delivery of specific outcomes? Are faiths at the public table to bring their values and ideals to the fore? Or are they invited for the resources which reside within them? In practice, as with all the other interests which vie for a voice in the making of civil society, it is likely to be somewhere between the two. The production of civil society is a contest conducted through the various mechanisms of rational debate, heated argument and downright political manoeuvring.

As a process, on the other hand, participation is regarded as 'a powerful vehicle for social inclusion and for mobilising new energy and resources for overcoming poverty' (Gaventa, 1998, p. 50). This is the primary emphasis of policy relating to governance – the re-engagement of a society of individuals considered to have lost interest in the processes of decision-making. A key political task has come to be understood as the need to 'construct policy discursively' (Barry and Hallett, 1998, p. 19) – in other words, to include more people, including faiths, in decision-making.

But such a discursive policy construction has been shown to be very difficult to achieve across general populations. Why should it be any easier amongst faiths? Alongside the challenges for participants themselves, cause also lies in the relationship between participation and power. It has been suggested in general contexts that 'the idea of public participation ... has been pursued with varying degrees of vigour since the 1960's' (Burns et al., 1994, p. 153) but that 'little has been achieved by way of a fundamental shift of power' (Boaden et al., 1982, p. 179). Burns et al. reject the equation of participation with power or control on the grounds that it is 'at best partial since it opens up the participant to a whole range of unknowns dictated by national economic policy' (Burns et al., 1994, p. 155). Therefore they argue, for example, that 'the apparent control offered by neighbourhood committees can also be an illusion' (ibid., p. 155). They suggest that public institutions need to decide whether they want to 'invite citizens behind the scenes. If [it does] not want to move in this direction it should not pretend that it does' (ibid., p. 156). Indeed, it is argued that 'there is a critical difference between going through the empty ritual of participation and having the real power needed to affect the outcome of the process' (Arnstein, 1971, p. 176).

Arnstein sets out a helpful tool for analysing power in relation to participation in her 'ladder of participation' (see Table 12). This is useful in interrogating experiences of participation in practice.

The division of the ladder into sections of 'control', 'tokenism' and 'non-participation' has been highly influential in analyses of participation ever since. Though Arnstein stresses that the ladder is a simplification, 'it still provides a helpful starting point for discussion of citizen empowerment' (Burns et al., 1994, p. 158). Though no formal data currently exist which analyse the experiences of faiths in this way, there have been criticisms from others that they are disproportionately privileged to be at the public table at all. In this case the form that participation takes becomes a secondary factor. Others have observed obstacles to the participation of faiths once they are at the public table (in this case in neighbourhood renewal), including

> an inadequate understanding of what faith communities can bring to the regeneration table. Faith communities...referred to a sense of feeling stigmatised by professional regenerators, thought to stem from prejudice based on purely secular attitudes and approaches towards development and renewal. Not infrequently, faith-based organisations reported being turned away by potential funders because they were considered to be seeking funding for essentially religious activities, which were not eligible for public funding. [And

Table 12   Arnstein's ladder of participation

8	Citizen control	Degrees of citizen power
7	Delegated power	same as above
6	Partnership	same as above
5	Placation	Degrees of tokenism
4	Consultation	same as above
3	Information	same as above
2	Therapy	Non-participation
1	Manipulation	same as above

Source: Arnstein, 1971, pp. 176–82.

there are problems with] Religious illiteracy on the part of regeneration professionals. (Angoy, 2004, p. 22)

Burns et al. propose a revised ladder (see Table 13) which they suggest is 'more tuned to the needs of the public sphere...' (Burns et al., 1994, p. 161). This is in response to their key criticisms in two directions. First, that Arnstein's ladder is culturally specific to national government in the US and that it therefore needs to be adapted for local contexts in the UK and elsewhere. For faiths in particular this contextual specificity may apply intensely. A 'faith participation' ladder might look very different to the experiences of participants outside of faiths, in part at least for some of the reasons given by Angoy above. Indeed, 'ladders' might vary significantly between traditions and at different parts of the public table. And participation certainly differs dramatically between the US and the UK because of the policy parameters which form their contexts.

Second, 'the rungs of the ladder should not be considered to be equidistant' (ibid., p. 161). They suggest that it is far easier to 'climb the lower rungs of the ladder than to scale the higher ones' (ibid., p. 161). They therefore introduce some further rungs while also recognising that 'some public institutions will have their feet on several rungs at once' (ibid., p. 164). Again, for faiths the experience may differ depending on where the participation takes place. A preponderance of faith participation at national level in the UK in the work of the Faith Communities Consultative Council may appear to be highly influential and yet it is not really clear how far up the ladder this goes in terms of actual power. There is no simple relationship between being at the centre of national

Table 13 Burns et al. ladder of participation

12	Interdependence	Citizen control
11	Entrusted control	same as above
10	Delegated control	same as above
9	Partnership control	Citizen participation
8	Limited decentralisation	same as above
7	Effective decision-making	same as above
6	Genuine advisory bodies	same as above
5	High-quality consultation	same as above
4	Information and customer care	Citizen non-participation
3	Poor information	same as above
2	Cynical consultation	same as above
1	Civic hype	same as above

Source: Burns et al., 1994, pp. 162–3.

government and being at the top of the ladder. Similarly, significant levels of participation in LSPs at local level do not guarantee concomitant levels of influence.

There are questions to be asked, therefore, about what kind of participation faiths are having at the public table and how these experiences might differ from tradition to tradition and depending on which bit of the public table is being occupied.

What of faiths and democracy?

Participation has implications for democracy and how participation may be exercised in democratic terms. This operates in two directions. First, participation requires participants and where the number of those participants is restricted, as in the case of extensions of formal dimensions of governance, the identification of those participants requires a process of some kind. Can such a process be in itself democratic in some way? What is the proper relationship between the selection of participatory representatives and the democracy in which they participate?

Second, participation in governance is itself an alteration to the processes of democracy. Are faiths amenable to such democratic forms or do they tend instead towards the 'conversation stopping certainties' about which many are concerned (see Keane, 2000, p. 9)?

I have noted that the representation of faiths at the public table is unlikely to sit well with forms of direct democracy as championed by Rousseau who argued for 'unmediated popular government' (in Weale, 1999, pp. 132–141). Direct democracy is concerned with ensuring democratic rights for the whole community as well as for the community as a whole. The already crowded public table does not have space for this and faiths find themselves managing with very small numbers of what they call 'representatives'. But are they actually representatives? Representative democracy draws on the liberal notion of the individual who has a right but not an obligation to participate in politics. Here, the role of the state is to safeguard individuals' rights to self-fulfilment and liberty and to represent those rights on behalf of individuals. In this sense, democracy is understood as the aggregation of individual preferences. During the nineteenth century, these positions were in continuing competition for hegemony. Petitions, marches and protests can be construed as forms of direct democracy, though they are largely no longer aligned to power as direct forms were in the classical Athenian polis in which citizens would come together in the literal public square to debate and decide on public issues. Such forms have since been subjugated to the representative so that democracy is largely exercised through the processes of elections. For faiths something 'in between' is happening. Their public table representatives are by no means 'elected'. But neither are they cut off from their constituency. Rather, they are delegated as trusted voicers of the generalised interests of faiths at the public table.

This reflects the struggle between direct and representative forms of government. J. S. Mill observed direct democracy through the lens of the Athenian polis at its end, when the collective aggregation of individual views resulted in a democracy so diverse that it added up to 'little more than anarchy' (in Anschutz, 1953, p. 24). This gives rise to debates about the boundaries of participation which resonate in the renegotiation of the public table to include faiths. There is a leaning towards some of the characteristics associated with direct forms of democracy in the extension of participative forms. These include a desire in policy to hear from faiths at the grass roots direct, the assertion of the value of local voices being heard, the empowerment of the oppressed and a concentration on the 'ordinary' and the 'minority'. At the same time, there is tension since the ability of structures of governance to accommodate direct forms is highly limited and in practice it is representatives who give voice. The public table is a place then, which celebrates direct participative forms of governance on the one hand but which necessarily requires representative modes in practice. It therefore practices a form of delegated democracy – a hybrid table at which all are welcome but where there is only room for so many. The 'all' must negotiate the 'few'. For faiths, whose 'communities' are themselves contested ideas, what and who is represented, and by whom are highly vexed questions.

Faiths, participation, democracy and community

Grugel argues that democracy has become divorced from community, wherein the aggregation of the will and rights of individuals is mediated in a direct way. This results, it is argued, in an attachment to liberalism instead, wherein individuals have the right, but not the obligation, to be citizens. Thus representative democracy is extended and entrenched as conceptions of the polis 'shift from the city to the nation state' (Grugel, 2002, p. 36). He argues that democracy thus becomes an administrative function. Grugel thus identifies a shift from democracy being an ideology or theory to its being a description; what he calls 'empirical democratic theory' (ibid., p. 42). Thus politics becomes an arena of academic interest preoccupied with systems of power rather than with notions of the 'good' society; no longer a moral endeavour but an administrative process. This settlement of democracy may be fundamentally challenged by the extended forms of participative governance with which faiths are involved, one aspect of which could be the revalorisation of ideological dimensions at the public table. This might be as much a concern as a benefit, depending on what those ideologies are and how they are negotiated.

What is clear, then, is that the shape of democracy has been changing. What is not clear is in what directions. What can be argued, nevertheless, is that it is far from the Schumpeterian notion of a 'realist' theory in which representative democracy is accepted as best because to expand participative democracy would be unrealistic and eventually detrimental to effective government. Rather, democracy is extending in the direction of its participative forms. How far up Arnstein's ladder that goes is as yet unknown and is, in any case, likely to differ from context to context. It has also been suggested that it represents the development of consensus by 'competing elites' (Gramsci in Bell, 1986, p. 16). Yet this pluralist representation of difference and conflicting social interests is criticised by Dahl as falsely assuming that pluralism hears all groups equally (Dahl, 1989). Dahl refers to Lukes' classic discussion of power (Lukes, 1974) to identify massive inequalities between competing groups. This is particularly true for faiths whose capacities vary significantly, as we have seen.

Direct or participatory theories of democracy, on the other hand, start with the idea that democracy should be understood as the development of reciprocal relations of trust between individuals in very local environments. In this way, participatory democracy requires a change in people's consciousness so that they regard themselves and each other as citizens within a community of other citizens. Faiths are often assumed strong on these dimensions of trust and reciprocity. Yet, once again, these ideas take little account of power and capacity imbalances between actors which often mean that the most powerful voices dominate. Faiths are also more likely than some hotly to debate these imbalances from the position of committed theological stances. What might this mean for the deliberations they must certainly engage in as they negotiate their place at the public table and the things they say once seated?

Associative and deliberative forms of democracy

The trajectory of public policy is in the direction of more associative and deliberative forms of democratic participation and the extension of the public table with new forms of governance is an expression of this.

Associative democratic forms were a feature of political ideology in the early twentieth century, where they were understood by emerging Labour movements as a possible transformative basis for a whole new society. They arise out of the view that 'representative democracy is failing badly by the standards of liberal democratic political theory' (Hirst, 1997, p. 3) and that contemporaneously there were 'few means of authoritatively determining and responding to citizens' wishes about the course of...policy whilst [governments are] in office' (ibid., p. 5). These are the same sorts of preoccupations of many Western democracies, including the UK, the US and Canada, which they describe in the terms of a 'democratic deficit'. People seem disengaged from politics.

Associations in communities were seen thus, as the locus of a 'continuous flow of information between governors and the governed' (ibid., p. 20) wherein the wishes of the people would be expressed through the agenda of self-governance of local communities arising out of the needs and issues known locally. This certainly resonates with the rhetoric of extended forms of participative governance which make space for faiths. It is at least in part a response to the development of state-provided social welfare after the Second World War. This perspective has come to understand the public provision of welfare as having resulted in the attempted uniformity of state policy through 'big' government and the 'imposition of common rules and standard services' (ibid., p. 5). A burgeoning of government, from military protector, through provider of social welfare to macro-economic manager, is seen as having drawn with it a type of democracy which is hierarchical, inflexible and uniformly representative. Contemporary forms of associative democracy respond to this by seeking the introduction of flexible, responsive government via the extension of the mixed economy of welfare into the voluntary and community sectors. Here, associations of issue-focused people and groups become stakeholders in government by contributing to an ever-emerging agenda for social change and development. At the same time they identify and provide services and activities which reflect what are asserted as the real wishes of people at very local levels. Thus 'voluntary self-governing associations might contribute to providing facilities for different communities and also serve as a means of lessening tension between such communities in the public sphere' (ibid., p. 11).

In this sense, associationalism is understood as a part of the production of democracy via the expression and consolidation of consensus from the grass roots of public space – 'a vital supplement...that enables the defects [of existing institutions] to be meliorated' (ibid., p. 12). Associationalism thus makes accountable representative government by 'embedding the market system in a social network of coordinative and regulatory institutions' (ibid., p. 12). The strength of such a system of democracy is that it provides citizens with '...a political community that will allow them to be different and not one that exhorts them to be the same' (ibid., p. 14). An associative democracy thus sees the state as facilitator of self-governing communities and protector of the entitlements, standards and equity which are their preconditions.

These are recognisable conditions in the rhetoric of new forms of governance and faiths are clearly engaging within them. And yet, the more associative and deliberative forms with which they engage require an openness of mind and readiness for debate which faiths have also sometimes shown themselves to be poor at. It is possible that discourse about the extension of associative and deliberative forms conceals or ignores the contests which are really going on within faiths. As we have seen, there can be no assumption in the first place of an associational continuity in the relationships between worshipping communities, clergy, community projects, service users, strategic partners and anyone else coming into contact with a so-called faith community. And this means that they cannot either be assumed to be safe sites for the deliberation which is necessary for the participation of many interests at the public table. There is evidence that, like any community, faith traditions can fall out amongst and between themselves, and with others (see Furbey et al., 2006). There is concern, too, that faiths are also capable, not only of disinterest in participation in the democratic processes of governance but also sometimes actively in their overthrow (see Hussein, 2007).

This reflects considerable concern – perhaps prejudice – about faiths' capacity for rational deliberation at all. It is also possible that where the rational forms of deliberation are challenged, deliberative discussion may lead to 'intellectual war – the escalation of conflict rather than its resolution' (Elster, 1998, p. 10). Others have found something of a middle way, for example in 'congregational development' which offers a tool for identifying, acknowledging and mediating differences within worshipping communities so that change and development can take place. It acknowledges in a Christian setting that

> something that holds churches back is an atmosphere of 'niceness' and politeness – the feeling that, because we are all Christians, we all have to get on in a happy kind of way. Whereas, sometimes, the situation demands a kind of seriousness that's not really compatible with what is being 'polite'. (in Furbey et al., 2006, p. 43)

Governance, participation and gender

Even where faiths are generally quite good at associating and at the deliberation required of participation, they are not always so good at ensuring the participation of the women amongst them. Important critiques of democracy and faith come from feminism, where it is suggested that both treat women systematically as inferior. Our study on faith and social capital found that

> Many of our interviewees observed that women do most of the work in [faith] community activity. Nevertheless they become less visible the further one moves from grassroots activity, and the higher one goes up the ladder of decision making. (ibid., p. 30)

It also refers to one woman who said that 'the overwhelming experience was of being blocked when she tried to have an influence at strategic and policy levels' (ibid., p. 30). Another tells the story of a church 'constitution [which] allows women to be active in all aspects, including being ministers, but not to be members of the decision-making pastoral council. This leads to the anomaly of a woman minister not being part of the pastoral council that governs her church' (ibid., p. 31). And in a part of East London, UK, we heard the story of how

> Muslim women have been working together to change the cultural restrictions that prevented them from participating in the community processes. The timing and venues for the meetings meant that they could not attend as they were expected to be in the home. (ibid., p. 31)

At the same time, even where women's participation has been strong and women have achieved high office within democratic processes, it is suggested that there is generally '...a gender bias in democratic theory itself' (Mendus, 1992, p. 37) since the abstract 'individual' of liberal thought does not encompass the experience of women. For them, democratisation means, not only introducing and developing structures for the election of leaders and legitimisation of governments but also the eradication of authoritarian social practices through the hearing of oppressed voices. Thus feminist critiques challenge understandings of democracy which arise out of patriarchal discourses in the first place. In addition, there is a challenge to the assumption that there is an equal distribution of power or, at least, of opportunities for power. It is observed that the reality is inequality.

Faith in governance?

The participative-governance edifice is based in part, then, on the recognition by communitarian theorists (Beck, 1998; Etzioni, 1993; Giddens, 1998a, 2000, 2002; Held, 1993) that 'markets and contracts...do not create any social cohesion in and of themselves' (Beck, 1998, p. 13) and that what is required is 'an interventionist project of recreating "social solidarity" through recasting the relationship between the state and society' (Chandler, 2001, p. 174), particularly at the very local level, where it seems most relevant to people. Faiths are regarded as particularly well placed to support this. It requires 'the re-politicisation of municipal policy, indeed a rediscovery and redefinition of it by mobilising programmes, ideas and people' (Beck, 1998, p. 16). So the state is cast in a new, much more socially engaged, position. Thus the guidance calls for 'consultation and participation to be embedded into the culture of all councils' (DETR, 1998, para 4.6). Local authorities have taken on coordinating and strategic roles as 'enablers' of the existing matrices in the community, bringing together the private, voluntary, community and statutory sectors in partnerships under cooperatively devised 'community plans'. They are no longer providers of public services but enablers of it – in partnership with some of those who are seen as already amongst the best at doing it, including faiths.

At the same time, participation itself is expanded to include any actors whom it is felt have a useful contribution to make. Thus faiths are welcomed as 'repositories' of resources associated with service provision and community cohesion, as we have seen. They are regarded as sites of those elements which communitarianism values: social capital, family and community values and commitment to addressing issues of social justice.

But this recasting has impacts on all at the public table. In the first instance, it requires faiths to identify representatives and leaders who can give voice at that table. The processes for selecting them give rise to debates within and between faith traditions and communities which are as likely to be divisive as otherwise. Faiths enjoy a whole range of approaches and understandings of leadership, some of which are focused on a professional clergy and hierarchical systems of organisation while others operate much more 'horizontally'. The relationship between leadership and how the views of wider communities are represented in the context of limited space at the public table is fragile and sensitive. Many are likely to feel de-legitimated, unvoiced or even silenced by some of the processes of extended participation in governance.

Participative governance for faiths also highlights important differences in their capacity and power. Organisational and financial capacities are one part of this, affecting how, where and with what impacts different faiths are heard. Theological outlooks and motivations are another, informing and sometimes constraining the way in which power is exercised and with what aims. The minority faiths are also often aligned with the minority ethnicities and thus their over-representation in indices of deprivation is likely to be doubly compounded. This is also true of the experience of women within faith traditions, whose experiences frequently mirror and extend those of women more generally as they seek to participate. We might consider the impacts of discrimination on gay people, young people and people with disabilities in this regard too. The engagement of women is often funnelled in the direction of informal ex officio roles, the bonding rather than the bridging and linking activities and sometimes excluded altogether on the basis that they must focus on their function within the family as lead caregiver and parent.

The processes of participative governance can for these reasons, also result in an actual distancing of people from the governance to which they are expected better to connect. At local level, the promise was of 'a radical change in local councils' relationships with their communities and with central government' (DETR, 1998, para 1.7). This would be understood as 'the rebirth of democratic local government...vital to building a modern Britain and a decent society' (ibid., preface). This was seen to be necessary in order to tackle the problems of social disengagement with community affairs, a 'culture of apathy', by 'bringing government to the people' (ibid., p. 2). In practice, this has meant that local councillors have been reinvented as 'community champions' (ibid.) and the decision-making of councils given much more focus in cabinets led by mayors or chief executives. Decisions about the exact structures have been opened up to local referenda, many of the results of which have shown a marked disinclination for elected mayors in the UK (with the exception of London where the office is significantly more powerful). There is a tension in the reform of governance, therefore, between a desire to devolve power on the one hand and an effect which has seen decision-making taken further away from local people, concentrated in practice in fewer and fewer hands. This has been described as having in effect '... [decapitated] what power councillors once had' by removing the decision-making level up to cabinets, leaders, managers and mayors (Chandler, 2001, p. 178). The chamber becomes a place for the views of the people made by their representatives, but the power is largely elsewhere so that local government is effectively 'split in two, institutionalising a sharp distinction between the executive and representative roles' (ibid., p. 181). This is what Chandler describes as 'more participation, less democracy' (ibid.). Rao goes on that 'perversely it is the "in touch" councillors that will have much less say in policy formulation' (Rao, 2000, p. 36).

These processes might be reflected in some of the experiences of faiths as they join the public table, too – that as they take up the challenges and opportunities of the voice they now have, at the same time, in identifying and mandating leaders and representatives they also find themselves handing over much of that new power to the few. The processes of devolving power thus end up in taking power further away from participants whose roles are minimised as decision-making is handed over to a small number of representatives.

And extended opportunities for people to join new kinds of decision-making processes call forth new kinds of responses from faiths, who find themselves needing to 'gear up' to make sure that they can participate effectively. In the examples of neighbourhood management boards in NDC and LSPs, these can require an active engagement and a genuine lived participation which can make it all the more meaningful to those who take part. But it is precisely this that also makes the 'more participation, less democracy' effect a very personal and painful one in these domains. Investigations of local people's experiences of participation in new forms of governance have suggested that it frequently ends up as little more than tokenism (see Dinham, 2005b) and that this can result in a disappointment which rapidly results in disengagement (see Dinham, 2006). For faiths this resonates with debates about the mix of instrumentalism and idealism in policies directed towards their involvement. The danger is that participatory tokenism in pursuit of policy-focused outcomes may diminish faiths' enthusiasm for engagement. Policy could end up killing the goose that lays the golden eggs – or at least disrupting its laying.

New forms of participative governance in the end fundamentally recast the relationship between person and state, encouraging people to take a social role as well as a private one and to draw the boundaries between private, family, community and national life differently.

They envisage a shift in the line between private and public domains in which faiths return as a public category – a formal participant at the public table.

We will turn now to how this is formalised in the rhetoric of active citizenship and the strengthened community.

8
Faiths, Active Citizens and Strengthened Communities

When I started school, aged five, Margaret Thatcher had just become prime minister in the UK. It was not until I had more or less finished at school and was sitting my exams for university that she stepped down, and it was another seven years after that until I finally knew that governments could come from the Labour Party as well as from the Conservative. This long predominance of the right (at that time for me, a lifetime) was mirrored in the US too, where the Reagan–Thatcher relationship came to embody there, and in much of the world, the dominance of the free market over all other forms of public life. In Alberta, Canada, where much of this book was written, there has been a conservative (or 'social credit') government for most of the province's century-long history and there too, even when the rest of the country has shown more of a taste for the taking of turns between liberals and conservatives, free-market conservatism has been the dominant political force. It was in this context that I, like millions of others of my generation, got used to the idea that individuals would have to look after themselves and there was, in that infamous observation of Thatcher's, 'no such thing as society'.

It was against this view that the Anglican report, *Faith in the City* (ACUPA, 1985), emerged to remind politics that society *does* matter. And it was also in this context that the left-of-centre Labour Party in the UK and the Democrats in the US embraced the ideas of communitarianism in the early 1990s, embarking upon a rhetoric which placed community at its heart. Far from there being no such thing as society, it suggested, its neglect was the very cause of an individualistic temperament which had rendered public spaces and social life impoverished, threatening and threadbare. What was needed, it was felt, was a new vision of society which celebrated communities and the people within them.

What emerged was the policy notion of the 'active community'. The language has ranged round various associated ideas so that at times the focus has been on 'active citizens', 'strengthened communities', and more recently 'resilient communities'. What these have in common is their reticence to the notions of individualism which had gone before and their embodiment of social capital and community cohesion. What is envisaged is a revalorisation of the social through celebration and magnification of the community.

This chapter considers the idea of active communities and citizens as the overall organising principle for the re-emergence of faiths at the public table. It is in this broad political landscape that the role of faiths has been re-emerging as a public category and it is within it that their participation is encouraged.

From this perspective it is overall an instrumentalist landscape made up of three dimensions of the 'usefulness' of faiths to civil society, as we have seen. The first seeks the activation of people in communities through their participation in the building of community cohesion (as we saw in Chapter 5). The second invites such activation through their participation in the provision of services (as we saw in Chapter 6). The third calls it forth through participation in extended forms of governance (as we saw in Chapter 7). Each is a part of the reactivated community which has been so vigorously sought. They are expressions of a renewed taking of responsibility, alongside government, for the things which happen between us in public, and not only within ourselves or our families. The rhetoric, if not the practice, marks a new relationship between people in their everyday encounters and between people and the state. It recasts the boundaries between government, citizen and person, and calls us into a new relation within the construction of communities. As we have seen, such imaginaries or constructions are enormously difficult to pin down, but the emergence of a discourse which appeals to them represents a significant shift, at least in the thinking behind the practice.

The emergence of a discourse

As the fundamental backdrop to policies about communities, including faith communities, communitarianism has borne a great deal of weight in recent years. As I observed in Chapter 4, it represents a response to the individualism of the preceding period by emphasising the responsibilities of people in their communities as well as their rights as individual citizens. Thus in 2003, the UK Home Secretary asserted a key set of purposes associated with this:

> To support strong and active communities in which people of all races and backgrounds are valued and participate on equal terms by developing social policy to build a fair, prosperous and cohesive society in which everyone has a stake.
>
> To work with other departments and local government agencies and community groups to regenerate neighbourhoods and to support families; to develop the potential of every individual; to build the confidence and capacity of the whole community to be part of the solution; and to promote good race and community relations, combating prejudice and xenophobia.
>
> To promote equal opportunities both within the Home Office and more widely and to ensure that active citizenship contributes to the enhancement of democracy and the development of civil society. (Home Office, 2003, p. 1)

Elsewhere, it has been noted that what government has called 'civil renewal' depends upon '...a revitalised democracy, more responsive public services, more active and sustainable communities, local people engaged in decision making... [that] depends on active citizens' (Woodward, 2004, p. 3).

It is also part of a broader agenda in government for self-help in 'the key areas of public service delivery, philanthropy, volunteering, building strong communities and social enterprise' (Home Office, 2006, p. 2), domains which are clearly seen as linked. They are understood as the backbone of newly reactivated communities emphasising, as each does, the tradition of community life and self-help which are regarded as a palliative to rampant individualism.

The UK Home Office's Citizenship Survey 2005 (ibid.) explored the activities people undertake in the public spaces of civil society. It demonstrates government's thinking about what constitutes 'active citizenship' through its choice of things to measure. By focusing on volunteering, charitable giving, civil activism, civic consultation and civic participation, government gives an implicit indication, or definition, of the things which it thinks matter in civil society. Its definitions of each are instructive. It describes informal volunteering as 'giving unpaid help as an individual to someone who is not a relative' (ibid., p. 4), and formal volunteering as 'unpaid help given as part of groups, clubs or organisations to benefit others or the environment' (ibid., p. 6). Charitable giving is defined in terms of people 'living in England who had given money to charity in the four weeks before ...' (ibid., p. 15).

In terms of the broader category of civil renewal, it defines this as 'the development of strong, active, and empowered communities, in which people are able to do things for themselves, define the problems they face, and tackle them in partnership with public bodies' (ibid., p. 18). It further divides this activity into civic activism, civic consultation and civic participation, which are defined in explicit and concrete terms:

> ... civic activism, which refers to involvement either in direct decision-making about local services or issues, or in the actual provision of these services by taking on a role such as a local councillor, school governor or magistrate; civic consultation, which refers to active engagement in consultation about local services or issues through activities such as attending a consultation group or completing a questionnaire about these services; and civic participation, which covers wider forms of engagement in democratic processes, such as contacting an elected representative, taking part in a public demonstration or protest, or signing a petition. (ibid., p. 18)

Civic participation is also defined as

> undertaking at least one of the following activities: contacting a local councillor; contacting an official working for the local council; contacting an MP; contacting a government official; contacting an elected member of the Greater London Assembly (for people living in London); contacting an official working for the Greater London Assembly (for people living in London); attending a public meeting or rally; taking part in a public demonstration; and signing a petition. (ibid., p. 26)

There was also a phase in which government talked about 'vibrant communities' in which people can 'shape their own future and whose voice is heard by government at all levels' (DETR, 2000, foreword). In a study on faith in rural communities (Farnell et al., 2006) this is located in the notion of social capital and it is noted in relation to 'vibrancy' that '... some aspects of local rooted-ness come from the presence and involvement of the church at crucial stages of life' (ibid., p. 6). They add that '... notions of the home church, rites of passage, the significance of graveyards, the church building as a special sacred space and the annual church cycle of prayer and celebration contribute to a sense of belonging and well-being' (ibid., p. 6).

The agenda is also brought together in the government White Paper, *Communities in Control: Real People, Real Power* (CLG, 2008). This promises to extend active citizenship by 'enhancing the power of communities and helping people up and down the country to set and meet their own priorities' (ibid., foreword) and

> helping citizens to get involved when they want to on their own terms – paving the way for a new style of active politics that not only gives people a greater say but ensures that their voices are heard and that their views will make a difference. (ibid., foreword)

It is predicated on the assumption that 'With the right support, guidance and advice, community groups and organisations have a huge, largely latent, capacity for self-government and self-organisation' (ibid., p. iii). In other words, it returns us once more to a rhetoric about inactive passive individuals with huge potential to be reactivated as 'active citizens'. Thus, in a section called 'Supporting you in becoming a more active citizen or volunteer' the focus is split into two parts: the first is on the tangible activities of volunteering in the Third Sector, indicative of the value placed on volunteering as a key aspect of civic participation; the second is on the citizenship it is assumed this will produce.

The remainder is about 'providing you with more access to information' (ibid., p. 4), 'making sure your petitions are heard – and acted upon' (ibid., p. 5), 'increasing your chance to influence council budgets and policies' (ibid., p. 5), 'giving you more say in your neighbourhood' (ibid., p. 5), 'giving older and young people a stronger voice' (ibid., p. 6), 'enabling you to hold those with power to account' (ibid., p. 7), 'providing you with redress when things go wrong' (ibid., p. 8), 'making it easier for you to stand for office' (ibid., p. 9) and 'ownership and control' (ibid., p. 10).

In a section called 'The role of faith-based groups' (ibid., pp. 43–5), it is stated that 'Among the voluntary organisations we want to help in different ways to build stronger communities, there is a particular role for faith based groups' (ibid., p. 43). The emphasis is on volunteering, which it is assumed will produce citizenship, and this in turn is located in an instrumentalist preoccupation with faiths as repositories of resources. Thus it states 'we intend to work with faith communities to clarify the issues and to remove the barriers to commissioning services from faith-based groups' (ibid., p. 45). And the conclusion to the White Paper has as its title 'unleashing genius and talent'. Once again the agenda is for a reactivation of passive people in individual or family settings as active citizens in communities.

Faiths and the civic

In each of these areas what data there are (though much of it is 'grey') suggest that faiths are highly engaged. So by the government's definition of 'activism' – direct decision-making, being a councillor and so on – there are clear indications of the participation of faiths, notably in Local Strategic Partnerships, Primary Care Trusts (PCTs), in Crime Reduction Partnerships and in other forms of governance bodies, as we saw in Chapter 7. A survey of 222 faith communities in 2006 produced interesting data in this regard (see Figure 6) showing upwards of 35 per cent participation rates in an albeit small sample (84 out of 222). They are also present on neighbourhood boards in areas of urban disadvantage as Richard Farnell records (Farnell 2001).

In public consultations, faiths have shown themselves particularly active, making 186 responses to the UK national government's consultation on a new 'interfaith dialogue and social action' framework, including 48 multi- or interfaith submissions. The distribution of submissions by tradition is once again indicative of the differing capacities of traditions, as shown in Table 14. This also demonstrates considerable capacity for organising responses which give voice of some kind to faiths in communities (in so far as we can know what that means). At

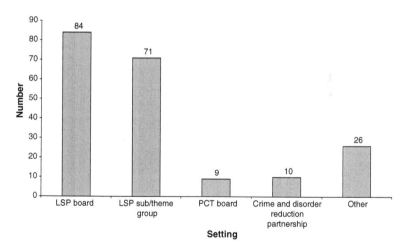

Figure 6 Faith representation by setting

Source: Chart based on and adapted from data in Berkeley, N., Barnes, S., Dann, B., Stockley, N. and Finneron, D. (2006) *Faithful Representation: Faith Representatives on Local Public Partnerships*, Church Urban Fund and the Faith Based Regeneration Network, UK.

Table 14   Respondents to the UK government's consultation for faiths, Face to Face and Side by Side, 2008

Classification	Number of responses
Academic	11
Baha'i	0
Buddhist	2
Christian	40
Hindu	0
Interfaith body	33
Jain	0
Jewish	2
Local authority	13
Multi-faith group	15
Muslim	4
Not given	8
Non-religious	34
Pagan	4
Regional faith forum	8
Sikh	2
Unclassified	10
Zoroastrian	0
Total number received	**186**

Source: Face to Face and Side by Side: A framework for interfaith dialogue and social action consultation – summary of responses CLG July 2008 available at www.communities.gov.uk/documents/communities/pdf/898791.pdf

the same time, the numbers of returns per faith tradition highlight the differences in power and capacity between them.

We might also speculate that on participation – wider forms of engagement such as contacting an MP or councillor, signing a petition, attending a public meeting and so on – faiths make available an otherwise diminishing space in which people can come together around a particular kind of wisdom or world view and in relations which have become less widely available, popular or familiar. This was an observation made by the *Faith and Social Capital* study (Furbey et al., 2006) where there are data to show that a particular and distinctive kind of psychosocial space can be generated by communities of faith which is dependent upon a combination of their buildings, motivations, theologies, staff and volunteers and activities.

For government, the types of activities which are highlighted include decision-making roles in young people's services, regeneration and tenants' committees, initiatives for crime, education and health, and

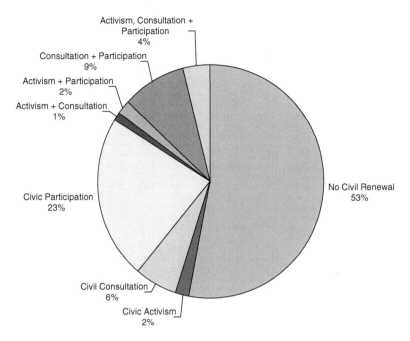

Figure 7 Participation in civil renewal strands in the 12 months before interview by British people

Source: Home Office, 2006, *The Citizenship Survey 2005*, London: Home Office.

acting in forms of governance, for example as a school governor, a local councillor or a magistrate (see Home Office, 2006, p. 21: see Figure 7). Again, faiths can demonstrate their participation in each of these activities. Overall, the Citizenship Survey 2005 found that 47 per cent of British people had taken part in some kind of active citizenship through 'civil renewal' in the previous 12 months (see Table 14 and ibid., p. 41). The majority of those had undertaken either civic participation, informal volunteering or formal volunteering, with fewer than a fifth (19 per cent) of people having not undertaken any activities at all. This has given policy-makers strong grounds for assuming that an already active core of citizens of faith can both extend their own participation and also help extend that activity much more widely amongst the remaining 53 per cent. Faiths are regarded as having particular potential for doing so. It is widely agreed that they have demonstrated their strengths in delivering precisely the sorts of social capital which these activities embody, as suggested in Chapter 5 (see Furbey et al., 2006).

Indeed, the data also show that '23% have participated in volunteering in a faith-based context' (Home Office, 2005) and that, for example, though 'Taking all volunteering activity, religious affiliation itself does not make much difference...those who actively practice a religion are more likely than others to volunteer' (Dinham and Lowndes, 2008).

The survey also asks about attitudes towards and experiences of the institutions of civil society within which active citizenship takes place. It asked about people's sense of efficacy in political decision-making, trust in institutions (police, courts and Parliament), views of local services, fear of crime and perceptions of discrimination and concludes that

> There was evidence that negative perceptions of the political system were common. The majority of people did not think that they could influence decisions affecting their local area, and even fewer felt that they could influence decisions affecting Britain. Levels of trust in Parliament remained fairly low...although there was a rise in the proportion of people who trusted their local council. Younger people were more likely than older people to trust Parliament and the local council, although they were less likely to think that they could influence decisions affecting their local area or Britain. (Home Office, 2006, p. 41)

The UK government has been interested, therefore, in extending opportunities for active engagement with those institutions too, as we saw in Chapter 7. It has also indicated its intention to look 'beyond opportunities for individuals, to the importance of strengthening society' (Home Office, 2005, foreword), suggesting that

> This is not something that the Government can do alone, but it is an issue on which we can give a lead: helping people come together from different backgrounds; supporting people to contribute to society; and taking a stand against racism and extremists who promote hatred. As a society, I believe we need to give more attention to what binds us together if we are to achieve the economic and social progress that benefits all. (Home Office, 2006, foreword)

What is envisaged is partnership between state and person, mediated through activity in communities. It is a key aspect of the communitarian call to 'rights with responsibilities'. Government desires active citizenship because 'Progress on increasing life chances for all is a fundamental element of building strong, cohesive communities and a dynamic society and economy' (ibid., p. 17) and because

> ...a strong society relies on more than simply good individual life chances. Experience suggests that people also need a sense of common belonging and identity, forged through shared participation in education, work and social activities. (ibid., p. 18)

It is nothing less than '...a greater focus on helping build a stronger sense of common belonging and social participation, at national and local levels, in partnership with civic organisations and communities themselves' (ibid., p. 19): all of which are things which faiths are seen as 'good at'. And who could argue with that?

A threat to strengthened communities?

And yet at the same time, since 9/11 in the US and 7/7 in the UK, there is a growing interest in threats to strengthened communities from religious extremists. This, too, has entered the rhetoric of policy in terms of 'citizenship', as well as in assorted policies about 'prevention of extremism', emanating primarily from a security milieu. Thus it is suggested that

> While their influence should not be overstated, extremist organisations – whether political or religious – can undermine inclusion and fuel resentment. We have therefore recently introduced legislation to make incitement to religious hatred an offence, while protecting free speech, responding to the way that racist organisations have increasingly turned their focus on followers of certain faiths. (Home Office, 2005, p. 11)

The turn to faith as a potential problem is quite understandable in the post-9/11 context. But it presents policy with a conflict. How are we to reconcile the instrumentalisation of faiths in civil society with their vilification as proponents of terror within it? Faiths will not withstand being cast as both heroes and villains for long. It is a position which can only fragment and polarise. And the perceived lines of fracture are likely to lie along the boundaries between faith traditions. This demands that we accept the Orwellian notion of 'some faiths good, some faiths bad'. And yet the reality seems to be rather that the 'good' or 'bad' of faith at the public table is contingent upon individuals and groups within traditions, and across them, and that we cannot single out particular or whole traditions as dangerous.

The UK's Commission on Integration and Cohesion recognises this nuance in the role of public faith, suggesting that

> We do not underplay the importance of ethnicity and faith in the context both of individual and community lives, and nor do we fail to recognise that there are times when ethnic or religious identity can be linked to tensions. The priority in a number of areas may well be to address relationships between different ethnic or religious groups. (Commission on Integration and Cohesion, 2006, p. 18)

Yet much of the debate about faiths in terms of 'resilient communities' has been formed in the light of a rhetoric about 'prevention of extremism', as we saw in Chapter 5. As noted, this has frequently tended to focus on Muslims as a particular problem within this. This 'othering' of Islam involves a paradox: such fracture is both what government precisely hopes to avoid and at the same time what policy, by singling Muslims out, risks causing.

Faiths and active citizenship

Though the policy agenda for the active citizen is in many ways simple, its implications for citizenship are not. Surprise, surprise – the idea of 'citizenship' is an essentially contested concept in this sea of contested concepts.

In the tradition of liberal and social rights, citizenship is expressed in terms of the rights of the individual (Oldfield, 1990). Here, citizenship emphasises rights, not duties, and locates these rights in such devices as the Bill of Rights, the Constitution, the Human Rights Act and the Geneva Convention. It is citizenship based in membership of an otherwise exclusive group, usually a nation, from which are derived rights but to which the only duty owed is to act within the law. It is notable that faiths are often interested in ideas and issues which blur the certainties of law, and there are instances where faith feeling is sufficiently strong that it conflicts with it, for example in relation to what politicians often call 'issues of conscience', such as abortion, sexuality and a range of medical interventions. This kind of 'rights' based citizenship is citizenship by status. T. H. Marshall (Marshall, 1950) describes it as citizenship which is civil or legal. This he conceives as 'the rights necessary for individual freedom... and the right to justice... and to defend all one's rights' (ibid., p. 92). And yet it is palpably the case that in relation to faith, policy-making and popular debate are anxious about the conferral of such rights without condition. Concerns about religious extremism in the UK, Canada, the US – and for that matter in the struggling democracies of Afghanistan and Iraq – are ensuring that debates and practices in relation to rights are circumscribed under certain conditions. *Habeas Corpus* itself is suspended under certain conditions in the name of the protection of citizens. Put another way, the rights of citizenship for some are suspended in the interests of the rights of citizenship of the rest. This is a difficult terrain.

Such a rights-based citizenship of status is only available to some, therefore. And in any case, as I suggested in Chapter 2, the make-up of faiths in the UK, Canada and the US is highly diverse and citizenship allegiance is, in some cases, more likely to be experienced as within the faith tradition, or across some transnational boundary, than in terms of membership of the nation itself. It is also the case that many people of faith, especially among those faiths which are newer to these countries, may not have the sort of status citizenship which confers such rights upon them in the first place. This may be particularly true for people of faith who are immigrants with unresolved or illegal status. In such circumstances, how are faiths to exercise active citizenship where its very basis may be questioned for some or many of its members? Status citizenship is anyway un-conducive to active citizenship since it precisely implies a 'rest on your laurels' *in*activity in relation to public space and civil society. The rights are already won, or conferred, and no further action is necessary.

There has also been much debate about a shift from the politics of state to the politics of identity, and it is likely that faiths are almost always at home in terms of identity. And the 'faith community', as we have seen, is a nebulous, heterogeneous and contested idea. It is identification with a group, a creed, a space or a combination of these, which determines what might be called 'membership'. Nationhood is unlikely to rank very high on lists of allegiance to define people of faith in the UK, US or Canada.

Rather, active citizenship is better located in the ideas of citizenship by practice. Aristotle defines the citizen as 'someone who participates in public affairs' through the innate natural order of homo politicus, which ethically requires it (Aristotle in Germino, 2000). Such a concept focuses on the mutuality of membership and the shared life of the polis. Broadly it is this to which 'active citizenship' appeals. It is a form of citizenship in which people take part. They do not merely assert or exercise rights but participate, for example in provision of services, or in decision-making and governance. In the act of doing so, it is envisaged that communities will be strengthened and grow. At the same time, it is hoped that this can be directed towards greater community cohesion as people work together and come to better understandings of one another's differences.

However, the Aristotelian understanding of practice citizenship relates specifically to practice as political, and therefore to active citizenship as productive of community. But it has been observed that

> classical understandings of the political, which understand politics as an aspect of ethics, morality, self-completion and beauty, contrast with contemporary ones which are characterised by the artifice of party politics in a context of an increasingly significant politics of identity. (Knox, 1994, p. 167)

Modern politics are not necessarily directed towards the 'good' or the 'ethical', as in the classical conception, but to the 'productive'. Therefore, to transpose the classical image of political participation into a twenty-first-century definition of citizenship would be folly. And yet, is it possible that precisely what is hoped for from faiths is a re-moralisation of the political; a rediscovery of the ethical and the good as a pursuit of society – social justice, not just as a matter of economic distribution but also of the well-being of spirits, souls or whatever other language is comfortable for people to use. Certainly this can be detected in the US Faith Based Initiative, as I have argued (in Chapter 6). And yet at the same time, there is grave concern among many US liberals (as distinct from Clinton's democrats, who instigated the Faith Based Initiative) that religious morality is precisely the sort of thing that should be kept away from the public table. In the UK too, there is confusion about how much 'faith' faiths should be allowed to bring.

In addition to these 'status' and 'practice' citizenships, Marshall proposes two others (Marshall, 1950). First, he suggests there is citizenship as political. This is described as 'the right to participate in the exercise of political power' (ibid., p. 92). This has been controversial across academic disciplines since Marx where it is noted that 'political citizenship operates exclusively as well as inclusively' (Kain, 1993, p. 35). In other words, some people are in. Others are out. Marshall gives no account of the under-representation of disadvantaged groups in the political polis. These are serious obstructions to a citizenship of the political and are issues of relevance to the participation of faiths at the grass roots where they are seen as most valuable to civil society, for example in the challenges of child care, transport, time and the sheer energy to participate. It also highlights the challenges of power and capacity differentials between faiths, as we have seen. Political citizenship nevertheless finds a conceptual middle way between citizenship by status and by practice, requiring those included in suffrage (now only children and those deemed mentally unfit are excluded in the UK) to practice actively and in a sense extending the influence of suffrage, not through more voting but through more participation.

Second, Marshall suggests that citizenship may be social. This he describes as 'the whole range from the right to a modicum of economic welfare and security to the right to share to the full in social heritage and to live the life of a civilised being, according to the standard prevailing in society' (Marshall, 1950, p. 93). This is clearly problematic viewed from a practice perspective, not least in its implication that opportunity is a sufficient precondition for social citizenship, when subsequent critiques of participation are clear that people may not wish to participate in a prescribed society but might prefer one of their own making. Might this be the case for certain faith traditions or groups within them? It also assumes that an objective conception of 'civilisation' can be attained and in so doing fails to account for postmodern critiques and the rise of constructed diversity. Again, given the immense differentiation of faiths and traditions, meanings of 'civil society', and understandings of allegiance within them, are likely to vary enormously.

As if the debates were not complex enough, it is also suggested that the dichotomy between status and practice has been superseded, not only in the rise of the idea of participation as a form of citizenship, wherein 'local people work together to improve their own quality of life' (Pahl, 1995, p. 15) in an 'active citizenship', but also in the way in which status (rights) can be defended or extended through practice (agency). Thus citizenship may be understood, not as an absolute, but as a continuum so that people are citizens to greater or lesser extents and can gain (or lose) rights, status and agency according to what they do.

At the same time, Barry and Hallett (1998) suggest that in territorial and nationalistic terms, citizenship may be seen to operate, in practice, absolutely, for example in the exclusion of asylum seekers or the deportation of foreign nationals. Against this they postulate the potential of a human rights perspective to transcend the exclusionary power of citizenships through the assertion of local, regional, national, supranational and global citizen states. Thus have developed certain 'international citizenship obligations' such as the tackling of child poverty and aspects of the environmental movement. In this way, citizenship may be said to consist, not only in rights, practice and society but also in chosen membership of bodies such as NSMs.

This is important if citizenship discourse is not to be trapped in the absolutism of status and practice based on homogeneity and exclusion, which would be a disaster for public faith. Lister thus proposes the concept of 'differentiated universalism' (Lister, 1998, p. 53). This describes the universal right to rights, but to rights which are capable of varying meanings across diverse groups and individuals. Only in this way can they be inclusive. Applied to status citizenship this constructs rights as capable of particularisation to take account of the situations of specific groups. Thus status citizenship may be reactive (countering past disadvantages such as disability discrimination) or proactive (affirming diversity such as multicultural language policies). It is suggested that this has the secondary effect of anchoring rights in needs which are interpreted and translated into rights responsively, thereby reflecting and valuing diversity.

Applied to practice citizenship, too, 'differentiated universalism' proposes that people 'come together with a commitment to a universalistic orientation to the positive value of difference within a democratic political process' (Yeatman, 1993, p. 231) which amounts to an active politics of difference. Thus, in seeking common ground, difference is to be valued and respected, not repressed. This is understood in a pluralist account of community as an arena in which a transversal politics can be played out through the processes of dialogue and transaction. This may be something that many faiths are already good at. But experience suggests that it is also something that others have seriously compromised.

Policy for the active citizen is compelling then. It envisages the reactivation of people within their communities through participation in projects, initiatives and systems of governance. It recasts individuals as community members and as partners, with state, in the creation of a thriving civil society. Within this, it is anticipated that faiths have particular gifts to offer because they already value community, generate social capital, emphasise the neighbour and, by extension, the neighbourhood and are rich in the resources which support civil society.

But the paradox of faiths as heroes and villains is likely to confuse the notion of 'citizenship' and the active role which citizens of faith play. It highlights the presence of a boundary around the 'citizen' in 'active citizenship' which people are either within or without. Active citizenship is inclusive in so far as anyone can be a citizen who complies with its parameters but is highly and perhaps increasingly exclusive where people fall outside of them. While the terms may not be clear, citizenship is thus circumscribed within the terms of a set of 'practices' which are acceptable and another which are not. There is no 'rights' or 'status' based citizenship in the realm of the 'active citizen'. It is a citizenship based in practice.

'Active citizenship' also fails to acknowledge competing citizenship identities within the same person. Insistence on the quite tightly boundaried notion of the 'active citizen' as the predominant identity may conflict for some with elements they feel to have other importance for them, whether they compete, conflict or complement. For example, where the person of faith is highly identified with what they see as the land of their religion, which may be foreign to the land of their domicile, or indeed of their birth, perhaps they will feel predominantly aligned with a global community of faith; their citizenship claims may compete with those of the 'active citizen' which national policy requires of them.

Some other debates about the 'active citizen'

The notion of active citizenship is also problematic because it implies its opposite – the *inactive* citizen. This locates policy in the notion that people are apathetic and need to be re-motivated as 'active'. But Richards suggests that where people appear to have disengaged, there is 'more to this break down than ignorance and indifference' (Richards, 2000, p. 28). It is argued that the UK is now a 'post-traditional society' in which social homogeneity, immobility, class and community allegiance have broken down and that politics is suffering from the end of membership. If the problem is not so much a democratic deficit than a different *kind* of politics, then it cannot be addressed by re-engaging citizens within the existing processes of decision-making, nor by simply extending them *per se*. Richards' argument that politics has, rather, become a matter of single issues is reflected in other analyses such as Crossley's where the rise of a politics of identity is seen as a key cultural shift affecting the engagement of local people in public activity (Crossley, 2002). A different kind of politics requires a different kind of democratic engagement which works with the rise of identity over ideology.

This is especially pertinent to faiths since it has been observed, as we have seen (in Chapter 3), that faith is increasingly a key or even primary marker of identity, especially where there are other visible or highly conscientised aspects of identity competing within the one person or community, such as ethnicity or race. For second-generation immigrants in particular, the contests between alternative identities is increasingly being resolved in favour of faith so that young people, especially, are frequently identifying themselves as Muslim, Hindu or Sikh rather than in terms of their ethnicity as Asians, Middle Eastern or otherwise.

Yet faiths also occupy an intermediate space between private and public identities and may be in a position to mediate the trend towards single and identity politics to a political system which is struggling to come to terms with the shift from ideology to identity. This is partly because of the manner in which faiths look both ways – inwards to the private interior life of devotion, faith and fellowship; and outwards to the public exterior life of social justice, love, neighbourhood and compassion to which they are often directed, theologically if not in practice. It is also due to the way in which they are able to reintroduce perspectives about the significance of person, the self and society to a polis which seemed to have forgotten, or rejected, them. Might faiths be particular reminders of the responsibility humans have to one another and to society, and thereby find themselves in a position to render relevant people's preoccupations to a polis which had forgotten them?

At the same time, the notion of active citizenship has been criticised for the way in which this locates local people as the architects of their own disadvantage (Lister, 1998) rather than asking structural questions about how society oppresses the poor. The assumption that people have 'switched off' is also matched by a number of subsequent assumptions: that 'switching them on' is a matter of re-energising existing structures; that this will stimulate 'active citizenship'; that active citizens are the necessary precondition for cohesive community; and that communities are the site for the reintegration of a fragmented society (as though community itself is an uncontested idea). It is by no means clear that these positions correctly identify or understand the issues about the 'fragmentation of society' and yet they form the planks underpinning policies for community and participative governance.

This is reflected, too, in policies for welfare reform, which are closely related in two ways: first, as a mechanism for generating a sense of active citizenship rather than dependant subject; and second, as an aspect of fiscal discipline, ensuring an active economy which is able to sustain welfare realistically. It assumes that structural reform of welfare is essential for four main reasons: first, in order to address key challenges (such as child poverty); second, to cut out perverse policies (such as higher benefits than wages); third, to repair damage caused by under-investment (as in housing); and fourth, to combat 'moral dependency'. This last relates directly to the constitutional reform ambition of pushing down power in order to energise communities of active citizens rather than passive recipients.

Yet in drawing faiths, and others, increasingly into partnership in the delivery of public services, in the management and governance of civic initiatives, and in daily life as active citizens, the relative positions of person and state are fundamentally changed. The relationship is reconstructed in terms of the citizenship of people (how they belong to a state as well as exist in themselves) and the democracy through which they mediate it. It begins with an appeal to the participation of local people which in itself constructs them as citizens within a democratic polis. Each of these ideas is contested in itself. And in the end the relationship between the idealism which invites faiths, and others, to an extended public table of active citizens, is cut dramatically across, both by the instrumentalism which sees them as repositories of resources and the tension between their construction as both heroes and villains.

9
Conclusion: Policies, Problems and Controversies

Putting a book like this one together is a bit of a juggling act. This is not because of inefficiency on my part alone, though in this area of faiths at the public table I do sometimes feel that I am running up and down a line of spinning plates (to mix my circus metaphors). But public faith sits at the intersection of a number of arenas, both material and conceptual. It is this vantage point which makes it such an interesting phenomenon when thinking about the public table. In negotiating the range of civil society encounters, faiths illuminate many of the questions raised by the extension of the public table more generally. In doing so, they have a great deal of complexity to contend with to keep the plates spinning.

Faiths at the intersection

So what are the arenas at this intersection? First there is the sheer range and diversity of faith traditions to take into account, as the data show in Chapter 2. This demands a nuanced understanding of faiths as heterogeneous, located and contingent. It is partly for this reason that I have used the plural 'faiths' throughout the book. (I also use it to indicate that it is the organised contexts of 'faiths' as well as the fact of 'belief' itself which are the significant presence at the public table). These contingencies are a feature, not only between faith traditions but also within and beyond them too. Frustratingly for anyone who wants to 'hear the voice of faith' in civil society there is no such apprehendable 'thing'. Rather, there are many voices and many faiths. Starting where they are, in all their locatedness, is the best hope for their sustained engagement at the public table, as I suggested in Chapter 2. This approach is reflected in the UK policy context in the government document *Face to Face and*

Side by Side: A Framework for Working Together in Our Multi-faith Society (CLG, 2008). This emphasises the role of local interfaith and multi-faith encounters in delivering the triplets of strengthened community, resilience and community cohesion and active citizens.

Second, there are all sorts of degrees and types of belief, and faith is not a neatly observable phenomenon which it is simple to pin down. The growing trend in Europe and Canada is towards believing without belonging. This is reflected in wider trends towards the politics of identity over issues, and people are aligning themselves much more personally than organisationally around the things which feel important to them. Alongside this, the data observe an appetite – even a hunger – for a spiritual fulfilment which many feel eludes them. Often this finds expression in a turn to non-theistic, spiritualist traditions which do not bind adherents to liturgical, organisational or dogmatic forms of belonging. This is especially significant in the context of the indigenous 'first nations' traditions of North America which emphasise 'spirituality' in their theologies and devotional practices. The idea of spirituality also has greater currency in the literature on well-being than does the narrower notion of 'faith'. While 'spirituality' is a given dimension in many of the mainstream well-being definitions, including that of the World Health Organization, 'faith' is never used. As a more palatable theme in social science the idea of 'spirituality' may help lend respectability to faith as a public category, though for many 'faith' remains the unacceptable face of 'spirituality', where the connection is made between the two at all. Spirituality is palatable while faith has baggage.

In the US, the trends are different. There is a growth in belonging which Pippa Norris and Ronald Inglehardt ascribe to a lack of psychological security (Norris and Inglehardt, 2004) – a different kind of spiritual hunger perhaps. They point to fear about the world after 9/11, awareness of a gap between the rich and the poor and a fear of apocalypse and annihilation linked to nuclear arms and to the endangered environment. In either case, the assumption by secularism that the age of belief was over has been seriously and comprehensively challenged. Yet the forms of religious belief have shifted from formality to something much more personal and informal.

Third, there is the approach faiths take to each other and to others outside their traditions, both believers and non-believers. Sometimes this takes an interfaith character, seeking common ground between and beyond traditions. At other times the emphasis is on a multi-faith encounter, focusing more on common action than on common ground. Some see a way forward through theoretical wranglings, for example in the 'scriptural reasoning' encounters promoted by an inter-faith dialogue project at Cambridge University, wherein people from the Abrahamic faiths meet to consider points of intersection between the holy books of their traditions. Others are committed to a more practical and grounded approach, seeing a way forward through shared action in communities. There are those, too, who prefer to bunker down within their own traditions and communities, as discussed in Chapter 3. They are focused, not on the world around, but on the world within. Whatever the choice of *modus operandi*, it will be determined by the heady mix of theology, need, personality and policy in which activities of faiths emerge. Within this, as we have seen, some faith communities have been good at bonding, bridging and linking. Others have not.

Fourth, there is the intersection between different disciplines which come to bear. Primary among these are the social sciences and theology. These are sometimes presented as representing a supposed breach between science and religion. Many have sought to polarise the one as rational and the other as fantastical; a domain of madness and delusion (e.g., see Dawkins, 2006; Harris, 2006). Yet in the countries considered, each uses similar academic techniques and conventions, operates in the same overall philosophical and epistemological milieu of postmodernism and relativism, and in many cases explores similar sorts of questions, albeit in very different vocabularies. Neither can claim the sort of neutrality which secularised rationalism thought it had achieved. As I noted at the start of this book, nobody starts from nowhere.

Fifth, faiths encounter each other and the rest of civil society at an intersection of sectors and activities. Public faith crosses the public, voluntary and community sectors, engages with service delivery, with community cohesion and in governance. In each of these arenas it encounters, and is encountered by, a whole range of differing values, goals, practices and languages. The challenge is to respond in a context of mutuality, reciprocity and trust if the shared meal at the public table is not to result in indigestion. Faiths may have an especial mountain to climb in this regard because of a popular concern (perhaps prejudice) that they seek only to engage in 'conversation stopping certainties' (Alexander, 2001). For some this is the case. But for the majority experience suggests that it is not, as demonstrated in the plethora of inter and multi-faith work discussed in Chapter 2, and in the example of congregational development in Chapter 4. Theirs is to demonstrate skill and grace in the agonistic processes of deliberation which accept dispute, concede to other interests and, yes, sometimes get their way (see Norval, 2007). And debates about faiths' predilection for deliberation and debate can be appraised in the light of their relatively high levels of civic participation and in the phenomena of regional and local multi-faith forums, many of which have been forged out of years of careful inclusion and deliberation across faith traditions. Assumptions about faith, certainty and dogma are challenged by the evidence.

Theirs, too, is to think through the implications of engaging in the language of 'sectors' at all. There are risks in public faith becoming associated with – even subsumed within – a 'sector' (most likely the voluntary and community sector). What becomes of their critical edge – what theologians have called their 'prophetic voice'? The perils of enlistment within a public policy matrix are that faiths lose their independence, their nuance, their responsiveness to local need and their credibility as forces for human well-being. This argument has been applied to the language of social capital, too, in cautions against accepting the logic of 'capital' as a defining lens of the faith contribution. Perhaps faiths are more interested in human interactions than in capitalist transactions. Might this be part of any distinctiveness faiths bring to the public table?

These are the contexts within which faiths appear at the public table. They find themselves in a contentious position at the intersection of a range of issues and interests. These call into question their very legitimacy as participants at the public table among many who consider faith a private, not a public, matter; an irrational realm, against a rational one; and value-laden versus neutral, prone to moral partisanship, ready to spill over into evangelical fervour and dogma. No wonder, then, that this book has been about 'policies, problems and controversies'. How might these be summarised, and what are the debates which are raised?

Three policy paradoxes

The making of binary opposites between private–public, rational–irrational and partisan–neutral may be understandable in a context which thought that faith had been relegated by science. So it has been fascinating to observe a notable eating of words in more recent debates about secularism, as we saw in Chapter 1. As I observed there, it is to the surprise of many that faith is back. And that has been the starting point of this book. But these conceptual surprises are not the only paradoxes in the story of faiths at the public table. They are reflected in the policies which pertain, too.

Policies for faiths in each of the three countries considered are primarily associated with the idea of faiths as repositories of resources. This is a discourse of 'usefulness' and its legitimacy is disputed. For politicians it is likely to seem eminently reasonable to seek to draw faiths into the production of civil society since they have already shown themselves to be so good at civic participation, as we saw in Chapters 5 and 8, and at service provision, as we saw in Chapter 6. But for others at the public table the presence of faiths is concerning. Will they preach? What moral agenda do they want to push? Why should faiths be privileged in policy? For some their participation is positively an outrage against the rationalism of the twenty-first-century West; something about which thinking people ought to know better. They fear the sharing of power and influence with people whose past they regard as inhabited by the ghosts of dogma, inquisition, oppression and crusade. In the UK and Canada the moral or theological dimensions of public faith are explicitly excluded in the rhetoric. Faith at the public table must be inclusive, open to all and come without strings. In the US, the formal separation of religion and state is countered in places by a greater intertwining of the values of religious belief with public services. For some, this is regarded precisely as one of the benefits of public faith, though it is also the cause of heated debate between conservatives and liberals. This is the first of three paradoxes of public faith – that faith is both embraced and repelled. The role of the 'faith' which underpins 'public faith' is hotly disputed. For some public faith is a matter strictly of instrumentalising existing resources in the interests of civil society. For others there is a more idealistic understanding of public faith as a revalorisation of particular theological and moral concerns at the public table.

It is the instrumentalist public service dimension which is most emphatic in policies and practices of public faith in all three countries. The community and neighbourhood level activities of faiths in meeting local need are highly valued at the public table and it is this which assures their place. Yet faiths are valued, too, for the 'community' which they are so highly regarded for producing. The consensus is that faiths are 'good at community' and that, if handled properly, their commitment to love, family and neighbourhood can be made to rub off on wider society.

Yet here is a second paradox. While there is plenty of evidence that faiths are capable of contributing to community cohesion, as we saw in Chapter 5, it is also the case that they can shatter it. Faiths can be good for society. But there is a dark side too. The rise of extremism along religious lines has been a noted aspect of life after 9/11 and whether we treat faiths as heroes or villains in this regard will to some extent determine the way they engage in other arenas of public life. One simple response is that it is not a confusion which results in this paradox but a reality: that some faith is heroic while in the case of others it is villainous. The risk for public policy is that, in dealing with the villains, it alienates the heroes, or at least confuses them.

It is precisely this which has given impetus to renewed efforts to engage faiths in extended forms of participative governance – our third arena of public faith. This started as a theme within a generalised desire to produce 'active citizens' across the piece, as we saw in Chapter 8. More recently it has taken an additional turn in the direction of empowering minorities, thereby hitching them to the civil society wagon before they can be alienated from it. And herein lies our third paradox. Faiths (and others) are offered greater opportunities for participation in decision-making. Yet at the same time the citizenship which this enjoins is increasingly circumscribed within the terms of nationhood (e.g., 'Britishness'), a citizenship ceremony which pledges allegiance to the State – in the UK to the Queen – and a requirement to pass a citizenship test and to speak English. The multicultural settlement, which recognised differentiated citizenships, has been *unsettled*. Opportunities for participation are extended, but the civil society in which people participate has narrowed. So too have the gateways into it.

Positive disruptions, not negative eruptions!

The thing about tables, whether public or otherwise, is that they bring people face to face with a purpose, whether to eat (as it were, to share in the cultural traditions and 'tastes' of each others' milieux), to talk and debate or to confront. It is difficult to be at a table and to remain disengaged from the others at it. That takes some effort and is usually uncomfortable. Whether our analogy is about eating, talking or confronting, the public table ensures a coming together of people and interests in the production of civil society. This requires negotiation and deliberation. This engagement is frequently characterised in the terms of conflict, as in the case of the representative and delegated models of democracy with which the West is familiar. Here people compete to represent or voice interests and, once selected, do so in competition with other representatives and delegates. It is about asserting and winning the hegemony of 'your' interests and is fundamentally associated with the winning and holding of power.

Collaboration or conflict?

Though conflict has sometimes been a corollary of faith, the experiences of many, especially the faith-based community projects which predominate, has been of partnership and collaboration. As we have seen, in the forming of inter and multi-faith work, the coming forth of local and regional faith bodies, in response to crises, and in provision of services, faiths have been working within, between and beyond their traditions in collaboration, not conflict. The instrumentalisation of public faith poses a risk to this by setting faiths up in competition with one another for scarce resources in a mixed economy of welfare and in the competitive processes associated with some of the elected governance roles with which they are involved. These sorts of processes which many civil society bodies are used to might pose particular challenges to faiths as their public mechanisms and capacities move from relative fragility towards a greater robustness.

And at the same time, conflict is the form of involvement which most frightens those who are concerned about faiths at the public table in the first place. For them, the presence of faiths introduces an illegitimate claimant of power which can only translate, if successful, into the hegemony of beliefs and practices which oppress women, vilify gay people, forbid birth control and medical research, and generally inhibit the liberalism which post-Enlightenment society affords.

There are undoubtedly places and times where faiths have asserted themselves in just these ways. In our own times, the Taliban in Afghanistan is just one such example. And Ed Hussein writes eye-openingly about the desire of some radicalised Muslims to usher in a global Islamic state, willed by God (Hussein, 2006). Yet in projects and initiatives in neighbourhoods and communities across the West, faith traditions are making a far more gentle contribution rooted in post-Enlightenment theologies, and what evidence there is suggests that these far outweigh the minority of radical interests which cause such anxiety, as we have seen. In some cases faiths consciously challenge power relations and promote the voicing of the oppressed in the making of civil society, as in the example of congregational development in Chapter 4.

Remembering forgotten categories

So another take on the presence of faiths at the public table is that they introduce a new voice there; one which is unfamiliar both in tone and content. They insist on questions which have fallen out of fashion, about what it is to be human, how to interact as well as transact, the source and character of human value, the role of love and, yes, the meaning of life. Might this be some sort of reminder at the public table, in an age of 'capitals', of the importance of the *poetry* of human life as well as of the *prose*? Or, if such a claiming of the poetic is unfair to atheist poets, perhaps the idea of the 'God's eye view' might be an alternative?

Faiths might also magnify and refresh more familiar questions about concerns as wide ranging as neighbourhood renewal, human rights and education. The contentiousness of their involvement in these issues, and the range of perspectives which faiths can bring to bear, might help reinvigorate existing debates. Perhaps faiths can be the grit in the oyster in this way – a positively disturbing presence in an otherwise more comfortable and settled zone. Even where this is not their intent, perhaps the presence of a civil society actor whose interests are, in the end, ontological, can be a reminder. Seen this way, faiths at the public table are re-raising ontological questions which others had forgotten to ask.

Three challenges of faith at the public table

Since we seem to be doing things in threes, let's consider three challenges of faiths at the public table.

The first challenge consists is the surprise that faiths are there at all. As public actors struggle to understand each others' somewhat unfamiliar interests and vocabularies, anything which had hitherto been taken for granted is reappraised in the light of the surprising jolt of finding faiths at the public table. Looking up, public players are finding faiths there, large as life. Sitting up to take stock of them is perhaps a reminder to sit up and take stock more generally. Seen this way, faiths act as winds of change, refreshing the public table, even if they do blow some of the papers around while doing so.

Second, their presence produces – even demands – debate about public legitimacy in general. The right and role of public actors is questioned because the right and role of *faiths* is questioned. That which is acceptable and appropriate for public decision-making is bought smartly into question.

Third, once the surprise has worn off, these substantive deliberations can start to take place, as they have been doing in very many places. Seen this way, faiths are reintroducing themes and preoccupations which had been diminished, neglected or forgotten. They are reminders of ontological categories which the public table may have neglected and which have been bubbling to the surface elsewhere in a rather diffuse and unmet spiritual hunger in individuals and communities at large. These forgotten categories are concerned with broad existential and ontological questions about human being and how society should respond to it. Many of these had become caught up in the huge emerging machineries of policy, society and state which throughout the twentieth century increasingly converted human concerns about welfare, justice and equality into systemic and bureaucratic problems.

Faiths are a new voice at the public table: a disruptive presence. At their worst – and rarely, we should note – faiths challenge civil society to define itself against their threats. At their best, faiths join those who stand up for social justice and human fulfilment, insisting on their inclusion in a context which has neglected them.

Notes

Chapter 2

1. For a full list see *Religion (95) and Visible Minority Groups (15) for Population, for Canada, Provinces, Territories, Census Metropolitan Areas* at www.statcan.ca

Chapter 3

1. Faith in the City was a report of the Archbishop of Canterbury's Commission on Urban Disadvantage which identified the enormity of the challenge of inner-city poverty and deprivation and located it in a critique of the political landscape which was highly influential.
2. Local Strategic Partnerships (LSPs) were introduced by the New Labour government in the UK to bring together representatives from all the bodies and interest groups in relatively small areas to plan strategically for the deployment of public funding and activities in public services.
3. Theodicy is the problem of suffering – how a just or good God could allow or cause suffering and why good people suffer. On salvation, there is a theological systematic which sees history as a history of God's attempts to 'save' humankind from its fallen state and effect recovery to 'perfection' or 'completion' in union with God or the universe. Eschatology refers to ideas about the end of the world and time and of what that might consist.
4. LSP EXPAND.
5. NRU Boards EXPAND.

Chapter 4

1. Two regional faith based bodies providing support to local faith bodies to maximise their capacity for and engagement in community development.
2. For a discussion of bonding, bridging and linking see Putnam's study of social capital in Bowling Alone REF. For its application to faith communities see Furbey, Dinham, Farnell and Finneron (2006), *Faith as Social Capital: Connecting or Dividing?* Bristol: Policy Press.

Chapter 6

1. It should be noted that faith based philanthropy in this period is almost exclusively Christian because faith in general is almost exclusively Christian at that time.
2. Source: Dinham, A. (2007), *Priceless, Unmeasureable? Faith and Community Development in 21st Century England*, London: FbRN. It is probable that these are collapsible into a smaller number of categories overall and we hope that this report can inform a wider conversation about 'standardising' such

definitions nationally as part of the development of faith based frameworks which are more readily engageable with.

3. Popple, K. (2000) (4th ed.), *Analyzing Community Work: Its Theory and Practice*, Berkshire, Open University Press.
4. Angels and Advocates CRC, Yorkshire and the Humber (2005).
5. Faith in the North East.
6. Faith in the East of England EEFC and Cambridge University (2005).
7. Faith in Action in the South West.
8. Embracing the Present, Planning the Future.

References

ACUPA (1985), *Faith in the City: A Call for Action by Church and Nation,* London: Church House Publishing.

Adams, R. (1990), *Self-Help, Social Work and Empowerment,* London: Macmillan.

Ahmed, R., Finneron, D. and Singh, H. (2004), *Tools for Regeneration: A Holistic Approach for Faith Communities,* FbRNUK/CUF.

Alexander, A. (2002), *Rebuilding the Matrix: Science and Faith in the 21st Century,* Oxford: Lion Press.

Alinsky, S. (1971), *Rules for Radicals,* New York: Random House.

Allan, D. H. (1991), *The Struggle for Community,* Boulder, CO and Oxford: Westview Press.

Allingham, M. (2002), *Choice Theory: A Very Short Introduction,* Oxford: Oxford University Press.

Amin, A. (2002), 'Ethnicity and the Multicultural City: Living with Diversity', *Environment and Planning A,* vol. 34, no. 6, pp. 959–80.

Anderson, B. (1991), *Imagined Communities: Reflections on the Origin and Spread of Nationalism,* London: Verso.

Angoy, S. (2004), Faith Communities in the New Deal for Communities in Tower Hamlets (online only).

Angoy, S. (2005), *New Deal for Communities Faith Pilots Project,* ODPM, www.neighbourhood.gov.uk/publications.asp?did=1317

Anschutz, R. P. (1953), *The Philosophy of J S Mill,* Oxford: Clarendon Press.

Arnstein, S. R. (1971), 'A Ladder of Participation in the USA', *Journal of the Royal Town Planning Institute,* April: 176–82.

Baistow, K. (1995), 'Liberation and Regulation? Some Paradoxes of Empowerment', *Journal of Critical Social Policy,* no. 42, pp. 34–46.

Baker, C. and Skinner, H. (2006), *Faith in Action – The Dynamic Connection between Spiritual and Religious Capital,* Manchester: William Temple Foundation.

Baldock, P. (1974), *Community Work and Social Work,* London and Boston, MA: Routledge and Kegan Paul.

Barber, B. R. (1984), *Strong Democracy: Participatory Politics for a New Age,* Berkeley, CA and London: University of California Press.

Barnes, M. (1997), *Care, Communities and Citizens,* London: Longman.

Baron, S., Field, J. and Schuller, T. (2000), *Social Capital: Critical Perspectives,* Milton Keynes: Open University Press.

Barry, M. and Hallett, C. (1998), *Social Exclusion and Social Work,* Oxford: Russell House.

Bauman, Z. (2004), *Identity,* Cambridge: Polity Press.

Beck, U. (1998), *Democracy without Enemies,* Oxford: Polity Press.

Beckford, J., Gale, R., Owen, D., Peach, C. and Weller, P. (2006), *Review of the Evidence Base on Faith Communities,* London: Office of the Deputy Prime Minister.

Bell, P. (1986), *New Party, New Politics: Gramsci's Democratic Socialism,* London: Pamphlet.

Bellah, R. N. and Neelly, R. (1991), *The Good Society*, New York: Knopf (distributed by Random House).

Beresford, P. and Croft, S. (1986), *Whose Welfare? Private Care of Public Services*, Brighton: Lewis Cohen Urban Studies Centre.

Berger, P. (ed.) (1999), *The Desecularization of the World: Resurgent Religion and World Politics*, Washington, DC: Ethics and Public Policy Center and Eerdmands.

Berger, P., Durkheim, E., Stouffer, S. A. and Steward, J. (1968), *Perspectives in the Social Order: Readings in Sociology*, N.P.: McGraw Hill.

Berger-Schmitt, R. (2000), 'Social Cohesion as an Aspect of the Quality of Societies', EuReporting Working Paper No. 14, Mannheim, Centre for Survey Research and Methodology.

Berkeley, N., Barnes, S., Dann, B., Stockley, N. and Finneron, D. (2006), *Faithful Representation: Faith Representatives on Local Public Partnerships*, Church Urban Fund and the Faith Based Regeneration Network, UK.

Best Value ODPM Circular 03/2003: Best Value Performance Improvement, London: The Stationery Office, 13 March.

Bevir, M. and Rhodes, R. (2006), *Governance Stories*, Abingdon: Routledge.

Billings, A. and Holden, A. (2008), *The Burnley Project: Interfaith Interventions and Cohesive Communities – the Effectiveness of Interfaith Activity in Towns Marked by Enclavisation and Parallel Lives*, Department of Religious Studies: Lancaster University.

Black, A. E., Loopman, D. L. and Ryden, D. K. (2004), *Of Little Faith: The Politics of George W Bush's Faith-Based Initiatives*, Washington, DC: Georgetown University Press.

Boaden, N., Goldsmith, M., Hampton, W. and Stringer, P. (1982), *Public Participation in Local Services*, London: Longman.

Bourdieu, P. (1991), in Thompson, J. B. (ed.) (trans. Raymond, G. and Adamson, M.) *Language and Symbolic Power*, Cambridge: Polity Press.

Bourdieu, P. and Passeron, M. (1970), *Outline of a Theory of Practice*, London: Open University Press.

Bowpitt, G. (1998). Evangelical Christianity, Secular Humanism and the Genesis of British Social Work. *British Journal of Social Work*, Vol. 28 no. 5, pp. 675–93.

Bowpitt, G. (2007), 'Stemming the Tide: Welfare, Mission and the Churches' Response to Secular Modernity in Britain, 1850–1895', Seminar paper presented to the Faiths and Civil Society seminar, Anglia Ruskin University, 26 February 2008.

Bradley, M. B., Green, N. M., Jones, D. E., Lynn, M. and McNeil, L. (1992), *Churches and Church Membership in the United States, 1990*, Atlanta, GA: Glenmary Research Center.

Bretherton, L. (2008), 'The Churches, Broad-Based Community Organising and Pursuit of the Common Good', Paper given at the ESRC 'Faiths and Civil Society' seminar series, Anglia Ruskin University, Cambridge, 26 February.

Burns, D., Hambleton, R. and Hoggett, P. (1994), *The Politics of Decentralisation: Revitalizing Local Democracy*, London: Macmillan.

Cabinet Office (2004), *Social Enterprise Action Plan – Scaling New Heights*, www.cabinetoffice.gov.uk/third_sector

Calhoun, C. (ed.) (1994), *Social Theory and the Politics of Identity*, Oxford: Blackwell.

Cantle, T. (2005), *Community Cohesion: A New Framework for Race and Diversity*, Basingstoke and New York: Palgrave Macmillan.

Castells, M. (1991), *The Informational City: Information Technology, Economic Restructuring and the Urban Regional Process*, Oxford: Blackwell.

Castells, M. (1997a), 'The Contingent Value of Social Capital', *Administrative Science Quarterly*, vol. 42, pp. 339–65.

Castells, M. (1997b), *The Power of Identity*, Oxford: Blackwell.

Castells, M. (2000), *The Rise of the Network Society*, Oxford: Blackwell.

Chadwick, P. (2001), 'The Anglican Perspective on Church Schools', *Oxford Review of Education*, vol. 27, no. 4, pp. 475–86.

Chandler, J. (2001) (3rd ed.), *Local Government Today*, Manchester: Manchester University Press.

Church of England Church Statistics 2003/04 and 2004/05, London (www.cofe.anglican.org)

Cieslak, M. (1995), 'Being Creative: Diverse Approaches to Estimating Catholics', paper presented to the annual meeting of the Religious Research Association.

Clarke, J. and Newman, J. (1997), *The Managerial State: Power, Politics and Ideology in the Remaking of Social Welfare*, London: Sage.

CLG (2008), *Communities and Control: Real People, Real Power*, London: The Stationery Office.

Cohen, J. L. and Arato, A. (1992), *Civil Society and Political Theory*, Cambridge, MA and London: MIT Press.

Commission on Integration and Cohesion (2006), *Our Shared Future*, London: CIC.

Copson, A. (2006), 'Why Education Should Not Divide on Faith' in a speech to the Westminster Forum on 24 April 2006.

CRCYH (2002), *Angels and Advocates: Church Social Action in Yorkshire and the Humber*, Leeds: Yorkshire and the Humber Churches Regional Commission.

Crossley, N. (2002), *Making Sense of Social Movements*, Buckingham: Open University Press.

Dahl, R. A. (1989), *Democracy and Its Critics*, Yale: Yale University Press.

Davie, G. (1999), *Religion in Britain Since 1945: Believing without Belonging*, Oxford and Cambridge, MA: Blackwell.

Davis, J. A. and Smith, T. W. (serial), *General Social Surveys* [machine readable file].

Dawkins, R. (2006), *The God Delusion*, London: Bantam.

Dearlove, J. (1979), *The Reorganisation of British Local Government: Old Orthodoxies and a Political Perspective*, Cambridge: Cambridge University Press.

Della-Porta, D. and Diani, M. (1999), *Social Movements in a Globalising World*, Basingstoke: Macmillan.

Demaine, J. and Entwistle, H. (eds) (1996), *Beyond Communitarianism: Citizenship, Politics and Education*, Basingstoke: Macmillan.

DETR (1998), *Modern Local Government, In Touch with the People*, London: HMSO.

DETR (2000), *Our Countryside, Our Future: A Fair Deal for Rural England*, London: HMSO.

Dicenso, J. (1999), *The Other Freud: Religion, Culture, and Psychoanalysis*, London: Routledge.

Dinham, A. (2005a), 'Empowered or Overpowered: The Real Experiences of Local Participation in the UK's New Deal for Communities', *Community Development Journal*, vol. 40, no. 3, pp. 301–12.

Dinham, A. (2005b), *The Mustard Seed Effect: The Role of the Church Urban Fund in Areas of Urban Disadvantage*, London: CUF.

Dinham, A. (2006), 'Raising Expectations or Dashing Hopes?: Well-Being and Participation in Disadvantaged Areas', *Community Development Journal*, vol. 42, no. 2, pp. 181–93.

Dinham, A. (2007), *Priceless, Unmeasureable: Faith Based Community Development in 21st Century England*, London: FbRN.

Dinham, A. (2008), 'From Faith in the City to Faithful Cities: The "Third Way", the Church of England and Urban Regeneration', *Urban Studies*, vol. 45, no. 10, pp. 2163–74.

Dinham, A. and Lowndes, V. (2008), 'Religion, Resources, and Representation: Three Narratives of Faith Engagement in British Urban Governance', *Urban Affairs Review*, vol. 43, no. 6, pp. 817–45.

Dinham, A., Furbey, R. and Lowndes, V. (eds) (2009), *Faith in the Public Realm: Problems, Policies, Controversies*, Bristol: Policy Press.

Doward, J. (2006), '£10m state cash for first Hindu school', *The Guardian*, 24 December 2006, p. 6.

DTI (2005), *Social Enterprise: A Strategy for Success – An Introduction*, London: DTI/HMSO.

Edin, K. and Levin, L. (1997), *Making Ends Meet: How Single Mothers Survive Welfare & Low Wage Work*, New York: Russell Sage Foundation.

Elster, J. (ed.) (1998), *Deliberative Democracy*, London: Cambridge University Press.

Etzioni, A. (1993), *The Spirit of Community: Rights, Responsibilities and the Communitarian Agenda*, NY: Crown Publishers.

Eyerman, R. and Jamieson, A. (1991), *Social Movements: A Cognitive Approach*, Cambridge: Polity Press in association with Basildon.

Farnell, R. (2001), 'Faith Communities, Regeneration and Social Exclusion: Developing a Research Agenda', *Community Development Journal*, vol. 36 no. 4, pp. 263–72, Oxford: Oxford University Press.

Farnell, R., Furbey, R., Shams Al-Haqq Hills S., Macey, M. and Smith, G. (2003), *Faith in Urban Regeneration: Engaging Faith Communities in Urban Regeneration*, London: Policy Press.

Farnell, R., Hopkinson, J., Jarvis, D., Martineau, J. and Ricketts, Hein J. (2006), *Faith in Rural Communities: Contributions of Social Capital to Community Vibrancy*, Coventry, Applied Centre for Sustainable Regeneration: Coventry University.

FCWTG (1989), *What is Community Development?* FCWTG.

Field, J. (2003), *Social Capital*, London: Routledge.

Fine, B. (1999), 'It Ain't Social and It Ain't Capital ESRC', in Morrow (ed.) (2001) *An Appropriate Capital-isation? Questioning Social capital*, London: Gender Institute LSE.

Finneron, D. and Dinham, A. (2002), *Building on Faith: The Use of Faith Buildings in Areas of Urban Regeneration*, London: CUF.

Finneron, D., Green, L., Harley, S. and Robertson, J. (2001) *Challenging Communities: Church Related Community Development & Neighbourhood Renewal*, London: CUF/CCWA.

Freire, P. (1985), *Pedagogy of the Oppressed*, Harmondsworth: Penguin.

Freire, P. and Shor, I. (1987), *A Pedagogy for Liberation: Dialogues on Transforming Education*, Basingstoke: Macmillan.

Fremeaux, I. (2005), 'New Labour's Appropriation of the Concept of Community: A Critique', *Community Development Journal*, vol. 40, no. 3: pp. 265–74.

Fukuyama, F. (1992), *The End of History and the Last Man*, London: Hamilton.

Fukuyama, F. (1995), *Trust: The Social Virtues and the Creation of Prosperity*, London: Penguin.

Furbey, R. and Macey, M. (2005), 'Religion and Urban Regeneration: A Place for Faith?', *Policy and Politics*, vol. 33, no. 1, pp. 95–116.

Furbey, R., Dinham, A., Farnell, R. and Finneron, D. (2006), *Faith as Social Capital: Connecting or Dividing?* Bristol: Policy Press & Joseph Rowntree Foundation.

Galbraith, J. K. (1992), *The Culture of Contentment*, Boston, MA: Houghton Mifflen.

Gaventa, J. with Estrella, M. (1998), *Who Counts Reality? Participatory Monitoring and Evaluation: A Literature Review*, University Sussex: Institute of Development Studies.

Germino, D. (ed.) (2000), *Plato and Aristotle, in Order & History*, vol. 3, Baton Rouge: LSU Press.

Giddens, A. (1998a), *The Third Way: The Renewal of Social Democracy*, Cambridge: Polity Press.

Giddens, A. (1998b), *Conversations with Anthony Giddens: Making Sense of Modernity*, Stanford, CA: Stanford University Press.

Giddens, A. (2000), *The Third Way and Its Critics*, Cambridge: Polity Press.

Giddens, A. (2002), *Where Now for New Labour?* Cambridge: Polity Press.

Gilchrist, A. (2004), *The Well-Connected Community: A Networking Approach to Community Development*, Bristol: The Policy Press.

Gillard, D. (2001), *Glass in Their Snowballs: The Faith Schools Debate*, http://www.dg.dial.pipex.com/articles/educ22.shtml

Gillies, P. (1998), 'Effectiveness of Alliances and Partnerships for Health Promotion', in *Health Promotion International*, vol. 13, no. 2, pp. 99–120.

Goldsmith, S. (2002), *Putting Faith in Neighborhoods: Making Cities Work through Grassroots Citizenship*, Noblesville, IN: Hudson Institute.

Grace, G. (2001), 'The State and Catholic Schooling in England and Wales: Politics, Ideology and Mission Integrity', *Oxford Review of Education*, vol. 27, no. 4, pp. 489–98.

Grammich, C. (2004), 'Many Faiths of Many Regions: Continuities and Changes among Religious Adherents across US Counties, WR-211 December 2004', Working Paper of the RAND Labor and Population working paper series.

Greater London Enterprise (GLE)/London Churches Group (LCG) (2002), *Neighbourhood Renewal in London: The Role of Faith Communities*, London: LCG for Social Action/GLE.

Green, G., Grimsley, M. and Stafford, B. (2005), *The Dynamics of Neighbourhood Sustainability*, York: Joseph Rowntree Foundation.

Grugel, J. (2002), *Democratisation: A Critical Introduction*, Basingstoke: Palgrave.

Habermas, J. in Norris, P. and Inglehart, R. (2004), *Sacred and Secular: Religion and Politics Worldwide*, Cambridge: Cambridge University Press.

Halman, L. (2001), *The European Values Study: A Third Wave Sourcebook of 1999/2000 European Values Study Survey*, Tilburg: WORC Tilburg University.

Halsey, A. H. (ed.) (1997), *Education: Culture, Economy and Society*, Oxford: Oxford University Press.

Harris, S. (2006), *The End of Faith: Religion, Terror and the Future of Reason,* London: The Free Press.

Held, D. (1993), *Democracy and the New International Order,* Stanford: Institute for Public Affairs.

Henderson, P. and Thomas, D. N. (2001) (3rd ed.), *Skills in Neighbourhood Work,* London: Routledge.

Hirst, P. (1997), *From Statism to Pluralism,* London: UCL Press.

Home Office (2003), Citizenship Survey: People, Families and Communities, Home Office Research, Development and Statistics Directorate.

Home Office (2004), *Working Together: Co-operation between Government and Faith Communities,* London: The Stationery Office.

Home Office (2005), *Improving Opportunity, Strengthening Society: The Government's Strategy to Increase Race Equality and Community Cohesion,* London: Home Office.

Home Office (2006), *The Citizenship Survey 2005,* London: Home Office.

Home Office (2007), *Preventing Violent Extremism: Winning Hearts and Minds,* London: Stationery Office.

Hussein, E. (2007), The Islamist, XXX.

James, H. (ed.) (2007), *Civil Society, Religion and Global Governance: Paradigms of Power and Persuasion,* London and New York: Routledge.

Jelen, T. and Wilcox, C. (1995), *Public Attitudes toward Church and State,* Georgetown: SSSR

Johnson, D. W., Picard, P. R. and Quinn, B. (1974), *Churches and Church Membership in the United States,* 1971, Washington, DC: Glenmary Research Center.

Jones, D. E., Doty, S., Grammich, C., Horsch, J. E., Houseal, R., Lynn, M., Marcum, J. P., Sanchagrin, K. M. and Taylor, R. H. (2002), *Religious Congregations and Membership in the United States,* 2000, Nashville, TN: Glenmary Research Center.

Kain, P. (1993), *Marx and Modern Political Theory: From Hobbes to Contemporary Feminism,* Lanham, MD: Rowman & Littlefield.

Keane, J. (2000), 'Secularism?', in Marquand D. and Nettler R. L. (eds), *Religion and Democracy,* Oxford: Blackwell, pp. 5–19.

Knox, B. M. W. (1994), *Backing into the Future: The Classical Tradition and Its Renewal,* New York, London: W.W. Norton.

Kosmin, B. A., Mayer, E. and Keysar, A. (2001), *American Religious Identification Survey, 2001,* New York: The Graduate Center of the City University of New York.

Lash, S. with Heelas, P. and Morris, P. (eds) (1996), *Detraditionalisation: Critical Reflections in Authority and Identity,* Oxford: Blackwell.

Lash 1994 in Mayo, M. (2000), *Cultures, Communities, Identities: Cultural Strategies for Participation and Empowerment,* Basingstoke: Palgrave.

Lemann, N. (1996), *Kicking in Groups,* Atlantic Monthly April, 1–9.

Lewis, J. with Randolph-Horne, E. (2001), *Faiths, Hope and Participation: Celebrating Faith Groups' Role in Neighbourhood Renewal,* London: New Economics Foundation/CUF.

Lewis, A. Coser (1977) (2nd ed.), *Masters of Sociological Thought: Ideas in Historical and Social Context,* Fort Worth: Harcourt Brace Jovanovich, Inc.: pp. 136–9.

Lister, R. (1998). 'In From the Margins: Citizenship, Inclusion and Exclusion', in Barry, M. and Hallett, C. (eds), *Social Exclusion and Social Work,* Lyme Regis: Russell House.

Loomis, C. P. (ed.) (2002), *Gemeinschaft und Gesellschaft (Community and Society)*, Mineola, NY: Dover Publications.

Lowndes, V. and Smith, G. (2006), *Faith Based Voluntary Action*, London: NCVO.

Lowndes, V. and Sullivan, H. (2004), 'Like a Horse and Carriage or a Fish on a Bicycle: How Well Do Local Partnerships and Public Participation Go Together?', *Local Government Studies*, vol. 30, no. 1, pp. 52–74.

Lukes, S. M. (1974), *Power: A Radical View*, London: Macmillan.

MacIntyre, A. C. (1981), *After Virtue: A Study in Moral Theory*, London: Duckworth.

Marris, P. (1987), *Meaning and Action: Community Planning and Conceptions of Change*, London: Routledge and Kegan Paul.

Marshall, T. H. (1950), *Citizenship and Social Class, and Other Essays*, Cambridge: Cambridge University Press.

Mayo, M. (2000), *Cultures, Communities, Identities: Cultural Strategies for Participation and Empowerment*, Basingstoke: Palgrave.

McKinnon, Andrew M. (2005), 'Reading "Opium of the People": Expression, Protest and the Dialectics of Religion', *Critical Sociology*, vol. 31, no. 1/2, 15–38.

McTernan, O. (2003), *Violence in God's Name: Religion in an Age of Conflict*, London: Darton, Longman and Todd.

Mean, R. (1988), *Community Care before and after the Griffiths Report*, Association of London Authorities, Oxford: Blackwell.

Meer, N. (2007), 'Muslim Schools in Britain: Challenging Mobilisations or Logical Developments?', *Asia Pacific Journal of Education*, vol. 27, no. 1, pp. 55–71.

Mendus, S. (1992), 'Losing the Faith: Feminism & Democracy', in Dunn, J. (ed.), *Democracy: The Unfinished Journey*, Oxford: Oxford University Press.

Millar, J. (1989), *Poverty and the Lone-Parent Family: The Challenge to Social Policy*, Aldershot: Avebury.

Modood, T. (1997), 'Culture and Identity', in Modood, T. (ed.), *Ethnic Minorities in Britain*, London: Policy Studies Institute, pp. 290–338.

Monsma, S. V. (1996), *When Sacred and Secular Mix: Religious Non Profit Organizations and Public Money*, Lanham, MD: Rowman & Littlefield.

Morrow, V. (1999), 'Conceptualising Social Capital in Relation to the Well-Being of Children and Young People: A Critical Review', *The Sociological Review*, vol. 47 no. 4, pp. 744–65.

Morrow, V. (ed.) (2001), *An Appropriate Capital-isation? Questioning Social capital*, Gender Institute LSE.

Musgrave, P. (1999), *Flourishing Communities*, London: CUF.

Neitzsche, F. in Kaufman, W. (trans.) (1966) (14th ed.), *Thus Spoke Zarathustra: A Book for None and All*, New York and London: Penguin.

Newman, J. (2007), 'Rethinking "the Public" in Troubled Times', *Public Policy and Administration*, vol. 22, no. 1, pp. 27–46.

Norris, P. and Inglehart, R. (2004), *Sacred and Secular: Religion and Politics Worldwide*, Cambridge, MA: Cambridge University Press.

Norval, A. J. (2007), Beyond Deliberation: Agonistic and Aversive Grammars of Democracy – The Question of Criteria, Personal correspondence.

Olasky, M. (1992), *The Tragedy of American Compassion*, Lanham, MD: Regnery Gateway.

Oldfield, A. (1990), *Citizenship and Community: Civic and the Modern World*, London: Routledge.

Ousely, H. (2001), *Community Pride Not Prejudice*, Bradford: Bradford Vision.

Pahl, R. E. (1995), *After Success: fin de siecle Anxiety and Identity*, Cambridge: Polity Press.

Parekh, B. (2006) (2nd ed.), *Rethinking Multiculturalism: Cultural Diversity and Political Theory*, Basingstoke: Palgrave Macmillan.

Performance and Innovation Unit (2002), *Social Capital: A Discussion Paper*, London: Cabinet Office.

Phillips, D. L. (1993), *Looking Backward: A Critical Appraisal of Communitarian Thought*, Princeton, NJ: Princeton University Press.

Phillips, S. D. (2006), 'The Intersection of Governance and Citizenship in Canada: Not Quite the Third Way', *IRPP Policy Matters*, vol. 7, no. 4, pp. 3–31.

Popple, K. (1995), *Analysing Community Work*, Buckingham: Open University Press.

Prochaska, F. (2006), *Christianity and Social Service in Modern Britain*, New York: Oxford University Press.

Putnam, R. (1995), 'Bowling Alone: America's Declining Social Capital', *Journal of Democracy*, vol. 61, pp. 65–78.

Putnam, R. (1996), *Who Killed Civic America?* Prospect.

Quinn, B., Anderson, H., Bradley, M., Goetting, P. and Shriver, P. (1982), *Churches and Church Membership in the United States, 1980*, Atlanta: Glenmary Research Center.

Rao, N. (2000), *Reviving Local Democracy: New Labour, New Politics?* Bristol: Policy Press.

Rawls, J. (1980), 'Kantian Constructivism in Moral Theory', *Journal of Philosophy*, vol. 77, pp. 515–72.

Richards, P. (2000), *Is the Party Over? New Labour and the Politics of Participation*, London: Fabian Society.

Robinson, D. (2005), 'The Search for Community Cohesion: Key Themes and Dominant Concepts of the Public Policy Agenda', *Urban Studies*, vol. 42, no. 7, pp. 1411–27.

Ruthven, M. (2004), *Fundamentalism: The Search for Meaning*, Oxford: Oxford University Press.

Saegert, S., Phillip, Thompson J. and Warren, M. R. (eds) (2001), *Social Capital and Poor Communities*, New York: Russell Sage Foundation.

Sandel, M. J. (1982), *Liberalism and the Limits of Justice*, Cambridge: Cambridge University Press.

Scott, J. (1991), *Social Network Analysis: A Handbook*, London: Sage.

Sen, A. (1987), 'Rational Behaviour', *The New Palgrave Dictionary of Economics*, vol. 3, pp. 68–76, Basingstoke: Palgrave.

SEU (1999), *Bringing Britain Together: A National Strategy for Neighbourhood Renewal*, London: HMSO.

Sherman, A. (2002), *Fruitful Collaborations: A Survey of Government-Funded Faith-Based Programs in 15 States*, Harlottesville: Hudson Institute.

Smith and Randolph-Horne, D. (2000), *Faith Makes Communities Work*, London: GLE.

Soloman, L. and Vlissides, M. J. Jr (2001), 'In God We Trust? Assessing the Potential of Faith-Based Social Services', *Policy Report*, Progressive Policy Institute, 1 February 2001.

Stacey, M. (1969), 'The Myth of Community Studies', *British Journal of Sociology*, vol. 20, no. 20, pp. 137–47.

Stewart, M. and Taylor, M. (1995), *Empowerment and Estate Regeneration*, London: Polity Press.

Thomas, D. N. (1983), *The Making of Community Work*, London: Allen & Unwin.

Touraine, A. (1981), (trans. Duff, A.) *The Voice and the Eye: An Analysis of Social Movements*, Cambridge: Cambridge University Press.

Trevillion, S. (1999) (2nd ed.), *Networking and Community Partnership*, Aldershot: Ashgate.

Twelvetrees, A. (2001) (3rd ed.), *Community Work*, Basingstoke: Palgrave.

Valins, O. (2003), 'Defending Identities or Segregating Communities? Faith-Based Schooling and the UK Jewish Community', *Geoforum*, vol. 34, pp. 235–47.

Walford, G. (2001), 'Evangelical Schools in England and the Netherlands', *Oxford Review of Education*, vol. 27, no. 4, pp. 529–41.

Ward, K. (2004), *The Case for Religion*, Oxford: One World.

Watts, F. N. and Williams, M. (2007), *The Psychology of Religious Knowing*, Cambridge: Cambridge University Press.

Weale, A. (1999), *Democracy*, Basingstoke: Macmillan.

Weller, P. (ed.) (2007), *Religions in the UK Directory 2001–03*, London, Multi-Faith Centre at the University of Derby, Derby and Inter Faith Network for the United Kingdom.

Wesley (1771), See http://www.archive.org/details/standardsermonsc01wesluoft.

White, S. and Pettit, J. (2004), *Participatory Approaches and the Measurement of Human Well-Being*, UN University/World Institute for Development Economics Research (WIDER) 2004/57, New York.

Whitman, L. and Trimble, G. (1956), *Churches and Church Membership in the United States: An Enumeration and Analysis by Counties, States, and Regions*, New York: National Council of Churches of Christ.

Williams, R. (1976), *Keywords: A Vocabulary of Culture and Society*, London: Croom Helm.

Williams, C. L. (1989), *Gender Differences at Work: Women and Men in Non-traditional Occupations*, Berkeley: University of California Press.

Wilson, B. (1966), *Religion in a Secular Society*, London: Watts.

Winnicott, D. W. (1971), *Playing and Reality*, London: Tavistock Books.

Woodward, V. (2004), *Active Learning for Active Citizenship*, London: Home Office.

Wuthnow, R. (2004), *Saving America? Faith-Based Services and the Future of Civil Society*, Princeton, NJ and Oxford: Princeton University Press.

Yeatman, A. (1993), *Feminism and the Politics of Difference*, St Leonards: Allen and Unwin.

Younghusband, E. L. (1959), *Report of the Working Party on Social Workers in the Local Authority Health and Welfare Services*, London: HMSO.

Younghusband, E. L. (1968), Community Work and Social Change: Report of a Study Group on Training, set up by the Calouste Gulbenkian Foundation, London and Harlow: Longmans.

Index

Note: *Italic* page numbers indicate tables and figures.